**WITHDRAWN**

# Criminal Procedure and Evidence

Titles currently available in the HBJ Criminal Justice Series:

**Criminal Procedure and Evidence**  Rolando del Carmen

**Legal Aspects of Evidence**  Robert W. Ferguson and Allan H. Stokke

**Criminal Investigation**  Jerry L. Dowling

Books on the following topics are now in preparation for the series: Criminology, Criminal Law, Police Organization and Administration, Community Relations, Juvenile Delinquency, Police Report Writing, Probation and Parole, Law Enforcement.

**HBJ CRIMINAL JUSTICE SERIES**

# Criminal Procedure and Evidence

**Rolando del Carmen**
Sam Houston State University

**HARCOURT BRACE JOVANOVICH, INC.**

New York  San Diego  Chicago  San Francisco  Atlanta

This book is lovingly dedicated to my wife, Josie,
and to my daughter, Jocelyn.

Copyright © 1978 by Harcourt Brace Jovanovich, Inc.

All rights reserved. No part of this publication may be reproduced or transmitted in any form or by any means, electronic or mechanical, including photocopy, recording, or any information storage and retrieval system, without permission in writing from the publisher.
Requests for permission to make copies of any part of the work should be mailed to: Permissions, Harcourt Brace Jovanovich, Inc., 757 Third Avenue, New York, N.Y. 10017.

ISBN: 0-15-516100-8

Library of Congress Catalog Card Number: 79-88649

Printed in the United States of America

# PREFACE

A knowledge of criminal procedure is important for anyone involved in the administration of criminal justice, since procedure encompasses the methods established under our system of justice for dealing with those who run afoul of the law. Its rules—as set by the Constitution, by statutes, and by judicial decision—must be learned well by students of criminal justice and personnel of criminal justice agencies. Ignorance of them has serious implications for society at large, as well as for those directly involved in the administration of justice.

The study of law can be difficult and frustrating, particularly for beginners. The field is broad, and the language is often strange and technical. One must understand abstract concepts, yet at the same time know details and specifics. Moreover, laws are often vague; court decisions often leave gaps, and sometimes they conflict.

This text, for undergraduate students of criminal procedure, has been written with these realities in mind. It strives to use simplified language that is easy to understand yet accurate. The examples that illustrate abstract legal concepts are based on recognizable factual situations. Only leading cases are cited, and legal citations are held to a minimum. The format makes transitions and connections easy to see and to follow, aiding students' comprehension and retention of the material.

Chapters I through X deal with the various aspects of criminal procedure, including the structure of the court system and criminal process and the significant issues at each stage of that process—from initial questions of probable cause through sentencing and postconviction challenges. At the same time, however, certain rules of evidence inevitably relate to and influence the issues and concepts of criminal procedure. Chapters XI through XV present these evidentiary rules, and their separate treatment gives the text maximum flexibility. This material, or portions of it, may be assigned as a regular part of the course or may be used by students as a convenient reference if evidence is covered more fully in a separate course. The entire text is written in outline form, and each chapter ends with a summary of the major points covered.

The book's format is patterned after publications that have enjoyed great success and a high reputation among law students for being easy to understand. Because of the complex nature of criminal procedure, this format should find even greater acceptance among undergraduate students of criminal justice.

Rolando del Carmen

# CRIMINAL PROCEDURE AND EVIDENCE

I. SOURCES OF RIGHTS AND STRUCTURE OF THE COURT SYSTEM ...... 1
   A. **Sources of Rights** ................................................. 1
      1. Constitutions ................................................... 1
      2. Statutes ........................................................ 1
      3. Court Rules .................................................... 1
   B. **The "Incorporation Controversy"** .................................. 1
      1. The Bill of Rights .............................................. 1
         a. Original applicability ..................................... 1
         b. Effect of the 14th Amendment .............................. 1
      2. "Total Incorporation" vs. "Selective Incorporation" .............. 1
         a. Definition of "fundamental" rights ......................... 2
         b. Rights held "fundamental" ................................. 2
         c. Rights not incorporated .................................... 2
      3. Result of Selective Incorporation ............................... 2
   C. **Structure of the Court System** .................................... 2
      1. Dual Court System .............................................. 2
         a. The federal court system .................................. 2
         b. The state court system .................................... 3
   D. **Jurisdiction vs. Venue** ............................................ 3
      1. Jurisdiction Equals Power ....................................... 3
      2. Venue Equals Place ............................................. 3
   E. **Federal vs. State Jurisdiction** .................................... 4
   F. **Summary** ........................................................... 4

II. AN OVERVIEW OF THE CRIMINAL PROCESS ................................. 5
   A. **In General** ........................................................ 5
      1. Procedure Relates to Felony Cases ............................... 5
      2. Variation Among States .......................................... 5
      3. Variation Within a State ........................................ 5
      4. Theory vs. Reality .............................................. 5
   B. **Procedure Prior to Trial** ......................................... 5
      1. Filing of Complaint ............................................. 5
      2. Arrest .......................................................... 5
         a. Arrest with a warrant ..................................... 6
         b. Arrest without a warrant .................................. 6
            (1) Summons or citation ................................... 6
      3. "Booking" at Police Station ..................................... 6
      4. Appearance Before Magistrate After Arrest ....................... 6
         a. Duty to bring arrested person before a magistrate .......... 6
         b. Proceedings before the magistrate .......................... 6
            (1) Arrestee advised of his rights ........................ 6
            (2) Misdemeanors .......................................... 6
            (3) Felonies .............................................. 6
            (4) Temporary disposition ................................. 7
               (a) Bail ............................................. 7
                  1) Setting of bail .............................. 7
                     a) Misdemeanors .......................... 7

i

|  |  |  |  |  |
|---|---|---|---|---|
|  |  | b) | Felonies | 7 |
|  |  |  | 1/ Amount of bail | 7 |
|  |  |  | 2/ Judicial review | 7 |
|  |  | 2) | Modification of bail | 7 |
|  |  | 3) | Bail bondsmen | 7 |
|  |  | 4) | Bail reform | 7 |
|  | (b) | Release on defendant's own recognizance | | 8 |
|  | (c) | Non-bailable offenses | | 8 |
| 5. | Preliminary Examination | | | 8 |
| a. | Purposes of examination | | | 8 |
|  | (1) Determination of probable cause | | | 8 |
|  | (2) Discovery | | | 8 |
|  | (3) Decision on "bind over" | | | 8 |
| b. | Cases in which preliminary examination is not required | | | 8 |
|  | (1) Indictment prior to preliminary examination | | | 8 |
|  | (2) Misdemeanor cases | | | 9 |
|  | (3) Waiver of preliminary examination | | | 9 |
|  | (a) A plea of guilty | | | 9 |
| c. | Scope of preliminary hearing | | | 9 |
| d. | Ruling | | | 9 |
|  | (1) "Hold defendant to answer" | | | 9 |
|  | (2) Discharge the accused | | | 9 |
|  | (3) Reduce the charge | | | 9 |
| 6. | Filing of Accusatory Pleadings | | | 9 |
| a. | Indictment proceedings before grand jury | | | 9 |
|  | (1) Grand jury distinguished from <u>trial</u> (petit) jury | | | 9 |
|  | (2) Defendant's right to grand jury indictment | | | 10 |
|  | (3) Procedure | | | 10 |
|  | (a) Bill of indictment | | | 10 |
|  | (b) Hearings | | | 10 |
|  | 1) Secrecy | | | 10 |
|  | 2) Evidence | | | 10 |
|  | 3) No right to counsel | | | 10 |
|  | (c) Disposition | | | 10 |
| b. | Filing of information | | | 10 |
|  | (1) Requirement of prior preliminary examination | | | 10 |
|  | (2) Contents of the information | | | 10 |
| 7. | Arraignment | | | 11 |
| a. | Accused must be present | | | 11 |
| 8. | Plea by Defendant | | | 11 |
| a. | Types of pleas | | | 11 |
|  | (1) Guilty pleas | | | 11 |
|  | (2) Nolo contendere plea | | | 11 |
|  | (3) Plea of not guilty | | | 11 |
| b. | The guilty plea | | | 12 |
|  | (1) Nature of the guilty plea | | | 12 |
|  | (a) Theory behind requirement | | | 12 |
|  | (b) Guilty plea to avoid death penalty not involuntary | | | 12 |
|  | (c) Plea entered with denial of guilt | | | 12 |
|  | (2) Plea bargaining | | | 12 |

     (a) Plea bargaining results in a guilty plea ..................... 12
     (b) Involuntary plea if bargain coerced ........................ 12
     (c) Right to have bargain kept ................................ 12
    (3) Withdrawing a guilty plea ..................................... 13
     (a) Involuntary pleas ........................................ 13
     (b) Voluntary pleas ......................................... 13
      1) State practices vary ................................. 13

**C. Procedure During Trial** .................................................... 13
 1. Selection of Jurors .......................................................... 13
  a. Jury panel ............................................................. 13
  b. Examination of jurors ................................................. 13
  c. Challenges ............................................................ 14
   (1) Challenge for cause ............................................. 14
   (2) Peremptory challenge ........................................... 14
 2. Opening statements ........................................................ 14
  a. By the prosecution .................................................... 14
  b. By the defense ........................................................ 14
 3. Presentation of Government's Case ........................................ 14
  a. Order of examination of witnesses .................................... 14
 4. Presentation of Defendant's Case .......................................... 14
 5. Motions Prior to Verdict .................................................. 15
  a. Motion for acquittal ................................................... 15
  b. Motion for directed verdict of acquittal ............................... 15
  c. Motion for a mistrial .................................................. 15
 6. Argument After Presentation of Evidence .................................. 15
  a. Order of closing argument ............................................. 15
   (1) Prosecution argument ........................................... 15
   (2) Defense argument ............................................... 15
 7. Instructing the Jury ...................................................... 16
  a. Instructions are given by the judge .................................... 16
  b. Requested instructions ................................................ 16
  c. Ruling on requested instructions ...................................... 16
 8. Jury Deliberations ........................................................ 16
  a. Choice of foreman .................................................... 16
  b. Jury deliberations are secret ........................................... 16
  c. Separation of jurors (sequestration) ................................... 16
 9. Conviction or Acquittal .................................................... 16
  a. Unanimous vote required in federal courts ............................. 16
  b. State courts may authorize non-unanimous vote ....................... 16
  c. Polling of jury ........................................................ 16
  d. Commitment of defendant ............................................. 16

**D. Procedure After Trial** ..................................................... 17
 1. Sentencing ................................................................. 17
 2. Appeal .................................................................... 17

**E. Summary** ................................................................... 17

**III. PROBABLE CAUSE** ........................................................ 18
 **A. What Constitutes Probable Cause** ..................................... 18
  1. Definition ............................................................. 18
   a. "Man of reasonable caution" ...................................... 18

   b. "Reasonable ground" .................................................... 18
   c. Practical requirement ................................................. 18
  2. Court Interpretation of Allegations ......................................... 18
 B. **When Probable Cause is Required** ............................................ 19
  1. Arrests WITH Warrant ........................................................ 19
  2. Arrests WITHOUT Warrant ..................................................... 19
  3. Search and Seizure WITH Warrant ............................................. 19
  4. Search and Seizure WITHOUT Warrant .......................................... 19
   a. In general ............................................................. 19
    (1) Search and seizure incidental to (i.e., immediately after) arrest . 19
    (2) Searches with consent ............................................. 20
    (3) Search where special factors justify the intrusion ............... 20
  5. Differences Among the Four Basic Areas ...................................... 20
   a. "With warrant" vs. "without warrant" ................................... 20
   b. "Arrest" vs. "search and seizure" ...................................... 20
  6. Advantages in Obtaining a Warrant ........................................... 20
  7. Consequences of Lack of Probable Cause ...................................... 20
 C. **How Probable Cause Is Established** .......................................... 20
  1. Officer's Own Knowledge of Particular Facts and Circumstances ............... 21
   a. Relevant factors ....................................................... 21
  2. Information Given by a Reliable Third Person (Informant) .................... 21
   a. Requirements ........................................................... 21
    (1) Reliability of informant .......................................... 21
    (2) Reliability of informant's information ............................ 21
   b. Need for specifics in affidavit ........................................ 21
  3. Information Plus Corroboration .............................................. 22
 D. **Probable Cause vs. Other Levels of Proof** ................................... 22
  1. Absolute Certainty .......................................................... 22
  2. Beyond Reasonable Doubt ..................................................... 22
  3. Clear and Convincing Evidence ............................................... 22
  4. Preponderance of Evidence ................................................... 22
  5. Probable Cause .............................................................. 22
  6. Reasonable Belief ........................................................... 22
  7. Reasonable Doubt ............................................................ 22
  8. Suspicion ................................................................... 22
  9. No Information .............................................................. 22
 E. **Summary** .................................................................... 22

IV. **ARREST, "STOP AND FRISK," AND OTHER FORMS OF DETENTION** .... 24
 A. **Arrest** ..................................................................... 24
  1. Definition .................................................................. 24
  2. Four Essential Elements of Arrest ........................................... 24
   a. Intention to arrest .................................................... 24
    (1) Examples of "non-arrest" .......................................... 24
    (2) Subjectivity ...................................................... 24
   b. Arrest authority ....................................................... 24
   c. Seizure and detention .................................................. 24
    (1) Actual ............................................................ 24
    (2) Constructive ...................................................... 24
   d. Understanding by the individual that he is being arrested .............. 25

iv

|  |  |  |  |  |  |  | |
|---|---|---|---|---|---|---|---|
|  |  |  |  | (1) | How conveyed | 25 |
|  |  |  |  |  | (a) Words | 25 |
|  |  |  |  |  | (b) Actions | 25 |
|  |  |  |  | (2) | Exceptions—understanding not required for arrest | 25 |
|  |  | 3. | Types of Authorized Arrests | | | 25 |
|  |  |  | a. | Arrests with warrant | | 25 |
|  |  |  |  | (1) | Complaint | 25 |
|  |  |  |  | (2) | Issuance of warrant | 25 |
|  |  |  |  |  | (a) Who may issue | 25 |
|  |  |  |  |  | (b) Contents of warrant | 26 |
|  |  |  |  | (3) | Service of warrant | 26 |
|  |  |  |  |  | (a) Service within state | 26 |
|  |  |  |  |  | (b) Service outside state | 26 |
|  |  |  |  |  |     1) "Fresh Pursuit" Act | 26 |
|  |  |  |  |  | (c) Time of arrest | 26 |
|  |  |  |  |  | (d) Possession of warrant | 26 |
|  |  |  |  | (4) | Announcement requirement | 26 |
|  |  |  |  |  | (a) Statutory requirement | 26 |
|  |  |  |  |  |     1) Effect of failure to announce | 26 |
|  |  |  |  |  |     2) Exceptions to the announcement rule | 27 |
|  |  |  |  |  |     3) Breaking into premises after announcement | 27 |
|  |  |  |  |  | (b) Constitutional requirement | 27 |
|  |  |  |  |  |     1) Scope of exceptions | 27 |
|  |  |  |  | (5) | Arrest warrant vs. other processes for arrest | 27 |
|  |  |  |  |  | (a) Summons or citation | 27 |
|  |  |  |  |  | (b) Search warrants | 27 |
|  |  |  |  |  | (c) Bench warrants | 28 |
|  |  |  | b. | Arrests without warrant | | 28 |
|  |  |  |  | (1) | Arrests by police | 28 |
|  |  |  |  |  | (a) Arrests by police for felonies | 28 |
|  |  |  |  |  | (b) Arrests by police for misdemeanors | 28 |
|  |  |  |  | (2) | Arrests by citizens | 28 |
|  |  | 4. | Use of Force During Arrest | | | 28 |
|  |  |  | a. | Use of reasonable force | | 28 |
|  |  |  | b. | What constitutes reasonable force | | 29 |
|  |  |  | c. | Use of deadly force | | 29 |
|  |  |  |  | (1) | In felony cases | 29 |
|  |  |  |  | (2) | In misdemeanor cases | 29 |
|  |  |  | d. | Handcuffing | | 29 |
|  |  | 5. | Disposition of Prisoner After Arrest | | | 29 |
|  |  |  | a. | "Initial appearance" | | 29 |
|  |  |  | b. | Purposes of initial appearance | | 29 |
|  |  |  | c. | "*Miranda* warnings" | | 30 |
| B. | "Stop and Frisk" | | | | | 30 |
|  | 1. | Definition | | | | 30 |
|  | 2. | Authorization for "Stop and Frisk" | | | | 30 |
|  |  | a. | By statute | | | 30 |
|  |  | b. | By judicial approval | | | 30 |
|  |  |  | (1) | Justification | | 30 |
|  | 3. | Guidelines | | | | 30 |

v

|   |   |   | | |
|---|---|---|---|---|
| | | a. | Circumstances | 30 |
| | | b. | What police officer must initially do | 30 |
| | | c. | Extent of what an officer can do | 31 |
| | 4. | Two Separate Acts Involved | | 31 |
| | | a. | A "stop" | 31 |
| | | b. | A "frisk" | 31 |
| | 5. | Other Considerations in a "Stop and Frisk" | | 31 |
| | | a. | Extent of risk | 31 |
| | | b. | Admissibility of evidence obtained | 31 |
| | | c. | No "fishing expeditions" allowed | 31 |
| | | d. | Drivers are subject to the practice | 31 |
| | 6. | Distinctions Between "Stop and Frisk" and Arrest or Search and Seizure | | 32 |
| C. | **Other Forms of Detention** | | | 32 |
| | 1. | Station House Detention | | 32 |
| | | a. | Purposes | 32 |
| | | b. | Can suspect be taken to police station? | 32 |
| | 2. | Roadblocks | | 32 |
| | | a. | Legality | 33 |
| | 3. | Airport Searches | | 33 |
| | 4. | Arrests by Bondsmen | | 33 |
| | | a. | Status of bondsman | 33 |
| D. | **Summary** | | | 33 |

## V. SEARCHES AND SEIZURES ... 34

|   |   |   | | |
|---|---|---|---|---|
| A. | **Definitions** | | | 34 |
| | 1. | "Search" | | 34 |
| | 2. | "Seizure" | | 34 |
| B. | **Types of Search or Seizure** | | | 34 |
| | 1. | Search WITH Warrant | | 34 |
| | | a. | General rule | 34 |
| | | b. | Basic requirements | 34 |
| | | | (1) Probable cause | 34 |
| | | | (2) Support by oath or affirmation | 34 |
| | | | (3) Particular description of place to be searched and person or things to be seized | 35 |
| | | | (4) Warrant must be signed by a magistrate | 35 |
| | | c. | Procedure for service of warrant | 35 |
| | | d. | Announcement requirement for searches and seizures | 36 |
| | | | (1) Statutory requirement | 36 |
| | | |    (a) Effect of failure to announce | 36 |
| | | |    (b) Exceptions to requirement | 36 |
| | | |    (c) Breaking into premises after announcement | 36 |
| | | | (2) Constitutional requirement | 36 |
| | | |    (a) Exceptions | 36 |
| | | e. | Oral warrants | 37 |
| | 2. | Searches WITHOUT a Search Warrant | | 37 |
| | | a. | Searches incident to a lawful arrest | 37 |
| | | | (1) The arrest itself must be lawful | 37 |
| | | | (2) The search must be limited in scope | 37 |
| | | |    (a) Suspect taken into custody—full search of person permitted | 37 |

|  |  |  |  |  |
|---|---|---|---|---|
|  |  | (b) | Suspect taken into custody—search of area within immediate reach permitted | 37 |
|  |  |  | 1) "Area" liberally defined | 38 |
|  |  |  | 2) Exigent circumstances | 38 |
|  |  | (c) | Relevant time frame | 38 |
|  |  | (d) | Suspect not taken into custody | 38 |
|  | b. | Searches with consent of accused |  | 38 |
|  |  | (1) | Consent must be voluntary | 38 |
|  |  | (2) | Consent to enter does not necessarily mean consent to search | 38 |
|  |  |  | (a) "Plain view" doctrine | 39 |
|  |  | (3) | Warning of rights not required | 39 |
|  |  | (4) | Scope of search | 39 |
|  |  | (5) | Revocation of consent | 39 |
|  |  | (6) | WHO may give consent to search | 39 |
|  |  |  | (a) Landlord—No | 39 |
|  |  |  | (b) Hotel clerk—No | 39 |
|  |  |  | (c) Co-occupant—Yes, with exceptions | 39 |
|  | c. | Situations where special factors justify intrusion without a warrant |  | 40 |
|  |  | (1) | Emergency searches or seizures justified by "exigent circumstances" | 40 |
|  |  | (2) | Automobile searches | 40 |
|  |  |  | (a) In general | 40 |
|  |  |  | (b) Reasons for permitting auto searches | 40 |
|  |  |  | (c) Specific situations | 40 |
|  |  |  |     1) Moving vehicles | 40 |
|  |  |  |         a) "Fleeting target" rationale | 41 |
|  |  |  |         b) Probable cause as to contents of car | 41 |
|  |  |  |         c) Delayed search of vehicle stopped on highway | 41 |
|  |  |  |     2) Example | 41 |
|  |  |  |     3) Vehicles impounded by police | 41 |
|  |  |  |     4) Vehicles parked in driveway or on street—items in "plain view" | 42 |
|  |  |  |         a) Seizure of evidence may require warrant | 42 |
|  |  | (3) | Searches in "hot pursuit" (or "fresh pursuit") of dangerous suspects | 42 |
|  |  | (4) | Goods in the course of transit | 42 |
|  |  | (5) | Mail searches | 42 |
|  |  | (6) | Border searches | 42 |
|  |  |  | (a) Persons searched | 42 |
|  |  |  | (b) "Border area" | 43 |
|  |  | (7) | "Stop and frisk" searches | 43 |
| C. | Items Subject to Search and Seizure |  |  | 43 |
|  | 1. | Contraband |  | 43 |
|  | 2. | Fruits of the Crime |  | 43 |
|  | 3. | Instrumentalities of Crime |  | 43 |
|  | 4. | "Mere Evidence" of the Crime |  | 43 |
| D. | General Guide in Search and Seizure Cases |  |  | 43 |
| E. | Summary |  |  | 44 |

## VI. PLAIN VIEW, OPEN FIELDS, ABANDONMENT AND ELECTRONIC SURVEILLANCE ... 45
### A. "Plain View" Doctrine ... 45
1. Requirements ... 45
   a. Items must be within officer's sight ... 45
   b. Officer must legally be in the place from which he sees the items ... 45
   c. Officer must have no prior knowledge that such items are present ... 45
   d. Items must be immediately recognizable as subject to seizure ... 46
   e. Items must actually be subject to seizure ... 46
2. Justification for Doctrine ... 46
### B. "Open Fields" Doctrine ... 46
1. Justification ... 46
2. Areas not Included in the "Open Field" Doctrine ... 46
   a. Houses ... 46
   b. Curtilage ... 46
      (1) Scope of coverage ... 46
         (a) Residential yards ... 46
         (b) Fenced areas ... 47
         (c) Apartment houses ... 47
         (d) Barns and other outbuildings ... 47
         (e) Garages ... 47
   c. Areas as to which there is a reasonable expectation of privacy ... 47
3. Comparison of "Open Fields" and "Plain View" ... 47
### C. Abandonment ... 47
1. Justification ... 48
2. When Items are Considered Abandoned ... 48
   a. Where the property is left ... 48
      (1) Property left in open field or public place ... 48
      (2) Property left in private premises ... 48
   b. Intent to abandon ... 48
3. Reasonable Expectation of Privacy ... 48
4. Comparison of Abandonment and "Plain View" ... 49
### D. Electronic Surveillance ... 49
1. Constitutional Limitations ... 49
   a. "Search" includes any form of electronic surveillance ... 49
      (1) Former rule ... 49
   b. Warrant requirements under the 4th Amendment ... 49
   c. Without warrant, police may listen in with consent of either party ... 50
   d. Transmission and recording with consent of either party ... 50
      (1) Limitation under state statutes ... 50
2. Statutory Limitations ... 50
### E. Summary ... 50

## VII. THE EXCLUSIONARY RULE ... 52
### A. Purpose ... 52
### B. Scope of Rule ... 52
1. Historical Development ... 52
   a. Federal courts ... 52
   b. State courts ... 52

|   |   |   | 2. | Does Not Apply to Private Searches | 52 |
|---|---|---|---|---|---|
|   |   |   | 3. | Does Not Apply in Grand Jury Investigations | 53 |
|   |   |   | 4. | May Not Apply to Parole Revocation Hearings | 53 |
|   |   |   | 5. | May Not Apply to Post-Conviction Sentencing | 53 |
|   |   | C. | **Exception to Exclusionary Rule—Illegally Obtained Evidence Admissible for Impeachment** | | 53 |
|   |   |   | 1. | Reason for Exception | 53 |
|   |   | D. | **What is Excluded Under the Rule** | | 53 |
|   |   |   | 1. | Illegally Seized Evidence | 53 |
|   |   |   | 2. | "Fruits" of the Illegal Search or Seizure | 53 |
|   |   | E. | **Procedure for Invoking the Exclusionary Rule** | | 53 |
|   |   |   | 1. | Motion to Suppress | 53 |
|   |   |   | 2. | Burden of Proof | 54 |
|   |   | F. | **Effect of Violation of Exclusionary Rule** | | 54 |
|   |   |   | 1. | Requirements to Demonstrate "Harmless Error" | 54 |
|   |   |   | 2. | "Other Sufficient Evidence" Not Enough | 54 |
|   |   | G. | **The Future of the Exclusionary Rule** | | 54 |
|   |   |   | 1. | Failure to Deter Misconduct | 54 |
|   |   |   | 2. | Possible Modifications | 54 |
|   |   | H. | **Summary** | | 55 |
| VIII. | **ADMISSIONS AND CONFESSIONS; IDENTIFICATION PROCEDURES** | | | | 56 |
|   | A. | **Admissions and Confessions** | | | 56 |
|   |   | 1. | Constitutional Requirement of Voluntariness | | 56 |
|   |   |   | a. | What constitutes "coercion" | 56 |
|   |   |   |   | (1) Current test | 56 |
|   |   |   |   | (2) Relevant factors | 56 |
|   |   |   | b. | Procedure for determining admissibility of alleged "involuntary" statements | 56 |
|   |   |   |   | (1) State procedures vary | 57 |
|   |   |   |   |     (a) New York rule | 57 |
|   |   |   |   |     (b) California rule | 57 |
|   |   |   |   |     (c) Massachusetts rule | 57 |
|   |   |   | c. | Effect of using involuntary or coerced confession—automatic reversal | 57 |
|   |   | 2. | Exclusion of Voluntary Statements | | 57 |
|   |   |   | a. | *Escobedo* rule | 57 |
|   |   |   | b. | *Miranda* rule | 57 |
|   |   |   |   | (1) Facts of the case | 57 |
|   |   |   |   | (2) Issue before the Court | 58 |
|   |   |   |   | (3) Decision | 58 |
|   |   |   |   | (4) Aftermath | 58 |
|   |   |   | c. | The *Miranda* warnings | 58 |
|   |   |   | d. | Waiver | 58 |
|   |   |   |   | (1) Waiver must be INTELLIGENT and VOLUNTARY | 58 |
|   |   |   |   | (2) Proof of voluntary waiver | 59 |
|   |   |   | e. | Stage at which *Miranda* warnings must be given | 59 |
|   |   |   |   | (1) When person is under arrest | 59 |
|   |   |   |   | (2) When person is not under arrest but is "deprived of his freedom in any significant way" | 59 |
|   |   |   |   |     (a) Questioning at the scene of the crime | 59 |

|          |           |           | (b) Questioning at police station | 60 |
|---|---|---|---|---|
|          |           |           | (c) Questioning in police cars | 60 |
|          |           |           | (d) Questioning in homes | 60 |
|          |           |           | (e) Questioning when defendant is in custody on another offense | 60 |
|          |           | f. | Situations in which no warnings required | 60 |
|          |           | (1) | General on-the-scene questioning | 60 |
|          |           | (2) | "Volunteered confessions" | 60 |
|          |           | (3) | Statements or confessions made to private persons | 60 |
|          |           | (4) | Appearance of potential criminal defendant before a grand jury | 61 |
|          |           | g. | Specific applications of the *Miranda* rule | 61 |
|          |           | (1) | Use of statements to impeach the accused | 61 |
|          |           | (2) | Subsequent questioning on unrelated offense | 61 |
|          |           | (3) | Voluntary statements | 61 |
|          |           | h. | Effects of *Miranda* rule on the voluntariness rule | 61 |
|          |           | i. | Unresolved questions on the *Miranda* rule | 62 |
|    B.    | Identification Procedures | | | 63 |
|          | 1. | Basic Types of Procedures | | 63 |
|          |           | a. | Lineups | 63 |
|          |           | b. | Showups | 63 |
|          |           | c. | Photographic identification (rogue's gallery) | 63 |
|          | 2. | Rights of Suspects During Identification Stage | | 63 |
|          |           | a. | Right to counsel | 63 |
|          |           | (1) | Lineups—may have right to counsel | 63 |
|          |           | (2) | Other identification procedures—no right to counsel | 63 |
|          |           |           | (a) Photographic identifications | 63 |
|          |           |           | (b) Pretrial interviews | 63 |
|          |           |           | (c) Showups | 63 |
|          |           |           | (d) Obtaining physical samples from suspect | 64 |
|          |           | b. | Privilege against self-incrimination | 64 |
|          |           | c. | Right to due process of law | 64 |
|          |           | (1) | What amounts to "unfairness" | 64 |
|          |           |           | (a) Compare—necessity for prompt identification | 65 |
|    C.    | Summary | | | 65 |

## IX. THE TRIAL ITSELF—CONSTITUTIONAL SAFEGUARDS AND LIMITATIONS .......... 66

|    A.    | In General | | | 66 |
|---|---|---|---|---|
|          | 1. | Rights Apply to All Criminal Proceedings | | 66 |
|          | 2. | Statutes May Supplement Constitutional Safeguards | | 66 |
|    B.    | **Right to Counsel** | | | 66 |
|          | 1. | Constitutional Basis for Right | | 66 |
|          |           | a. | Effect | 66 |
|          |           | b. | Underlying theory | 66 |
|          | 2. | Definition of "Right to Counsel" | | 67 |
|          |           | a. | Retained counsel | 67 |
|          |           | b. | Court-appointed counsel | 67 |
|          |           | (1) | Who an "indigent" is | 67 |
|          |           | (2) | How appointments are made | 67 |
|          |           | (3) | Indigent has no right to a specific attorney | 67 |
|          | 3. | Proceedings in Which Right to Counsel Applies | | 67 |

|  |  |  |  |
|---|---|---|---|
|  | a. | Where felony or actual imprisonment is at issue | 67 |
|  | b. | Effect | 67 |
|  |  | (1) Juvenile proceedings | 68 |
|  |  | (2) Parole or probation revocation | 68 |
| 4. | Proceedings at Which Right to Counsel (Retained or Appointed) Does NOT Apply | | 68 |
|  | a. | Grand jury | 68 |
|  | b. | Purely investigative proceedings | 68 |
|  | c. | Police lineup prior to charges being filed | 68 |
|  | d. | Prison discipline | 68 |
|  | e. | Military proceedings | 68 |
| 5. | Stages (as Opposed to Types of Proceedings) at Which Right to Counsel Applies | | 68 |
|  | a. | The trial itself | 68 |
|  | b. | Custodial interrogations | 69 |
|  | c. | Noncustodial interrogations after the accused has been formally charged | 69 |
|  | d. | A post-indictment "lineup" | 69 |
|  | e. | A preliminary hearing | 69 |
|  | f. | Sentencing | 69 |
| 6. | Right to "Effective Counsel" | | 69 |
|  | a. | What constitutes "effective counsel" | 69 |
|  | b. | Advising defendant to plead guilty | 69 |
|  | c. | Representation of defendant during trial | 69 |
| 7. | Effect of Denial of Right to Counsel | | 70 |
|  | a. | At trial, plea or sentencing—automatic reversal | 70 |
|  | b. | At earlier stages—judged by "harmless error" standard | 70 |
| 8. | Waiver of Right to Counsel | | 70 |
|  | a. | Constitutional right to act as own counsel | 70 |
|  | b. | Requirements for effective waiver | 70 |
|  |  | (1) Accused must be fully advised of right to counsel | 70 |
|  |  | (2) Waiver must be expressed | 70 |
|  |  | (3) Court must determine the competency of the accused | 70 |

**C. Right to A Speedy and Public Trial** .......... 70
   1. Constitutional Basis for Right .......... 70
      a. Speedy trial .......... 71
         (1) When right to speedy trial attaches .......... 71
         (2) Determining whether delay is unreasonable .......... 71
            (a) Length of delay .......... 71
            (b) Reason for delay .......... 71
            (c) Defendant's assertion or non-assertion of right .......... 71
            (d) Prejudice to defendant .......... 71
         (3) Only remedy is dismissal .......... 71
         (4) Statutory provisions .......... 72
      b. Public trial .......... 72
         (1) Exclusion of spectators from courtroom .......... 72
         (2) Who may object to such exclusions .......... 72

**D. Right to Trial by Jury** .......... 72
   1. Constitutional Basis .......... 72
      a. Size of jury .......... 72

|   |   |   | b. Unanimous verdict | 72 |
|---|---|---|---|---|
|   | 2. | Serious vs. Petty Offenses | | 73 |
|   |   | a. Standard used | | 73 |
|   | 3. | Waiver of Right | | 73 |
|   |   | a. Prosecution's right to a jury trial | | 73 |
|   | 4. | Selection of Jurors | | 73 |
|   |   | a. Must be from fair cross-section of community | | 73 |
| E. | **The Right to a Fair and Impartial Trial** | | | 73 |
|   | 1. | Constitutional Basis | | 73 |
|   | 2. | Prejudicial Publicity | | 74 |
|   |   | a. The problem | | 74 |
|   |   | b. Methods of controlling impact of prejudicial publicity | | 74 |
|   |   |   | (1) Change of venue | 74 |
|   |   |   | (2) Sequestration | 74 |
|   |   |   | (3) Continuance | 74 |
|   |   |   | (4) Control of participating counsel | 74 |
|   |   |   | (5) Control of the police | 74 |
|   |   |   | (6) Control of the press | 74 |
|   | 3. | Remedy if Right is Violated | | 75 |
|   | 4. | Right to Competent and Impartial Judge | | 75 |
|   |   | a. Competency—legal training | | 75 |
|   |   | b. Impartiality | | 75 |
| F. | **Right to Confrontation of Witnesses** | | | 75 |
|   | 1. | Constitutional Basis for Rights | | 75 |
|   | 2. | Proceedings in Which Right Exists | | 75 |
|   | 3. | Scope of Right | | 75 |
|   |   | a. Right of cross-examination | | 76 |
|   |   | b. Right to be physically present | | 76 |
|   |   |   | (1) Deliberate absence | 76 |
|   |   |   | (2) Disruptive conduct in courtroom | 76 |
|   |   | c. Right to know identity of prosecution witnesses | | 76 |
| G. | **Right to Compulsory Process to Obtain Witnesses** | | | 76 |
|   | 1. | Constitutional Basis for Right | | 76 |
|   | 2. | Scope of Right | | 76 |
|   |   | a. Intimidation by judge | | 76 |
|   |   | b. Exclusion of crucial evidence | | 76 |
| H. | **Privilege Against Self-Incrimination** | | | 77 |
|   | 1. | Constitutional Basis for Right | | 77 |
|   | 2. | Reason for Privilege | | 77 |
|   | 3. | Scope of Privilege | | 77 |
|   |   | a. Privilege applies only to natural persons (i.e., human beings) | | 77 |
|   |   | b. Protects only against testimonial self-incrimination | | 77 |
|   |   | c. Does not protect <u>production of records</u> | | 77 |
|   | 4. | Two Separate Privileges | | 77 |
|   |   | a. Privilege of the accused | | 77 |
|   |   |   | (1) Prosecutor cannot comment on assertion of right not to testify | 77 |
|   |   |   | (2) When privilege applies | 77 |
|   |   |   | (3) Waiver by taking witness stand | 78 |
|   |   | b. Privilege of a witness | | 78 |
|   |   |   | (1) When privilege applies | 78 |

|      |      | (2)  | Meaning of "tend to incriminate" | 78 |
|------|------|------|-----|----|
|      |      |      | (a) No protection if no danger of criminal liability | 78 |
|      |      | (3)  | Who decides whether answer "tends to incriminate" | 78 |
|      |      | (4)  | Effect of granting immunity | 79 |
|      |      | (5)  | Waiver of witness privilege | 79 |
|      |      |      | (a) Failure to assert | 79 |
|      |      |      | (b) Partial disclosure | 79 |
|      |      |      | (c) Accused taking the witness stand | 79 |
|      | **I.** | **Right to Proof of Guilt Beyond Reasonable Doubt** | | 79 |
|      |      | 1.   | Constitutional Basis for Right | 79 |
|      |      | 2.   | Scope of Right | 80 |
|      |      | 3.   | What Constitutes "Reasonable Doubt" | 80 |
|      |      | 4.   | Proceedings in Which "Reasonable Doubt" Standard Applies | 80 |
|      |      | 5.   | Presumptions—"Rational Connection" Required | 80 |
|      | **J.** | **Right to Protection Against Double Jeopardy** | | 80 |
|      |      | 1.   | Constitutional Basis for Right | 80 |
|      |      | 2.   | Scope of Protection | 80 |
|      |      | 3.   | When Double Jeopardy Attaches | 80 |
|      |      | 4.   | When Double Jeopardy is Deemed to be Waived | 81 |
|      |      |      | a. In mistrials | 81 |
|      |      |      | b. When verdict of conviction is set aside on defendant's motion or appeal | 81 |
|      |      |      | c. Where first trial ends in "hung" jury | 81 |
|      |      | 5.   | Double Jeopardy Applies Only to Prosecution for the "Same Offense" | 82 |
|      |      |      | a. What constitutes the "same offense" | 82 |
|      |      | 6.   | State Crimes vs. Federal Crimes—Separate Sovereignties | 82 |
|      |      | 7.   | Limitations on Consecutive Prosecutions—the Doctrine of Collateral Estoppel | 82 |
|      | **K.** | **Summary** | | 83 |
| **X.** | **SENTENCING** | | | 84 |
|      | **A.** | **General Considerations** | | 84 |
|      |      | 1.   | Court Imposes Sentences | 84 |
|      |      | 2.   | When Sentence Imposed | 84 |
|      |      | 3.   | Wide Discretion Allowed | 84 |
|      |      | 4.   | Pre-Sentence Investigation Report | 84 |
|      |      | 5.   | Types of Sentences | 84 |
|      |      | 6.   | Sentence Involving Imprisonment | 85 |
|      |      |      | a. Determinate sentences | 85 |
|      |      |      | b. Indeterminate sentences | 85 |
|      |      | 7.   | Concurrent or Consecutive Sentences | 85 |
|      |      | 8.   | Right of Accused During Sentencing | 85 |
|      |      |      | a. Right to counsel | 85 |
|      |      |      | b. "Right of allocution" | 85 |
|      |      |      | c. Other rights | 85 |
|      | **B.** | **Constitutional Limitations on Sentencing** | | 85 |
|      |      | 1.   | Prohibition Against Cruel and Unusual Punishment | 86 |
|      |      |      | a. Nature of punishment itself | 86 |
|      |      |      | b. Whether punishment fits the crime | 86 |
|      |      |      | c. Capital punishment | 86 |
|      |      | 2.   | Prohibition Against Double Jeopardy | 86 |

xiii

|   |   |   |   | |
|---|---|---|---|---|
|   |   | a. | Cannot increase sentence during imprisonment | 86 |
|   |   | b. | Can impose longer sentence after retrial | 87 |
|   |   |   | (1) When judge imposes longer sentence | 87 |
|   |   |   | (2) When jury imposes longer sentence | 87 |
|   |   | c. | Full credit given for time served | 87 |
|   | 3. | The Equal Protection Clause |   | 87 |
|   |   | a. | Inability to pay fine | 87 |
| C. | **Probation** |   |   | 88 |
|   | 1. | Convict Not Entitled to Probation as Matter of Right |   | 88 |
|   | 2. | Terms of Probation |   | 88 |
|   | 3. | Need for Acceptance by Probationer |   | 88 |
|   | 4. | Revocation of Probation |   | 88 |
|   |   | a. | Commission of a <u>new criminal offense</u> | 88 |
|   |   | b. | <u>Technical violation</u> | 88 |
|   | 5. | Rights of Probationer Concerning Revocation |   | 88 |
|   |   | a. | Minimal procedural due process | 88 |
|   |   | b. | Two-step procedure for revocation | 89 |
| D. | **Summary** |   |   | 89 |

## XI. KINDS OF EVIDENCE—PROCEDURE FOR ADMITTING OR EXCLUDING EVIDENCE ... 90

|   |   |   | |
|---|---|---|---|
| A. | **Evidence Defined** |   | 90 |
|   | 1. | "Admissible" vs. "Inadmissible" Evidence | 90 |
|   | 2. | "Evidence" vs. "Proof" | 90 |
|   | 3. | "Evidence" vs. "Testimony" | 90 |
| B. | **Forms of Evidence** |   | 90 |
|   | 1. | Real Evidence | 90 |
|   |   | a. Need for identification | 90 |
|   | 2. | Documentary Evidence | 90 |
|   |   | a. Need for identification | 90 |
|   | 3. | Testimonial Evidence | 90 |
|   | 4. | Judicial Notice | 91 |
| C. | **Types of Evidence** |   | 91 |
|   | 1. | Direct Evidence | 91 |
|   | 2. | Circumstantial Evidence | 91 |
|   |   | a. Admissibility | 91 |
|   | 3. | Cumulative Evidence | 91 |
|   | 4. | Corroborative Evidence | 92 |
| D. | **Basic Requirements for Admissibility of Evidence: Relevancy and Materiality** | | 92 |
|   | 1. | Relevancy | 92 |
|   |   | a. Tend to prove | 92 |
|   |   | b. Only relevant evidence is admissible | 92 |
|   | 2. | Materiality | 92 |
|   |   | a. When is a fact properly in issue | 92 |
|   | 3. | Modern trends | 92 |
| E. | **How Evidence is Introduced** | | 92 |
|   | 1. | Testimonial Evidence | 92 |
|   | 2. | Real or Documentary Evidence | 93 |
| F. | **How Question of Admissibility Arises** | | 93 |
|   | 1. | "Objection Sustained" | 93 |

  2. "Objection Overruled" ............................................................. 93
  3. Purposes Served by an Objection ............................................ 93
 G. **Rulings on Admissibility of Evidence in Trial Court** ......................... 93
  1. Preponderance of Evidence ...................................................... 93
  2. Weight and Credibility ............................................................. 93
  3. Where No Objection is Made .................................................. 93
   a. Exception ........................................................................... 94
 H. **Appellate Review of Trial Court Rulings on Admissibility** ................. 94
  1. Evidence Erroneously Admitted—Requirements for Reversal on Appeal . 94
   a. Specific objection ............................................................... 94
    (1) Reason for requirement ............................................... 94
   b. Timely made ..................................................................... 94
    (1) Motion to strike ......................................................... 94
     (a) Time of making motion ....................................... 95
   c. Ground for objection must be valid .................................. 95
   d. Prejudicial error in overruling objection ............................ 95
  2. Evidence Erroneously Excluded—Requirements for Reversal on Appeal.. 95
   a. Requisites for reversal ........................................................ 95
    (1) No valid ground for exclusion .................................... 95
    (2) Offer of proof made at trial ....................................... 95
     (a) Reason for requirement ........................................ 95
    (3) Prejudicial error ......................................................... 95
 I. **Summary** ............................................................................................. 96

XII. **WITNESSES AND PRIVILEGED COMMUNICATIONS** ..................... 97
 A. **Competency to Testify** ...................................................................... 97
  1. General Rules on Competency ................................................. 97
   a. Old English law ................................................................. 97
   b. Modern law ....................................................................... 97
  2. Basic Qualifications to be a Witness ........................................ 97
   a. Ability to <u>communicate</u> ..................................................... 97
   b. Understanding of duty to <u>tell the truth</u> ............................ 97
   c. <u>Personal knowledge</u> of the facts ........................................ 97
  3. Specific Examples of Competency ............................................ 97
   a. Children .............................................................................. 97
   b. Mentally impaired persons ................................................ 97
   c. Criminals ............................................................................ 97
 B. **Method and Scope of Examining Witnesses** ..................................... 97
  1. Direct Examination ................................................................... 98
   a. How presented ................................................................... 98
   b. Form of questioning .......................................................... 98
    (1) Questions calling for conclusions ................................ 98
    (2) Repetitive questions ..................................................... 98
    (3) Narrative questioning .................................................. 98
   c. Use of leading questions prohibited .................................. 98
    (1) Exceptions ................................................................... 98
   d. Effect of lack of memory .................................................. 98
    (1) "Present recollection revived" ..................................... 99
     (a) Anything may be used ......................................... 99
    (2) "Past recollection recorded" ........................................ 99

|   |   |   | (3) Distinctions between the above concepts | 99 |
|---|---|---|---|---|
|   | 2. | Cross-examination | | 100 |
|   |   | a. | Method of cross-examination | 100 |
|   |   |   | (1) Leading questions permitted | 100 |
|   |   |   | (2) Improper questions | 100 |
|   |   |   |    (a) Misleading questions | 100 |
|   |   |   |    (b) Compound questions | 100 |
|   |   |   |    (c) Argumentative questions | 100 |
|   |   |   |    (d) Questions which assume facts not in evidence | 100 |
|   |   |   |    (e) Conclusionary questions | 100 |
|   |   | b. | Scope of cross-examination | 100 |
|   |   |   | (1) Majority view—restricted scope | 100 |
|   |   |   | (2) Minority view—wide open | 100 |
|   | 3. | Redirect Examination | | 100 |
|   |   | a. | Scope of redirect examination | 101 |
|   | 4. | Recross Examination | | 101 |
| C. | **Opinion Testimony** | | | 101 |
|   | 1. | General Rule—Opinion Testimony <u>Not</u> Admissible | | 101 |
|   | 2. | When is Witness' Statement an "Opinion" | | 101 |
|   | 3. | Types of Opinion Testimony | | 101 |
|   |   | a. | Opinion testimony by lay witnesses | 101 |
|   |   |   | (1) Physical conditions | 101 |
|   |   |   | (2) Physical descriptions | 101 |
|   |   |   | (3) Identity of a person | 101 |
|   |   |   | (4) Sanity | 102 |
|   |   |   | (5) Handwriting | 102 |
|   |   | b. | Opinion testimony by experts | 102 |
|   |   |   | (1) Procedure to qualify witness as an expert | 102 |
|   |   |   |    (a) Factors considered | 102 |
|   |   |   |       1) Technical expertise and high education are <u>not</u> always required | 102 |
|   |   |   |       2) Key factor is helpfulness to jury | 102 |
|   |   |   | (2) Areas in which expert opinion may be needed | 102 |
|   |   |   | (3) Effect of expert opinion | 102 |
|   |   |   |    (a) Limitation | 102 |
| D. | **Impeachment of Witnesses** | | | 102 |
|   | 1. | Definition and Effect | | 102 |
|   | 2. | Methods of Impeachment | | 103 |
|   |   | a. | Cross-examination | 103 |
|   |   | b. | Use of extrinsic evidence | 103 |
|   | 3. | Grounds for Impeachment | | 103 |
|   |   | a. | Bias and interest | 103 |
|   |   | b. | Lack of character for honesty and truthfulness | 103 |
|   |   |   | (1) Conviction for any felony | 103 |
|   |   |   |    (a) Effect of juvenile adjudication | 103 |
|   |   |   |    (b) Effect of pardon | 103 |
|   |   |   | (2) Misconduct not the subject of criminal conviction | 103 |
|   |   |   | (3) Poor reputation for truthfulness | 104 |
|   |   | c. | Prior inconsistent statements | 104 |
|   |   |   | (1) "Laying a foundation" | 104 |

|   |   | d. | Defects in capacity | 104 |
|---|---|---|---|---|
|   |   | e. | Lack of knowledge | 104 |
|   |   | f. | Contradiction | 104 |
|   |   |   | (1) No impeachment on a collateral matter | 104 |
|   |   |   |     (a) Judge determines whether matter is collateral | 104 |
|   | 4. | Rehabilitation |  | 105 |
| E. | **Privileged Communications** |  |  | 105 |
|   | 1. | "Privilege" Defined |  | 105 |
|   | 2. | Purpose |  | 105 |
|   | 3. | Waiver of Privilege |  | 105 |
|   |   | a. | Failure to claim | 105 |
|   |   | b. | Voluntary disclosure or consent | 105 |
|   | 4. | What Communications are Privileged |  | 105 |
|   |   | a. | Lawyer-client privilege | 105 |
|   |   |   | (1) Basic rule | 105 |
|   |   |   |     (a) Reason for privilege | 105 |
|   |   |   | (2) Who is "holder" of privilege | 105 |
|   |   |   | (3) Requirements for exercising lawyer-client privilege | 106 |
|   |   |   |     (a) Client | 106 |
|   |   |   |     (b) Lawyer | 106 |
|   |   |   |     (c) "Communication" | 106 |
|   |   |   |         1) Consultation enough | 106 |
|   |   |   |         2) Documents | 106 |
|   |   |   |     (d) "Confidential" | 106 |
|   |   |   |         1) Presence of third persons | 106 |
|   |   |   |         2) Employees of attorney | 106 |
|   |   |   | (4) Exceptions to the privilege | 106 |
|   |   | b. | Privilege not to testify against spouse | 106 |
|   |   |   | (1) Basic rule | 106 |
|   |   |   |     (a) Reason for privilege | 106 |
|   |   |   | (2) Holder of the privilege | 107 |
|   |   |   | (3) Requirements for the use of privilege | 107 |
|   |   |   | (4) Exceptions | 107 |
|   |   | c. | Privilege for confidential marital communications | 107 |
|   |   |   | (1) Basic rule | 107 |
|   |   |   |     (a) Reason for privilege | 107 |
|   |   |   | (2) Distinguished from privilege against special testimony | 107 |
|   |   |   | (3) Holder of the privilege | 107 |
|   |   |   | (4) Requirements for use of privilege | 107 |
|   |   |   | (5) Exceptions to privilege | 108 |
|   |   | d. | Physician-patient privilege | 108 |
|   |   |   | (1) Basic rule | 108 |
|   |   |   | (2) Holder of the privilege | 108 |
|   |   |   | (3) Requirements for exercise of the privilege | 108 |
|   |   |   |     (a) "Communication" | 108 |
|   |   |   |     (b) "Physician" | 109 |
|   |   |   |     (c) "Confidential" | 109 |
|   |   |   | (4) Exceptions to privilege | 109 |
|   |   | e. | Psychotherapist-patient privilege | 109 |
|   |   | f. | Clergyman-penitent privilege | 109 |

xvii

|  |  |  |  |  |
|---|---|---|---|---|
|  |  | (1) | Basic rule | 109 |
|  |  | (2) | Holders of the privilege | 110 |
|  |  |  | (a) The penitent | 110 |
|  |  |  | (b) The clergyman | 110 |
|  |  | (3) | Requirements for exercise of the privilege | 110 |
|  | g. | Identity-of-informer privilege | | 110 |
|  |  | (1) | Basic rule | 110 |
|  |  |  | (a) Exception | 110 |
| F. | **Summary** | | | 110 |

## XIII. THE HEARSAY RULE AND ITS EXCEPTIONS ... 112

| | | | | |
|---|---|---|---|---|
| A. | **Statement of the Rule** | | | 112 |
| | 1. | What Constitutes "Hearsay" | | 112 |
| | 2. | Reasons for Excluding Hearsay | | 112 |
| | 3. | Forms of Hearsay | | 112 |
| | | a. | Oral statements | 112 |
| | | b. | Writings | 112 |
| | | c. | Assertive conduct | 112 |
| | 4. | Test to Determine Oral Hearsay | | 112 |
| B. | **Exceptions to the Hearsay Rule** | | | 112 |
| | 1. | Confessions | | 113 |
| | | a. | Definition | 113 |
| | | b. | Reason for admission | 113 |
| | | c. | How presented in court | 113 |
| | | d. | Requirements for admissibility | 113 |
| | | | (1) Confession must be voluntary | 113 |
| | | | (2) No violation of defendant's rights | 113 |
| | 2. | Dying declarations | | 113 |
| | | a. | Definition | 113 |
| | | b. | Reason for admission | 113 |
| | | c. | How presented in court | 113 |
| | | d. | Form | 113 |
| | | e. | Type of action in which admissible | 114 |
| | | f. | Requirements for admissibility | 114 |
| | | | (1) Victim must have given up hope of surviving | 114 |
| | | | (2) Declaration must concern the <u>cause of death</u> | 114 |
| | | | (3) Victim's personal knowledge | 114 |
| | | | (4) Victim must be dead | 114 |
| | | g. | Rebuttal and impeachment | 114 |
| | 3. | Spontaneous Declarations | | 114 |
| | | a. | Definition | 114 |
| | | b. | Reason for admission | 114 |
| | | c. | How presented in court | 114 |
| | | d. | Requirements for admissibility | 115 |
| | | | (1) Startling event | 115 |
| | | | (2) Declaration made contemporaneously | 115 |
| | | | (3) Personal knowledge of the facts observed | 115 |
| | | e. | The following are not required for admissibility | 115 |
| | | | (1) Declarant need not be competent | 115 |
| | | | (2) Declarant need not be unavailable | 115 |

(3) Declarant need not always be identified ........................ 115
            f.  Distinguished from res gestae .................................. 115
        4.  Previously Recorded Testimony ......................................... 115
            a.  Definition ..................................................... 115
            b.  Reason for admission ........................................... 116
            c.  How presented in court ......................................... 116
            d.  Type of previous proceeding .................................... 116
            e.  Requirements for use in criminal proceedings ................... 116
        5.  Past Recollection Recorded ............................................ 116
            a.  Definition ..................................................... 116
            b.  Reason for admitting ........................................... 117
            c.  How presented in court ......................................... 117
            d.  Requirements for admissibility ................................. 117
                (1) No present recollection ................................... 117
                (2) Recording made when events were fresh in mind ............. 117
                (3) Recording made by or under direction of witness ........... 117
                (4) Verification .............................................. 117
                (5) Authentication ............................................ 117
        6.  Business Records ...................................................... 117
            a.  Definition ..................................................... 117
            b.  Reason for admission ........................................... 117
            c.  How presented in court ......................................... 117
            d.  Requirements for admissibility ................................. 117
                (1) A business ................................................ 117
                (2) Entry made in the regular course of business .............. 117
                (3) Personal knowledge ........................................ 118
                    (a) Rule on police reports ............................... 118
                (4) Entry made at or near time of event ....................... 118
                (5) Authentication ............................................ 118
        7.  Official Records ...................................................... 118
            a.  Definition ..................................................... 118
            b.  Reason for admission ........................................... 118
            c.  Distinguished from "business records" exception ................ 118
            d.  How presented .................................................. 118
        8.  Other Exceptions to the Hearsay Rule Not Discussed .................... 118
    C.  **Summary** ............................................................... 119

XIV. **USE OF DEMONSTRATIVE, SCIENTIFIC AND DOCUMENTARY EVIDENCE AT TRIAL** ........................................................................ 120
    A.  **Demonstrative Evidence (Also Known as Real Evidence or Physical Evidence)** .. 120
        1.  Definition ............................................................ 120
        2.  Statement of the Rule ................................................. 120
        3.  Requisites for Admissibility .......................................... 120
            a.  Relevant ....................................................... 120
            b.  Authentic ...................................................... 120
                (1) Types of authentication ................................... 120
                    (a) By testimony ......................................... 120
                    (b) By establishing chain of custody ..................... 120
                (2) Purpose of authentication ................................. 121
        4.  Types of Demonstrative Evidence ....................................... 121

xix

   a. Direct evidence .................................................... 121
   b. Circumstantial evidence ............................................ 121
   c. Original evidence .................................................. 121
   d. Prepared evidence .................................................. 121
  5. Directionary Power of the Court to Admit or Exclude Evidence ......... 121
   a. Seldom reversed if admitted ........................................ 121
  6. Admissibility of Specific Types of Demonstrative Evidence ............. 122
   a. Diagrams, drawings, graphs, charts, models, casts, etc. ............ 122
   b. Photographs ........................................................ 122
   c. X-ray pictures, electrocardiographs, etc. .......................... 122
   d. Tape recordings .................................................... 122
   e. View of the scene .................................................. 122
   f. Exhibit of child in paternity suits ................................ 122
   g. Demonstrations ..................................................... 122

**B. Scientific Evidence** ........................................................ 123
  1. Statement of the Rule ................................................. 123
   a. Substantially similar conditions .................................... 123
   b. Done by expert if complicated ....................................... 123
   c. Probative value ..................................................... 123
  2. Where and When are Experiments Conducted ............................. 123
   a. In the courtroom during trial ....................................... 123
   b. Outside the courtroom before trial .................................. 123
  3. Qualifications of Witnesses ........................................... 123
  4. Discretionary Power of the Court ...................................... 123
  5. Judicial Notice ....................................................... 123
  6. Conclusiveness of Scientific Evidence ................................. 123
  7. Admissibility of Specific Scientific Evidence ......................... 124
   a. Lie detector (polygraph) tests ...................................... 124
    (1) Most courts exclude results ..................................... 124
   b. Breath or blood tests for intoxication .............................. 124
   c. Radar speedometer to determine speed ................................ 124
   d. Blood grouping tests ................................................ 124
    (1) To show identity ................................................ 124
    (2) To show paternity .............................................. 125

**C. Documentary Evidence** ...................................................... 125
  1. Definition ............................................................ 125
  2. Statement of the Rule ................................................. 125
   a. Relevant ............................................................ 125
   b. Authentic ........................................................... 125
  3. How to Authenticate Evidence .......................................... 125
   a. By direct evidence .................................................. 125
    (1) Through the testimony of a subscribing witness .................. 125
    (2) Through the testimony of other witnesses ........................ 125
    (3) Through handwriting verifications ............................... 126
     (a) Nonexpert opinion ........................................... 126
     (b) Expert comparison of writings ............................... 126
    (4) Voice identification ............................................ 126
   b. By <u>circumstantial</u> evidence .................................. 126
    (1) Admissions by an opposing party ................................. 126
    (2) Contents of the document ........................................ 126

|   |   |   |   | |
|---|---|---|---|---|
|   |   |   | (a) Style | 126 |
|   |   |   | (b) Reply letter doctrine | 126 |
|   |   | 4. | Self-Authenticating Documents | 126 |
|   |   |   | a. Public documents | 127 |
|   |   |   | b. Certified copies | 127 |
|   |   |   | c. Notarized documents | 127 |
|   |   | 5. | The Best Evidence Rule | 127 |
|   |   |   | a. Statement of the Rule | 127 |
|   |   |   | b. Reason for the Rule | 127 |
|   |   |   | c. What constitutes a "writing" under Best Evidence Rule | 127 |
|   |   |   | d. "Duplicate originals" may qualify under the Rule | 127 |
|   |   |   | e. Exceptions to Best Evidence Rule | 127 |
|   |   |   | (1) Official records | 127 |
|   |   |   | (2) "Collateral" writings | 127 |
|   |   |   | (3) Where opposing party admits contents of writing | 127 |
|   |   |   | f. Secondary evidence may be admissible | 128 |
|   |   |   | g. When secondary evidence may be introduced | 128 |
|   |   |   | (1) When original writing is lost or destroyed | 128 |
|   |   |   | (2) When original writing is unobtainable | 128 |
|   |   |   | (3) When original writing is too voluminous | 128 |
|   |   |   | (4) When original writing is in possession of opposing party | 128 |
|   |   |   | h. What type of secondary evidence is preferred | 128 |
|   |   | 6. | The Parol Evidence Rule | 128 |
|   |   |   | a. Statement of the Rule | 128 |
|   |   |   | b. Comparison of Best Evidence Rule and Parol Evidence Rule | 129 |
|   | D. | **Summary** | | 129 |
| XV. | **JUDICIAL NOTICE, BURDEN OF PROOF AND PRESUMPTIONS** | | | 130 |
|   | A. | **Judicial Notice** | | 130 |
|   |   | 1. | Definition | 130 |
|   |   | 2. | Nature | 130 |
|   |   | 3. | Reason for Judicial Notice | 130 |
|   |   | 4. | Procedure for Judicial Notice | 130 |
|   |   |   | a. Request usually made | 130 |
|   |   |   | b. Procedural safeguards | 130 |
|   |   | 5. | Effect of Judicial Notice | 130 |
|   |   |   | a. In civil cases | 130 |
|   |   |   | b. In criminal cases | 130 |
|   |   |   | (1) Reason | 130 |
|   |   | 6. | Matters Judicially Noticed | 130 |
|   |   |   | a. Mandatory judicial notice | 131 |
|   |   |   | (1) Universally known and indisputable facts | 131 |
|   |   |   | (2) All federal and state law | 131 |
|   |   |   | (3) Federal and state rules on practice and procedure | 131 |
|   |   |   | (4) Documents published in the Federal Register | 131 |
|   |   |   | (5) The true significance of all English words and phrases, and all legal expressions | 131 |
|   |   |   | b. Discretionary judicial notice | 131 |
|   |   | 7. | Matters Which Cannot be Judicially Noticed | 132 |
|   |   |   | a. Personal knowledge of the judge | 132 |

|  |  |  |  |
|---|---|---|---|
|  |  | b. Essential elements of a crime | 132 |
| B. | **Burden of Proof** | | 132 |
|  | 1. | Definition | 132 |
|  |  | a. "Burden of producing evidence" | 132 |
|  |  | b. "Burden of persuasion" | 133 |
|  |  | (1) Satisfaction of burden | 133 |
|  |  | (2) Differentiation of degree | 133 |
|  |  | (3) Allocation of burden | 133 |
|  |  | (4) Degrees of certainty | 133 |
|  |  | (a) Preponderance of evidence | 133 |
|  |  | (b) Clear and convincing evidence | 133 |
|  |  | (c) Beyond a reasonable doubt | 134 |
|  |  | 1) In criminal cases | 134 |
|  |  | (d) Creating "reasonable doubt" | 134 |
|  | 2. | Significance of Two-Part Concept | 134 |
|  | 3. | Comparison of Burden of Producing Evidence and Burden of Persuasion | 135 |
| C. | **Presumptions** | | 135 |
|  | 1. | Definition | 135 |
|  |  | a. Uses of presumptions | 135 |
|  |  | (1) Probability | 135 |
|  |  | (2) Practical convenience | 135 |
|  |  | (3) Public policy | 135 |
|  |  | b. Sources | 136 |
|  | 2. | Requirements of "Rational Connection" in Criminal Cases | 136 |
|  |  | a. What constitutes a "rational connection" | 136 |
|  | 3. | Operation of Presumptions | 136 |
|  |  | a. How proved | 136 |
|  | 4. | Classification of Presumptions | 136 |
|  |  | a. Conclusive and rebuttable presumptions | 136 |
|  |  | (1) Conclusive presumptions | 136 |
|  |  | (2) Rebuttable presumptions | 137 |
|  |  | (a) Presumptions of fact | 137 |
|  |  | (b) Presumptions of law | 138 |
|  | 5. | Inferences | 138 |
|  |  | a. Definition | 138 |
|  |  | b. Discretion of trier of fact | 138 |
|  |  | c. Comparison of inference and presumption | 138 |
| D. | **Summary** | | 138 |

# Criminal Procedure and Evidence

# I. SOURCES OF RIGHTS AND STRUCTURE OF THE COURT SYSTEM.

A. **SOURCES OF RIGHTS**

The rules governing criminal proceedings in the United States come from three basic sources: Constitutions, statutes and court rules.

1. **Constitutions**

    a. **Federal Constitution**: The U.S. Constitution contains the most important rights available to an accused in a criminal prosecution. These safeguards are enumerated in the Bill of Rights (the first ten amendments to the U.S. Constitution).

    b. **State Constitutions**: The constitutions of the various states also contain provisions designed to protect the rights of individuals in state criminal proceedings. These provisions are basically similar to those enumerated in the Bill of Rights, but apply only to that particular state.

2. **Statutes**: Federal and state statutes are the second major source of the law of criminal procedure. These statutes frequently cover the same rights mentioned in the U.S. Constitution, but in more detail.

3. **Court Rules**: The third major source of the law of criminal procedure consists of the various rules which have developed as a result of the courts' inherent supervisory power over the administration of criminal justice. Federal courts have inherent supervisory power over federal criminal cases, while state courts have similar power over state criminal cases.

B. **THE "INCORPORATION CONTROVERSY"**

1. **The Bill of Rights**: As stated above, the most important safeguards available to an accused person are found in the Bill of Rights of the U.S. Constitution. These rights were ratified as a group and made a part of the U.S. Constitution in 1791.

    a. **Original applicability**: Originally, the Bill of Rights was viewed as limiting only the federal government. State proceedings were therefore regulated by provisions of the state constitution or state laws.

    b. **Effect of the 14th Amendment**: In 1868, the 14th Amendment was passed. In part, it states: "No State shall make or enforce any law which shall abridge the privileges or immunities of citizens of the United States; nor shall any State deprive any person of life, liberty, or property, without due process of law; nor deny to any person within its jurisdiction the equal protection of the laws." This Due Process Clause of the 14th Amendment has been interpreted by the U.S. Supreme Court as "incorporating" most of the provisions of the Bill of Rights. In other words, those rights which are incorporated under the 14th Amendment apply to state as well as federal criminal proceedings.

2. **"Total Incorporation" vs. "Selective Incorporation"**: Advocates of "total incorporation" argue that the 14th Amendment Due Process Clause should incorporate all the rights given in the Bill of Rights. On the other hand, proponents of "selective incorporation" maintain that only those rights which are considered "fundamental" should be incorporated in the Due Process Clause so as to apply in state criminal proceedings. In its decisions, the U.S. Supreme Court has consistently rejected the "total incorporation" approach and relied on selective incorporation of fundamental rights.

a. **Definition of "fundamental" rights**: The Court has defined "fundamental" rights as "those principles implicit in the concept of ordered liberty," or "those principles of justice rooted in the traditions and conscience of our people." These rather vague phrases really mean that the Court will determine on a "case by case" basis whether a particular right should be incorporated.

b. **Rights held "fundamental"**: The Court in specific cases has held that the following provisions of the Bill of Rights apply in both federal and state proceedings:

(1) 1st Amendment protections of religion, speech, assembly, and petition for grievances;

(2) 4th Amendment provisions with respect to arrest, search and seizure;

(3) 5th Amendment privilege against self-incrimination and prohibition against double jeopardy;

(4) 6th Amendment rights to counsel, confrontation, and cross-examination of witnesses; speedy trial; public trial; compulsory process for witnesses; and jury trial in criminal prosecutions; and

(5) 8th Amendment prohibition against cruel and unusual punishment.

c. **Rights not incorporated**: Although required in federal proceedings, the states do not have to give an accused the following rights unless this is required by the state constitution or state law:

(1) 5th Amendment guarantee of grand jury indictment; and

(2) 8th Amendment prohibition against excessive bail and fines.

3. **Result of Selective Incorporation**: As a result of the 14th Amendment Due Process Clause, persons facing federal or state criminal charges <u>enjoy the same rights</u>, except as to grand jury indictment (used by the federal government and about 27 states) and excessive bail and fines (which is prohibited in many state constitutions or by state law).

## C. STRUCTURE OF THE COURT SYSTEM

1. **Dual Court System**: The United States has a dual (as opposed to a single) court system. In other words, there is one court system for <u>federal</u> cases and another for <u>state</u> cases.

   a. **The federal court system**

   (1) **U.S. Supreme Court**: This highest court is composed of one Chief Justice and eight associate justices. All are appointed for life by the President of the United States with the "advice and consent" of the Senate; and they may be removed only by impeachment. The Supreme Court is located in Washington, D.C. and always decides cases as one body, never in smaller groups.

   (2) **U.S. Courts of Appeals** (also referred to as Circuit Courts): These courts have a total of 97 judges and are located in eleven judicial "circuits" in different regions of the country.

   (a) Example: The Fifth Circuit Court of Appeal is located in New Orleans, Louisiana, and hears cases appealed from federal district courts in the states of Texas, Louisiana, Mississippi, Alabama, Georgia, and Florida.

(b) Judges of the Courts of Appeals are appointed by the President of the United States for life with the "advice and consent" of the Senate and can be removed only by impeachment. Courts of Appeals may hear cases as one body, or in groups of three or five judges.

(3) **U.S. District Courts:** On the trial level, the district courts have more than 400 judges located in 94 judicial districts in the United States and its territories. Judges are appointed by the President of the United States for life with the "advice and consent" of the Senate and can be removed only by impeachment. In practice, a recommendation for appointment is made by the senior U.S. Senator from that state if he belongs to the President's political party.

(a) **U.S. Magistrates:** Also under the federal system, but not considered a separate court, is the office of U.S. magistrate. There are currently 164 full-time and 323 part-time holders of this office. Magistrates are appointed by district court judges and must be lawyers. Their duties are limited: In addition to trying persons accused of minor offenses, magistrates perform various pretrial and other duties.

b. **The state court system:** The structure of the state court system varies from state to state. In general, however, state courts tend to follow the federal pattern. This means that most states have the following structure:

(1) **State Supreme Court (not always known by this name):** The highest state court makes final decisions on cases involving state laws and provisions of the state constitution.

(2) **Intermediate Courts of Appeals:** Less than half of the states have courts at this level. Where they do not exist, appealed cases go directly to the State Supreme Court.

(3) **Trial Courts:** Before any appeal, cases are originally tried in these courts. There is great variation in the names given to trial courts; they may be called district court, superior court, county court, municipal court, magistrate court, and justice of the peace court.

c. **Note:** The term "dual court system" is misleading. What we in fact have in the United States are 52 separate judicial systems representing the court systems in the 50 different states, the federal system, and the courts of Washington, D.C. These systems, however, have much in common and allow general discussion thereof.

## D. JURISDICTION VS. VENUE

Jurisdiction and venue are two terms which can be confusing and are sometimes used interchangeably. However, they are very different concepts.

1. **Jurisdiction** refers to the power of the government to try and punish a person for an offense. It is usually derived from statutes.

   a. **Example:** Texas law provides that felonies and all misdeameanors involving official misconduct must be tried in state district courts. All other cases are triable in lower state courts.

2. **Venue** means the place where the offense must be tried. This is also specified by statute which usually provides that the trial must be held in the place where the crime was committed.

a. Venue may be changed and the trial held in another place for causes specified by law. This is done to assure the accused a fair and impartial trial in cases where there has been massive pretrial publicity or a strong community prejudice against the accused such that it becomes difficult to select an impartial jury.

E. **FEDERAL VS. STATE JURISDICTION**

If a crime is committed, how do we know whether it will be tried in a federal or a state court? The basic rules are simple:

1. If an act is a violation of federal law, the trial will be held in a federal court. Conversely, if the act is a violation of state law, the trial will be held in a state court.

2. If the crime violates both federal and state laws (such as kidnapping, transportation of narcotics, counterfeiting, or robbery of a federally-insured bank), the crime can be tried in both federal and state courts if the authorities so desire.

   a. Example: X robs the Houston First National Bank. X can be prosecuted for the crime of robbery under Texas law and for robbery of a federally-insured bank under federal law. The prosecutions are for the same act, but involving two different laws. There is no double jeopardy because of the concept (really a fiction!) of "dual sovereignty." This means that the federal and state governments are considered sovereign in their own right, and that there is no double jeopardy because that rule applies only to successive prosecutions by the same sovereign.

   b. In the above example, the sovereign which first gets hold of the suspect is usually allowed to try him first. In most cases, this will be the state courts. Although the federal government can try X for the same offense in the above example, it will probably refrain from doing so if X has been convicted and sufficiently punished under state law (and vice versa).

F. **SUMMARY**

There are three basic sources of rights for persons involved in a criminal proceeding: United States and state constitutions, statutes passed by Congress and state legislatures, and Court rules. Originally, the Bill of Rights of the U.S. Constitution was applied only to federal criminal prosecutions; these guarantees (except for the right to grand jury indictment and the right against excessive bail) are now extended to state criminal cases as well. This has occurred through a process of "selective incorporation", by which those rights considered "fundamental" have been "incorporated" in state criminal proceedings through the Due Process Clause of the 14th Amendment.

The United States has a "dual" court system—i.e., one system of courts on the federal level and another system on the state level. The federal system consists of the U.S. Supreme Court, the Courts of Appeals, and the District Courts. State courts basically follow this general structure, although variations exist from state to state.

Jurisdiction and venue are two entirely different concepts. Jurisdiction refers to the power of the government to try and punish a person for an offense, while venue means the place where the offense is to be tried.

If an act violates a federal law, it is tried in a federal court. If it violates state law, it is tried in a state court. There are acts, however, which are punishable by both federal and state law. In such cases, the offender may be prosecuted and convicted twice without violating his constitutional right against double jeopardy.

# II. AN OVERVIEW OF THE CRIMINAL PROCESS

## A. IN GENERAL

The criminal process can be divided into three basic stages: Procedure before trial, procedure during trial, and procedure after trial (post-conviction procedure). Each of these stages is discussed below. At the outset, however, certain general points should be noted:

1. **Procedure Relates to Felony Cases:** The procedure outlined below applies mainly to felony cases. Misdemeanors and petty offenses are usually processed in a simpler way.

    a. Whether a crime is a felony or a misdemeanor depends on the law of the particular state and may therefore vary from one state to another. Generally speaking, however, a felony is a crime punishable by death or imprisonment in a state prison (as opposed to imprisonment in a local jail); or a crime for which the punishment is imprisonment for more than one year. All other criminal offenses are considered misdemeanors.

2. **Variation Among States:** The procedure discussed in this text applies in the federal courts and in most states. However, there are variations from state to state in the procedures prescribed in each state code of criminal procedure. For example, about half of the states use the grand jury for charging a person with a serious crime, while the remainder do not use the grand jury at all. As long as a particular procedure is not required by the U.S. Constitution (as interpreted by the Supreme Court), the states do not have to use it.

3. **Variation Within a State:** Likewise, there may be variations in procedure among different courts within a given state, even though all are governed by a single state Code of Criminal Procedure.

    a. For example, the procedure used in the courts of Houston, Texas to process felony or misdemeanor offenses may not be exactly the same as the procedure used in Dallas, Texas.

4. **Theory vs. Reality:** The procedures outlined below, as well as those found in codes and textbooks, are the prescribed procedures. However, there may be differences between the ideal (prescribed) procedure and the procedures actually used by local criminal justice agencies. Many such agencies have their own "convenient" and traditional ways of getting things done—and these are not always in keeping with procedures prescribed by law. Nevertheless, they continue to be tolerated, either because they have not been challenged or because they do not grossly prejudice the constitutional and statutory rights of the accused.

## B. PROCEDURE PRIOR TO TRIAL

1. **Filing of a Complaint:** A complaint is a charge made before a proper officer alleging the commission of a criminal offense. It may be filed by the offended party or by a police officer who has obtained information about or witnessed the criminal act. The complaint serves as the basis for issuing an arrest warrant.

    a. Where the accused has been arrested without a warrant (see below), the complaint is prepared and filed, usually by the arresting officer, at the defendant's initial appearance before the magistrate.

2. **Arrest:** There are two kinds of arrest:

a. **Arrest with a warrant**: In this type of arrest, a complaint has been filed and presented to a magistrate, who has read it and found probable cause to justify the issuance of an arrest warrant.

b. **Arrest without a warrant**: This usually happens when a crime is committed in the presence of a police officer or, in some jurisdictions, by virtue of a citizen arrest for specified offenses.

   (1) **Summons or citation**: Statutes in many states authorize the use of a citation or summons (i.e., a written notice to appear) rather than an arrest for less serious offenses. If the person fails or refuses to appear in court as scheduled, an arrest warrant is then issued.

3. **"Booking" at Police Station**: This involves making an entry in the police blotter or arrest book indicating the suspect's name, the time of arrest, and the offense involved. If the offense is a serious one, the suspect may also be photographed or fingerprinted.

4. **Appearance Before Magistrate after Arrest**: In some jurisdictions, this is known as an "initial appearance", "presentment", or "arraignment on the warrant".

   a. **Duty to bring arrested person before a magistrate**: In most jurisdictions, statutes or court rules require that an arrested person be brought before a judge, magistrate, or commissioner "without unnecessary delay." The meaning of the latter phrase varies from state to state, depending upon state law or court decisions.

      (1) In federal and most state proceedings, a delay of more than six hours in bringing the suspect before the magistrate for initial appearance is one factor to be considered in determining the voluntariness of any incriminating statements made by the accused.

      (2) Other jurisdictions do not specify the number of hours, but look at the surrounding circumstances and decide on a case-by-case basis whether a delay was unnecessary.

   b. **Proceedings before the magistrate**

      (1) **Arrestee advised of his rights**: The magistrate first advises the arrestee of his rights. This usually includes the so-called "Miranda warnings"—i.e., informing the suspect of his right to remain silent, the fact that anything he says can be used against him in a court of law, his right to counsel, that—if he is an indigent—counsel will be provided by the state, and such other rights as may be given by statute.

         (a) **Note**: If the police officer wants to question a suspect about the crime before taking him to a magistrate, the police officer must give him the Miranda warnings. Failure to do this makes the suspect's statements inadmissible in court.

      (2) **Misdemeanors**: If the charge is a misdemeanor, the arrestee may be arraigned at this time and required to plead to the pending charge. Many misdemeanor cases are disposed of at this stage either through a guilty plea or some type of diversionary procedure.

      (3) **Felonies**: If the charge is a felony, the arrestee ordinarily is not required to plead to the charge at this stage. Rather, he is held for preliminary examination on the felony charge.

(4) **Temporary disposition**: If the case is not finally disposed of at the time of arraignment, the arrestee is either sent back to jail, released on his own recognizance (ROR), or allowed to post bail in an amount determined by the magistrate.

  (a) **Bail**: Bail is the security required by the state and given by the accused to insure that the accused appears before the proper court at the scheduled time and place to answer the charges brought against him.

   1) **Setting of bail**: In theory, the only function of bail is to insure the appearance of the defendant at the time set for trial. In practice, however, bail has also been used to prevent the release of an accused who might otherwise be dangerous to society or whom the judges might not want to release. This latter practice is known as "preventive detention."

     a) **Misdemeanors**: Where the charge is merely a misdemeanor, most courts have bail schedules pursuant to which the arrested person can post bail with the police or clerk of court in an amount designated in the schedule, without having to see the magistrate.

     b) **Felonies**: If the offense is bailable and no bail has been set, the magistrate will fix the amount if there is enough evidence to justify charging the accused with a felony.

       1/ **Amount of bail**: The amount of bail is usually determined in light of the facts then known to the magistrate. These include the nature and seriousness of the crime, previous criminal record of the accused, likelihood of flight from the state, etc.

       2/ **Judicial review**: The magistrate's setting of bail is not subject to review by a higher court unless there is a gross violation of the constitutional guarantee against <u>excessive bail</u>. Unfortunately, the term "excessive bail" is <u>hard to define</u>; and this makes the constitutional right difficult to invoke.

   2) **Modification of bail**: In most states, the magistrate or any judge of the court in which the charge is pending can—for good cause shown—increase or decrease the amount of bail.

   3) **Bail bondsmen**: Bail is usually posted by a bail bondsman who demands cash payment of anywhere between 5 and 20 percent of the bail set. This amount is not refundable even if defendant shows up for trial. The bondsman also demands collateral in the form of property which he can confiscate should the accused "jump bail."

   4) **Bail reform**: Bail practices by bail bondsmen have been severely criticized in recent years; and several projects have attempted to make bail more available to and less damaging for the accused. One widely accepted project is a <u>court-administered bail</u> system, in which the state, (through the court) serves as bondsman but refunds the cash deposit (except for a small fee) if the accused shows up for trial. This may create a greater incentive for the accused to show up, knowing that he will get his refund.

(b) **Release on defendant's own recognizance**: By statute in a number of states, the magistrate or judge before whom the proceedings are pending may release any accused "on his own recognizance"—i.e., without monetary bail. This usually happens when the accused is one who, because of ties in the community, etc., will most likely appear for trial. If he fails to do so, however, a warrant may be issued for his arrest.

(c) **Non-bailable offenses**: Finally, the federal courts and most states deny bail to persons charged with a capital offense (offenses punishable by death or life imprisonment) when the proof of guilt is evident (i.e., strong).

5. **Preliminary Examination**: Where the accused is charged with a felony, he is usually entitled to a preliminary examination (sometimes called a "preliminary hearing" or "examining trial") held before a magistrate within a reasonably short time after his arrest. Preliminary examinations closely resemble trials, except that their purposes are more limited and the hearing officer is generally not the judge who will preside over the actual trial in the case. Representation by counsel and cross-examination of witnesses are both allowed.

    a. **Purposes of examination**: Preliminary examinations are usually held for three main purposes:

    (1) **Determination of probable cause**: The primary purpose of the preliminary hearing is to ascertain whether there is probable cause to support the charges against the accused. If not, the charges are dismissed. This prevents unsupported charges of grave offenses from coming to trial, and thereby protects persons from harassment, expense and damage to reputation.

    (2) **Discovery**: "Discovery" is a procedure used by either party to obtain information in the hands of the other party which is necessary or helpful in the case. Since the scope of discovery available to an accused in a criminal case is limited (compared with civil cases), the preliminary examination can give the accused some idea of the strength of the prosecution's case.

    (a) Generally, the prosecutor will reveal only as much of his evidence as he feels will be necessary to establish probable cause. On the other hand, the defense has no obligation to present any of its own case if it chooses not to do so.

    (3) **Decision on "bind over"**: Some states use the preliminary examination to determine if the accused shall be "bound over" for a grand jury hearing. In these states, there must be a finding of cause at the preliminary examination before a grand jury hearing will be held.

    (a) Other states use the preliminary examination to determine if the accused should be "bound over" for trial, bypassing grand jury proceedings altogether.

    b. **Cases in which preliminary examination is not required.**

    (1) **Indictment prior to preliminary examination**: When the grand jury has previously returned an indictment (usually because the case was referred to it before arrest), a preliminary examination is not required. The grand jury proceedings themselves constitute a determination that there is probable cause for the charges against the accused, so that he should stand trial therefor.

(2) **Misdemeanor cases**: In most jurisdictions, preliminary examinations are not required in misdemeanor cases because of the lesser penalties involved. The accused goes to trial directly on the complaint or information filed by the district attorney.

(3) **Waiver of preliminary examination**: Moreover, the accused may waive voluntarily (i.e., voluntarily give up) the right to a preliminary examination.

    (a) A plea of guilty to the charge generally operates as a waiver of the preliminary examination. The accused is thereupon "bound over" for sentencing to the court having jurisdiction over the crime involved.

c. **Scope of preliminary hearing**: In most jurisdictions, the prosecution must prove that there is competent evidence for each element of the offense on which the accused is held; and the accused must be given the opportunity to present any defense he wishes (evidence illegally obtained, etc.).

d. **Ruling**: After the preliminary hearing, the magistrate may do any of the following:

(1) **"Hold defendant to answer"**: If the magistrate finds probable cause—i.e., facts which would lead a person of ordinary caution or prudence to entertain a strong suspicion of the guilt of the accused—the accused is "held to answer" and bound over for trial in a court having jurisdiction over the offense charged (or for a grand jury hearing, in states where the preliminary examination is a prerequisite to the grand jury proceeding).

(2) **Discharge the accused**: If the magistrate does not find "probable cause," the accused is discharged.

(3) **Reduce the charge**: Most states allow the magistrate to reduce a felony charge to a misdemeanor based upon the results of the preliminary hearing. This serves to avoid cluttering grand juries or higher courts with cases that really belong in lower courts.

6. **Filing of Accusatory Pleadings**: A criminal prosecution is commenced by the filing of an accusatory pleading in the court having jurisdiction of the offense. Prior to this filing, the accused will have made an initial appearance before a magistrate to be informed of his rights and the posting of bail, and he will have had a preliminary examination to determine whether there is probable cause for him to be "bound over" for trial. However, the prosecution formally commences when the government files an indictment (grand jury) or information (no grand jury) in whichever court the defendant will be tried.

    a. **Indictment proceedings before grand jury**

        (1) **Grand jury distinguished from trial (petit) jury**:

            (a) Grand juries are usually composed of 16 to 23 members, with 12 votes required for an indictment. Trial juries are usually made up of 12 members, with a unanimous vote required for conviction.

            (b) Grand juries do not determine guilt or innocence: They merely return indictments or conduct investigations of reported criminality. Trial juries do decide guilt or innocence.

(c) Grand juries often retain the same membership for a month, six months, or a year, and may return several indictments during that period. Trial juries change membership in every case.

(d) Grand juries return indictments based upon "probable cause", whereas trial juries convict based upon evidence of guilt "beyond reasonable doubt."

(2) **Defendant's right to grand jury indictment**: A grand jury hearing is not a right guaranteed under the U.S. Constitution in all criminal prosecutions. Only about one-half of the states today use it, some on an optional basis. However, it is required in all federal felony prosecutions.

(3) **Procedure**

(a) **Bill of indictment**: The grand jury proceedings when a "bill of indictment"—a written accusation of the crime—is submitted to the grand jury by the prosecutor.

(b) **Hearings**: Hearings are then held before the grand jury, and evidence is presented by the prosecutor to prove the accusation.

1) **Secrecy**: Traditionally, these hearings are secret, the reason being that the charges may not be proved and it would thus be unfair to allow publication thereof. Unauthorized persons are excluded, and disclosure of the proceedings is generally prohibited.

2) **Evidence**: The accused has no right to present evidence in a grand jury proceeding. However, he may be given an opportunity to do so at the discretion of the jury.

3) **No right to counsel**: A witness appearing before the grand jury does not have a right to counsel—even if he is also the accused. The reasoning is that this is merely an investigation, not a trial.

(c) **Disposition**: If the required number of grand jurors (usually 12) believes that the evidence warrants conviction for the crime charged, the bill of indictment is endorsed as a "true bill" and filed with the court having jurisdiction of the offense as a formal accusation of the crime. If the jury does not so find, the bill of indictment is ignored and a "no bill" results.

b. **Filing of information**: An information is a written accusation of a crime prepared by the prosecuting attorney in the name of the state. This is done without going before a grand jury.

(1) **Requirement of prior preliminary examination**: To safeguard against possible abuse, most states provide that a prosecution by information may be commenced only after a preliminary examination and commitment by a magistrate, or waiver thereof by the accused. In that way, the "probable cause" assured in every grand jury indictment is supplied—in this case, by the reviewing magistrate.

(2) **Contents of the information**: The information must reasonably inform the accused of the charges against him, so that he has an opportunity to prepare

and present a defense. The essential nature of the offense must be stated, although the charges may (and usually do) follow the language of the <u>Penal Code</u> which defines the offense.

7. **Arraignment**: At a scheduled time and after prior notice, the accused is called into court, informed of the charges against him, and asked how he pleads. This is known as the arraignment.

   a. **Accused must be present**: The accused's presence during arraignment is <u>required</u>. If he has not been arrested, or if he is on bail and does not appear, a bench <u>warrant</u> (warrant issued by the judge) will be issued to compel his appearance.

      (1) **Exception**: In many states, an accused charged with a <u>misdemeanor</u> may appear through <u>counsel</u> at the arraignment. I.e., he need not be physically present.

8. **Plea by Defendant**

   a. **Types of pleas**: There are generally three kinds of pleas in modern criminal practice: (a) Guilty; (b) nolo contendere; and (c) not guilty.

      (1) **Guilty pleas** are discussed in detail below.

      (2) **Nolo contendere plea**: A nolo contendere plea means literally "no contest." The effect of this plea is the same as that of a guilty plea. However, the defendant may benefit in that the plea cannot be used as an admission in any subsequent <u>civil proceeding</u> arising out of the same offense.

         (a) Example: X pleads nolo contendere to a <u>criminal charge</u> of driving while intoxicated. This plea cannot be used as an admission of guilt in a subsequent <u>civil case</u> which an injured party might bring against X to recover damages. The injured party must prove the liability of X on his own and not simply rely on the nolo contendere plea.

            1) On the other hand, had X pleaded <u>guilty</u> to the charge of driving while intoxicated, the plea could be used by the injured party in a civil case to establish X's liability.

         (b) Nolo contendere pleas are permitted in federal courts and in the courts of about half the states.

         (c) Even where such pleas are permitted, however, the accused generally does not have an absolute right to enter same. Rather, it can be made only with the <u>consent of the prosecution</u> or, with the <u>approval of the court</u>. It is also generally used only for <u>misdemeanor offenses</u>.

      (3) **Plea of not guilty**: If the defendant pleads "not guilty", the case is usually set for trial within two or three weeks. The delay is designed to give both the prosecution and defense time to prepare their cases.

         (a) Where the defendant <u>refuses</u> to plead, or where the court is not sure of defendant's plea, the court will enter a <u>not guilty</u> plea.

         (b) Between the "not guilty" plea and the start of the trial, the defense often files a number of motions with the court. One of the most common is a "motion to supress" evidence which allegedly was illegally seized—requiring a hearing at which the police officer in question testifies on the facts surrounding seizure of the evidence, and a determination is made as to whether the evidence was in fact illegally obtained. Another common motion is for a change of venue where there has been prejudicial pretrial publicity against the accused.

b. **The guilty plea**

(1) **Nature of guilty plea**: Where defendant pleads "guilty", the record must affirmatively show that the plea was voluntary and that the accused had a full understanding of its consequences. Without these, the plea is invalid as a matter of constitutional law. [Boykin v. Alabama, 395 U.S. 238, 1968]

(a) **Theory behind requirement**: A plea of guilty has the effect of giving up several important constitutional rights (such as the right to trial by jury and the right against self-incrimination). Hence, there is a need to make sure the accused knew exactly what he was doing and was not coerced into making the plea.

(b) **Guilty plea to avoid death penalty not involuntary**: A plea of guilty that represents an intelligent choice among alternatives available to the defendant—especially where represented by competent counsel—is not involuntary simply because it is entered to avoid the possibility of the death penalty. If otherwise voluntary and informed, the plea is valid. [Brady v. U.S.; 397 U.S. 472, 1970]

(c) **Plea entered with denial of guilt**: Likewise, a plea is not invalid simply because the defendant does not admit guilt, or even continues to assert his innocence... provided that there is some basis in the record for his plea. All that is required for a valid guilty plea is a knowing waiver of the rights involved, not an admission of guilt. [North Carolina v. Alford, 400 U.S. 25, 1971]

(2) **Plea bargaining**: Frequently, a defendant is induced by the prosecutor to plead guilty to a lesser charge in order to save the time and expense (and uncertainty) of a trial. In these cases, the plea must be voluntary and the accused must have a full understanding of its consequences.

(a) **Plea bargaining results in a guilty plea**: Of course, not all guilty pleas are the result of plea bargaining. Many plead guilty for other reasons, without bargaining with the prosecutor.

(b) **Involuntary plea if bargain coerced**: Some forms of "inducement" may be so inherently unfair or coercive that a plea in reliance thereon is involuntary and therefore invalid. For example, a threat to prosecute the accused's wife as a co-defendant (despite lack of evidence), or to charge prior convictions (thereby increasing the possible sentence for the accused), would no doubt invalidate the plea because of improper pressure.

(c) **Right to have bargain kept**: If a plea is based to any significant degree upon a prosecutor's promise, that promise must be fulfilled. If not, the agreement or promise is either specifically enforced or the plea may be withdrawn. [Santobello v. New York, 404 U.S. 257, 1972]

1) To avoid this result, most prosecutors tell the accused that they will recommend a possible sentence in exchange for the guilty plea, but that the judge is not legally obligated to honor that recommendation.

(3) **Withdrawing a guilty plea**

    (a) **Involuntary pleas:** An involuntary plea may be withdrawn at any time, since it violates defendant's constitutional rights. What constitutes an involuntary plea is a difficult issue and must be determined by the court on the circumstances of each case.

    (b) **Voluntary pleas:** Federal procedure permits a voluntary guilty plea to be withdrawn only before sentence is imposed—except that the court may permit a withdrawal after sentencing—"to correct manifest injustice."

        1) **State practices vary.** Some states follow the federal procedure while others simply do not allow the withdrawal of voluntary pleas.

## C. PROCEDURE DURING TRIAL

The basic steps in a criminal trial are as follows:

—Selection of jurors.

—Indictment or information read to jury, and defendant's plea given.

—Prosecuting attorney makes an opening statement, after which defendant or his counsel may make an opening statement.

—Prosecutor presents his case against defendant, offering evidence in support of the charge.

—Defendant or his counsel presents the defense (which may, depending upon the law of the jurisdiction, include the making of an opening statement), offering his evidence in support thereof.

—The parties offer rebutting evidence.

—Each side makes closing argument to the jury, the government opening the argument and having the right to close—unless case is submitted on either or both sides without argument.

—Judge instructs or charges the jury.

—Jury deliberates in secret on the case.

—Verdict of conviction or acquittal, or a "hung jury", concludes trial.

1. **Selection of Jurors**

    a. **Jury panel:** A panel of jurors is assembled according to an established procedure—usually using voters' registration lists, municipal directories, telephone directories, or other available listings. The prospective jurors are then sent notification letters by the jury commissioner, with instructions to show up at a specified time and place for possible jury duty.

    b. **Examination of jurors** ("voir dire"): Prospective jurors may be questioned to determine whether there are grounds for challenge. This is known as "voir dire", meaning "to tell the truth".

        (1) In federal courts, the trial judge usually asks the questions—although he may permit counsel to conduct the examination or submit questions for the judge to ask the jury.

        (2) In state practice, counsel themselves often ask the questions.

c. **Challenges:** There are two types of challenges to prospective jury members:

   (1) **Challenge for cause:** Jurors can be dismissed for causes specified by law. These include actual bias, implied bias, or other factors which would prevent the juror from making a fair and impartial decision. Lack of residence, previous conviction, or insanity are also recognized challenges for cause.

   (2) **Peremptory challenge:** These are challenges for which no reason need be stated—i.e., they are entirely within the discretion of each party.

      (a) The number of peremptory challenges allowed a party varies from one jurisdiction to another, and may also depend upon the seriousness of the offense. The more serious the offense, the more peremptory challenges may be allowed.

2. **Opening Statements**

   a. **By the prosecution:** In his opening statement, the prosecutor acquaints the jury with the nature of the charge against the accused and gives some description of the evidence that will be offered to sustain the charge. Opinions, conclusions, references to the accused character, argumentative statements, or references to matters upon which evidence will not be offered are out of place, and the defense may object thereto.

   b. **By the defense:** There is a difference of opinion as to the tactical value of an opening statement by the defense. Some argue that the defense should not risk assuming the burden of proving something in the mind of the jury, which would occur if such a statement is made. Others note that failure to make a statement may imply a weak or hopeless defense.

      (1) It is generally considered best for the defense to make its opening statement after the prosecution has presented its entire case; and in some jurisdictions it can only be made at this time.

3. **Presentation of Government's Case:** After opening the case, the prosecutor offers evidence in support of the charge. While physical ("real") evidence may be introduced, most evidence tends to be in the form of witness testimony.

   a. Witnesses are examined in the following order:

      (1) Direct examination—by the prosecutor.

      (2) Cross-examination—by the defense lawyer.

      (3) Redirect examination—by the prosecutor.

      (4) Recross examination—by the defense lawyer.

   This procedure theoretically can continue back and forth, but the judge usually puts a stop to the examination of witnesses at this stage.

   b. After presenting all of its evidence, the government rests its case.

4. **Presentation of Defendant's Case:** When the prosecution has rested, the defendant or his lawyer opens the defense and offers evidence in support thereof.

a. Witnesses are examined in the order noted above (i.e., direct, cross, redirect, etc.)—with the defense lawyer conducting the direct examination and the prosecutor cross-examining the witness.

b. After presenting all the evidence, the defense rests its case.

5. **Motions Prior to Verdict**: Defendants can avail themselves of several different motions prior to jury deliberations and a verdict. The most common are:

    a. **Motion for acquittal**: The defense normally moves for a judgment of acquittal at the close of the prosecution's case on grounds of failure to establish a prima facie case. This motion alleges that the prosecution has failed to introduce evidence on a necessary element of the offense charged—such as intent in robbery, or death in homicide. If denied by the judge (as is usually the case), the defendant may renew the motion to acquit at the close of his case.

    b. **Motion for directed verdict of acquittal**: At the close of evidence in a jury trial, the defendant may ask the court for a directed verdict of acquittal—again on the ground that the evidence is legally insufficient to convict.

        (1) A few states do not permit a motion for directed verdict, on the theory that the right to a jury trial belongs to the prosecution as well as to the accused and hence that the judge cannot take the case away from the jury.

        (2) However, most states allow the judge to direct a verdict of acquittal as part of the court's inherent power to prevent a miscarriage of justice through conviction on insufficient evidence.

    c. **Motion for a mistrial**: Improper conduct at trial constitutes grounds for a mistrial, and a motion on this ground may be made prior to jury deliberations. Examples of grounds for a mistrial include the introduction of inflammatory evidence and prejudicial remarks by the judge or prosecution.

6. **Argument After Presentation of Evidence**

    a. **Order of closing argument**: In most jurisdictions, the prosecution first presents its closing argument; the defense replies; and the prosecution then has a final argument to rebut the defense.

        (1) **Prosecution argument**: The prosecution summarizes the evidence and presents theories on how the evidence should be considered to establish defendant's guilt. The prosecutor's summation sometimes may include improper remarks to which the defense may object and (if serious enough) even secure a mistrial, new trial, or reversal on appeal.

        (2) **Defense argument**: The closing argument by the defense is an important matter of tactics and strategy. Generally, the defense emphasizes the heavy burden of proof placed on the prosecution—i.e., proof of defendant's guilt beyond a reasonable doubt. The defense then stresses that this burden has not been met and hence that the defendant must be acquitted.

            (a) Like the prosecutor, defense counsel is not permitted to express a personal opinion as to defendant's innocence or guilt. The facts as presented must speak for themselves.

7. **Instructing the Jury**

   a. **Instructions are given by the judge**: The trial judge must properly instruct the jury on all general principles of law relevant to the charge and the issues raised by the evidence. Most states empower the trial judge to comment on the evidence. Some states, however, forbid such comment.

   b. **Requested instructions**: In most criminal cases, the parties—especially defense counsel—will request to the court that certain instructions be used.

   c. **Ruling on requested instructions**: The court must decide whether to give, refuse, or modify the instructions proposed by the parties, decide which additional instructions it will give, and advise counsel of its decision. Often an informal conference on instructions is held among the judge, prosecutor, and defense counsel.

8. **Jury Deliberations**

   a. **Choice of foreman**: The foreman of the jury is usually elected immediately after the jury has been instructed by the judge and has retired from the courtroom to start its deliberations. The foreman presides over the deliberations and gives the verdict to the court once a decision has been reached.

   b. **Jury deliberations** are conducted in secret; and jurors are not subject to subsequent legal inquiry regardless of the result arrived at.

   c. **Separation of jurors** (also known as sequestration): There is a conflict among the various jurisdictions as to whether a respective jury—during the trial and/or during its deliberations—should be kept together (sequestered) or allowed to return to their respective homes at night or during weekends. Most states permit the trial judge to order sequestration at his discretion.

9. **Conviction or Acquittal**: A jury verdict of guilty or a similar finding by the trial judge (in a bench trial) results in a conviction of the accused.

   a. **Unanimous vote required in federal courts**: In federal and most criminal trials, the jury vote for conviction or acquittal must be unanimous. Failure to reach a unanimous vote either way results in a hung jury and declaration of a mistrial.

      (1) The length of time a jury must deliberate before a hung jury will be declared is determined by the judge. If the jury is dismissed by the judge because it cannot agree on the result, the case may be tried again before another jury.

   b. **State courts may authorize non-unanimous vote**: The U.S. Supreme Court has held state laws providing for a less-than-unanimous vote for conviction are constitutional and will be upheld—at least in the case of a required 9-3 vote. The Court has yet to decide whether an 8-4 or 7-5 vote would also be valid.

   c. **Polling of jury**: After the jury has announced its verdict, the defendant has a right to have the jury polled. The jury must then express its vote in open court, either as a group or individually.

   d. **Commitment of defendant**: Following a conviction, the court may order the defendant committed to custody or released on bail pending imposition of sentence.

D. PROCEDURE AFTER TRIAL

1. **Sentencing**: Sentencing follows a verdict of conviction. This topic is discussed in Chapter IX, infra.

2. **Appeal**: Should the defendant so desire, he may appeal his conviction and sentence. The process of appeal is likewise discussed in Chapter IX, infra.

E. **SUMMARY**

The criminal process in our criminal justice system involves proceedings prior to trial, during trial, and after trial. Procedure prior to trial covers the time from the filing of the complaint up to the time of defendant's plea. Procedure during trial begins with the selection of jurors and ends with a verdict of conviction or acquittal (or a mistrial). Procedure after trial involves sentencing and appeals, both of which are discussed in Chapter IX.

The above procedure basically applies to felony cases (although misdemeanor offenses are referred to in several places). It should be noted that variations in procedures exist among the states and even within a state. While the procedure outlined here is the prescribed one, there may be some departure from it in the various local criminal justice agencies. These are generally tolerated by appellate courts as long as they do not unduly prejudice the rights of the accused.

The federal courts and practically all states follow a code of criminal procedure, which details the procedure to be used in processing offenders in that particular jurisdiction. It is important for a law enforcement officer to know exactly what is prescribed by law for his jurisdiction—since he will be held accountable for that procedure as prescribed by the legislature and interpreted by the courts of the state.

# III. PROBABLE CAUSE

The "probable cause" requirement in police work is based upon the 4th Amendment of the U.S. Constitution, which states:

> "The right of the people to be secure in their persons, houses, papers, and effects, against unreasonable searches and seizures, shall not be violated, and <u>no warrants shall issue, but upon probable cause.</u> (under-scoring supplied)

## A. WHAT CONSTITUTES PROBABLE CAUSE

1. **Definition:** Probable cause exists where the facts and circumstances within the knowledge of the arresting officers and of which they had reasonably trustworthy information are sufficient in themselves to warrant a man of reasonable caution in believing that an offense has been committed or is being committed (in case of arrest warrants) or that property could be found in a particular place or on a particular person (in case of search warrants). [Carroll v. U.S., 267 U.S. 132, 1925]

    a. **"Man of reasonable caution":** The term "man of reasonable caution" (some jurisdictions use the term "ordinarily prudent and cautious man") does not refer to a person with training in the law—such as a magistrate or lawyer. Instead, it refers to the <u>average "man in the street"</u> who, under the same circumstances, would believe that the person being arrested had committed the offense or that things to be seized would be found in a particular place.

    (1) However, the experience of the police officer must be considered in determining whether probable cause existed in a specific situation. In view of his work experience, training, and background, the police officer may be better qualified than the average man in the street to evaluate certain facts and circumstances.

    (2) Thus, what may amount to probable cause to an untrained person may be insufficient in the case of a police officer because of his training and background. This is particularly true in burglary or drug cases.

    b. **"Reasonable ground":** The terms "probable cause" and "reasonable ground" are used interchangeably in many jurisdictions.

    c. **Practical requirement:** In practice, probable cause exists when, in the <u>honest belief</u> of a <u>man of reasonable caution</u>, a <u>suspect's guilt</u> is <u>more probable than his innocence.</u> In mathematical terms, this means that the police officer (in cases of arrest or search without a warrant) or the magistrate (in cases of arrest or search with a warrant) is <u>more than 50%</u> certain that the suspect has committed the offense or that the items can be found in a certain place.

    (1) Since probable cause, if later challenged in court, must be established by police testimony, it is important that the police officer keenly observe and take careful notes of the facts and circumstances establishing that probable cause existed at the time he acted.

2. **Court Interpretation of Allegations:** The courts recognize that affidavits or complaints are often prepared hastily in the midst of a criminal investigation. Therefore, the policy is to interpret the allegations in a common-sense rather than overly-technical manner, and to uphold the sufficiency of the affidavit or complaint in close cases. [U.S. v. Ventresca, 300 U.S. 102, 1965]

B. **WHEN PROBABLE CAUSE IS REQUIRED**

Probable cause is required in four basic areas of police work:

Arrests with warrant;

Arrests without warrant;

Searches and seizures with warrant; and

Searches and seizures without warrant.

1. **Arrests WITH Warrant:** Before a warrant can be issued, there must be showing to the magistrate, through a complaint or affidavit, of facts sufficient for a man of reasonable caution to believe that the person to be arrested committed a crime. The complaint or affidavit can be filed by the offended party or by a police officer.

    a.  In arrest with a warrant, the police officer's concern is merely to serve the warrant. He does not worry about probable cause because that has been determined by the magistrate when he issued the warrant. However, the magistrate's determination can later be challenged by the accused.

2. **Arrests WITHOUT Warrant**

    a.  **In general:** The police officer must have probable cause to believe that the person to be arrested either:

    (1) Committed a crime (felony or misdemeanor) in his presence, or

    (2) Committed a felony, even though it was not committed in his presence.

    (3) Although the standard of probable cause for arrest is the same with or without warrant, in "close" cases an arrest with a warrant may be upheld on lesser evidence than an arrest without a warrant.

    b.  **Probable cause must exist before or at the time of arrest:** The arrest cannot be justified by facts which turn up after the arrest.

    (1) Example: X is arrested by the police on mere suspicion of having drugs. After his arrest, the police find several ounces of heroin in his pocket. The arrest and search are invalid despite the fact that X did have drugs—because the police acted on a mere suspicion which is insufficient for arrest.

3. **Search and Seizure WITH Warrant:** Probable cause is established if the magistrate finds that: (1) The items sought are connected with criminal activity, and (2) the items will be found in the place to be searched.

4. **Search and Seizure WITHOUT Warrant**

    a.  **In general:** This usually takes place when circumstances make it impractical or unnecessary for the police officer to obtain a search warrant. Some of these instances are:

    (1) **Search and seizure incidental to (i.e., immediately after) arrest:** Such searches are limited to the area of the arrestee's immediate control.

(2) **Searches with consent:** This is valid only when consent is voluntary, not forced.

(3) **Search where special factors justify the intrusion:** These would include vehicle searches, stop and frisk, hot pursuit, border searches, and the like.

5. **Differences Among the Four Basic Areas:** Although the definition of probable cause is the same in all four instances discussed above, there are certain differences which should be understood:

   a. **"With warrant" vs. "without warrant":** In arrests and seizures with a warrant, the determination of probable cause is made by the magistrate to whom the complaint or affidavit is presented.

   (1) By way of contrast, in arrests and searches and seizures without warrant it is the police officer who makes the determination, usually on the spot and in a very limited time. This determination is subject to review by the court if challenged at a later time, usually during the trial.

   b. **"Arrest" vs. "search and seizure":** In cases of arrest (with or without a warrant), the concern is whether an offense has been committed and whether the suspect did in fact commit the offense.

   (1) In cases of search and seizure (with or without warrant), on the other hand, the concern is whether the item or property to be seized can be found in a particular place.

6. **Advantages in Obtaining a Warrant:** Police officers are strongly advised to get a warrant whenever possible (for arrest or search and seizure) because of the following advantages:

   a. A warrant means a presumption of probable cause, since the affidavit or complaint has presumably been reviewed by the magistrate who found probable cause to justify issuance of the warrant. Hence, the arrest or search and seizure is considered valid unless the accused proves otherwise in court—and it is difficult for the accused to overcome the presumption of validity of the warrant.

   b. Having a warrant is likewise a valid defense in civil cases for damages brought against the police officer for alleged violation of defendant's constitutional rights. The only exception is where a warrant is served despite its being clearly invalid due to mistakes which the officer should have discovered—such as absence of a signature, or failure to specify the place or person subject to the warrant.

7. **Consequences of Lack of Probable Cause:** If probable cause for the arrest or search and seizure did not exist:

   a. The evidence obtained cannot be admitted in court during the trial, hence endangering the success of the prosecution; and

   b. The police officer may be subject to a civil action for damages or, in extreme cases, to criminal sanctions.

## C. HOW PROBABLE CAUSE IS ESTABLISHED

Probable cause may be established through: (1) The officer's own knowledge of particular facts and circumstances; (2) information given by a reliable third person (informant); or (3) information plus corroboration.

1. **Officer's Own Knowledge of Particular Facts and Circumstances:** This refers to knowledge obtained personally by the officer using any of his five senses (in contrast to knowledge given him by another person).

    a. **Relevant factors:** Factors which a police officer may take into account in establishing his belief that probable cause exists would include: Prior criminal record of the suspect, flight from the scene of the crime, highly suspicious conduct, admissions by the suspect, presence of incriminating evidence, unusual hour, resemblance of suspect to description of perpetrator, etc.

2. **Information Given by a Reliable Third Person (Informant):**

    a. **Requirements:** In *Aguilar v. Texas,* 378 U.S. 108, 1964, the Supreme Court established a two-part test for determining probable cause based upon information from an informant: (1) The reliability of the informant, and (2) the reliability of the informant's information.

        (1) **Reliability of informant:** The affidavit must describe underlying circumstances from which a neutral and detached magistrate can find that the informant is reliable.

            (a) If the informant's identity is revealed by the police, reliability is usually considered established.

            (b) But, if the informant's identity is not disclosed, the police must establish his reliability. This is usually done by stating in the affidavit that the informant has given accurate information many times in the past.

            (c) Note: The police need only testify as to the informer's reliability to show probable cause. I.e., unless the identity of the informant is directly material to the guilt or innocence of the accused, the police need not reveal the informer's identity in establishing probable cause for an arrest or search.[McCray v. Illinois, 386 U.S. 300, 1967]

        (2) **Reliability of informant's information:** The affidavit must also describe underlying circumstances from which the magistrate can find that the informant's information is itself reliable and not the result of mere rumor or suspicion.

    b. **Need for specifics in affidavit:** If the information relied on by the police officer comes from a third person, the officer must be specific in his affidavit in order to establish probable cause.

        (1) **Example of insufficient affidavit by police officer due to lack of specifics:** "Affiant has received reliable information from a credible person and believes that narcotics are being kept at 320 Jones Street, Apt. 5, for the purpose of sale and use contrary to the provisions of law." [Aguilar v. Texas, 378 U.S. 108, 1964]

        (2) **Example of sufficient affidavit:** "Affiant received information this morning from a trustworthy informant who has supplied information to the police during the past five years and whose information has proved reliable, resulting in numerous drug convictions, that he personally saw Henry Banks, a former convict, sell heroin worth $1000 to a buyer named Skippy Smith at ten o'clock last night in Banks' apartment located at 1300 Shady Lane, Apt. 10, and that Banks has been selling and continues to sell drugs from this location."

3. **Information Plus Corroboration:** If the police officer is unable to satisfy both parts of the *Aguilar* test—i.e., reliability of the informant and reliability of informant's information—and cannot establish probable cause, he may remedy this deficiency by conducting his own investigation to <u>corroborate</u> the information given by the informant. This may produce probable cause even if neither the informant's data or the corroborative findings standing alone would have been sufficient for issuance of a warrant.

   a. Example: An informant tells a police officer he has heard that X, a former convict, is selling drugs and that the sale is usually made at night in the apartment of X's girlfriend. This information alone probably would not establish probable cause. However, if the officer, acting on this information, puts the apartment under surveillance, sees people going in and out, and is in fact told by a buyer that he has just purchased drugs from X inside the apartment, there is a strong basis for probable cause either to arrest X without a warrant (if it would be impractical to obtain one) or to obtain a warrant from the magistrate. The information and subsequent corroboration demonstrates the existence of probable cause.

D. **PROBABLE CAUSE VS. OTHER LEVELS OF PROOF**

Ranked according to degree of certainty, the various levels of proof are as follows:

1. **Absolute certainty**—not required for any legal purpose.

2. **Beyond reasonable doubt**—needed for conviction in a criminal case.

3. **Clear and convincing evidence**—needed for certain civil judgments, and for denial of bail in capital punishment cases in some jurisdictions.

4. **Preponderance of evidence**—needed for judgment in civil cases and for affirmative criminal defenses.

5. **Probable cause**—needed for issuance of warrants, arrests and search and seizure without warrant, filing of indictments and informations, revocation of probation and parole, and the making of a citizen's arrest.

6. **Reasonable belief**—needed for "stop and frisk".

7. **Reasonable doubt**—sufficient for acquittal of accused.

8. **Suspicion**—needed to commence an investigation.

9. **No information**—not sufficient for any legal purpose.

E. **SUMMARY**

The term "probable cause" is taken from the 4th Amendment of the United States Constitution and applies to arrests and searches and seizures. It has been defined by the Supreme Court as a situation in which the facts and circumstances within the police officer's knowledge and of which he has trustworthy information are sufficient in themselves to warrant a <u>man of reasonable caution</u> to believe that an offense has been or is being committed, or that property subject to seizure can be found in a particular place or on a particular person. For practical purposes, there is probable cause when—in the honest belief of a man of reasonable caution—a suspect's guilt is more probable than his innocence.

In cases where an arrest or search warrant is issued, probable cause is determined by a magistrate through a filed complaint or affidavit. In other cases, the officer makes the determination; and it is subject to challenge and review by the accused in court.

The existence of probable cause is required in all arrests and searches, with or without a warrant. Although the standard for probable cause is the same in all situations, the person making the determination and the matters of concern may differ. A police officer is advised to obtain a warrant from a magistrate whenever possible, since this is a strong protection against civil liability and creates a presumption of the legality of the arrest or search.

Probable cause may be established through personal knowledge of the facts by the police officer, through information given by other persons, or by a combination of both sources.

# IV. ARREST, "STOP AND FRISK", AND OTHER FORMS OF DETENTION.

A. **ARREST**

1. **Definition**: An arrest is the taking of a person into custody so that he may be held to answer for the commission of an offense. While all arrests involve restraint of a person's liberty, not all restraints fall under the category of an arrest.

2. **Elements**: There are four essential elements which must be present for an arrest to take place. These are: (1) Intention to arrest; (2) arrest authority; (3) seizure and detention; and (4) an understanding by the individual that he is being arrested.

    a. **Intention to arrest**: Without the requisite intent, there is no arrest even if a person is temporarily stopped or inconvenienced.

        (1) **Examples of "non-arrest"**: Stopping a motorist for the issuance of a ticket, stopping a person to determine whether or not he has a weapon, stopping a motorist to check his driver's license, or stopping a person to warn him of possible danger do not involve an arrest. In all these cases, there may be temporary deprivation of liberty or a certain amount of inconvenience; but there is no intent on the part of the police officer to take the person into custody.

        (2) **Subjectivity**: The requirement of intention to arrest is essentially subjective—meaning that it exists in the mind of the police officer. Intention to arrest is always difficult to prove in court, except when the actions of the police officer clearly indicate that he intended to take the person into custody.

            (a) Example: When an officer places handcuffs on a suspect, the intent to effect an arrest likely exists. But if the officer merely blocks the way of a suspect, an intention to arrest is not clear.

    b. **Arrest authority**: Authority to restrain distinguishes arrest from deprivations of liberty (such as kidnapping or illegal detention) committed by private individuals.

        (1) Where there is proper authorization, the arrest is valid.

        (2) Where proper authorization is lacking, the arrest is invalid. This can arise where:

            (a) The police officer mistakenly thinks he has authority to arrest when he in fact does not; or

            (b) The officer knows that he is not authorized to make the arrest, but does so anyway.

    c. **Seizure and detention**: Restraint of the subject may be either:

        (1) **Actual**—accomplished by taking the person into custody with the use of hands, firearms (denoting use of force without touching the individual), or by merely touching the individual without the use of force; or

        (2) **Constructive**—accomplished without any physical touching, grabbing, holding, or the use of force. This occurs when the individual peacefully submits to the officer's will and control.

(a) Mere words alone do not constitute an arrest. The fact that a police officer tells a person, "You are under arrest," is not sufficient. The required restraint must be accompanied by actual seizure or by submission to the officer's will and control.

d. **Understanding by the individual that he is being arrested**

(1) **How conveyed**: Understanding may be conveyed through

(a) **Words**—as when the police officer says, "You are under arrest;" or

(b) **Actions** which strongly imply that a person is being taken into custody, even though the police officer makes no statement.

1) Example: When a suspected burglar is subdued by police and taken to a squad car, or when a person is being handcuffed to be taken to the police station, this understanding can be deemed to exist.

(2) **Exceptions—understanding not required for arrest**: The element of understanding is not required for an arrest where the suspect is:

(a) Drunk or under the influence of drugs, and does not understand what is going on.

(b) Insane.

(c) Unconscious following the commission of a crime.

3. **Types of Authorized Arrests**: There are two types of authorized arrest: (1) Arrest with a warrant, and (2) arrest without a warrant.

a. **Arrest with warrant**: Arrests may be made pursuant to a warrant issued by proper judicial authority.

(1) **Complaint**: To secure the issuance of a warrant, a complaint (filed by the offended party or by the police officer) must be filed before a magistrate, showing probable cause for arrest of the accused. I.e., it must set forth facts showing that an offense has been committed and the accused's responsibility therefor.

(2) **Issuance of warrant**: If it appears to the magistrate from the complaint and accompanying documents or testimony that probable cause exists for the charges made against the accused, he issues a warrant for his arrest.

(a) **Who may issue**

1) Most states insist that the issuance of arrest warrants is strictly a judicial function and must therefore be performed by a judge or judicial officer. The issuing party must also be "neutral and detached."

2) Some states hold that since the requirement of probable cause is designed to be applied by laymen (as when a police officer arrests a suspect without a warrant upon probable cause), a non-judicial officer—such as a court clerk—may properly issue warrants if empowered to do so by statute, and if he is otherwise "neutral and detached."

3) The term "neutral and detached" means that the issuing officer is not unalterably aligned with the police or prosecutor's position in the matter.

(b) **Contents of warrant:** The warrant must describe the offense charged and contain the name of the accused or, if unknown, some description by which he can be identified with reasonable certainty.

1) Thus, a "John Doe" warrant—one in which only the name "John Doe" appears, because the real name of the suspect is not known to the police—is valid only if it contains a particular description of the accused by which he can be identified with reasonable certainty. A "John Doe" warrant without such a description is invalid, since it could be used by the police to arrest almost anyone.

(3) **Service of warrant:** An arrest warrant is directed to, and may be executed by, any peace officer in the jurisdiction. In some states, a properly designated private person can also serve a warrant.

(a) **Service within state:** Inside the state of issuance, a warrant issued in one county or judicial district may be served by peace officers of any other county or district where the accused is found.

1) Some states, such as Texas and California, have statutes giving local peace officers state-wide power of arrest—thereby allowing the police officers in the county or district where the warrant was issued to make the arrest anywhere in the state.

(b) **Service outside state:** A warrant has no authority beyond the territorial limits of the state in which it is issued. Hence, an arrest in State A cannot be made on the basis of a warrant issued in State B.

1) **"Fresh Pursuit" Act:** However, most states today have adopted a uniform act authorizing peace officers from one state who enter another in fresh pursuit to arrest the suspect for a felony committed in the first state.

(c) **Time of arrest:** In general, felony arrests may be made at any time, day or night, but misdemeanor arrests usually must be made during daylight hours. In some states (like Texas), an arrest for any crime—felony or misdemeanor can be made at any hour of the day or night.

(d) **Possession of warrant:** The arresting officer need not have the arrest warrant in his possession at the time of the arrest as long as he shows it to the accused after the arrest, if so requested.

(4) **Announcement requirement**

(a) **Statutory requirement:** Federal and many state statutes require that an officer making an arrest or executing a search warrant must announce his purpose and authority before breaking into a dwelling. The idea is to allow voluntary compliance and avoid violence.

1) **Effect of failure to announce:** Under these statutes, breaking into premises without first complying with the announcement requirement invalidates the entry and any resulting search. As a result, any evidence obtained must be excluded at the defendant's trial.

2) **Exceptions to announcement requirement**: Announcement is not required by statute where it would be dangerous or futile to do so—as when there is danger that contraband or other property sought might be destroyed, danger to life or limb, or danger of escape.

   a) Some statutes permit a magistrate to authorize so-called "no knock" searches, particularly for drug cases. These mean exactly that—searches without having to announce entry. The constitutionality of such statutes has not been fully tested, although they have been upheld by some lower courts.

3) **Breaking into premises after announcement**: Most statutes provide that breaking into the premises is not permitted unless the officer has reason to believe that he has been refused admittance. This requires a showing that the occupant expressly refused to open the door, the occurrence of facts so indicating (such as the sounds of running away, attempted escape through the window, etc.), or simply the fact that the door was not opened after the occupant had adequate time to do so.

(b) **Constitutional requirement**: The Supreme Court has held that the announcement rule is also required by the U.S. Constitution, but subject to certain broad exceptions recognized by state law. [Ker v. California, 374 U.S. 23, 1964]

   1) **Scope of exceptions**: The Court in the *Ker* case did not enumerate the situations in which an announcement need not be given. However, a dissenting opinion by four justices (not the majority holding) argued that unannounced police entry into private dwellings should be limited to three situations, namely:

      a) Where the occupants already know of the officer's purpose and authority;

      b) Where officers reasonably believe that persons within the premises are in imminent peril of bodily harm; or

      c) Where persons within are reasonably believed to be engaged in the destruction of evidence or in an escape because they are aware of the presence of the police.

(5) **Arrest warrant vs. other processes for arrest**

(a) **Summons or citation**: Statutes in many states authorize the use of a citation or summons (written notice to appear) for less serious offenses such as traffic violations. A summons or citation means the offender does not have to be taken into custody for that offense at that time. In the event of failure to appear at the time and date indicated in the summons or citation, however, a warrant of arrest may then be issued.

(b) **Search warrants**: Search warrants are similar to arrest warrants, except that they authorize a search for property with instructions that it be seized if found. A search warrant is usually valid only for a stated period of time (most expire if not executed within 10 days), whereas an arrest warrant is good until executed or withdrawn.

(c) **Bench warrants:** Bench warrants are used to bring a <u>non-appearing defendant</u> before the court. Failure to appear is an offense against the court itself, and hence no complaint need be filed.

b. **Arrests without warrant:** There are two general categories of arrests without a warrant: (1) Arrests by the <u>police</u>; and (2) arrests by citizens.

(1) **Arrests by police:** Under various circumstances, police officers have a general power to arrest without a warrant. Statutes vary from state to state, but the following provisions are typical:

(a) **Arrests by police for felonies**

1) A police officer has power to arrest a person who has <u>actually committed</u> a felony, whether committed in the presence of the officer making the arrest or not.

2) A police officer also has the power to arrest a person if he has probable cause for believing that the person has committed a felony—even though the suspected person is in fact innocent or no felony was committed.

(b) **Arrests by police for misdemeanor**

1) The general view is that a police officer has the power to arrest without a warrant for a misdemeanor, but only if the offense is <u>actually committed or attempted in his presence</u> and the person arrested is actually <u>guilty</u>.

   a) "In the presence of" a police officer refers to knowledge gained first-hand by a police officer as a result of his five senses—sight, hearing, smell, touch, or taste.

2) Some states (like California) allow a police officer to arrest for a misdemeanor if he <u>reasonably believes</u> that the offense was being committed in his presence and that the person arrested was guilty thereof.

3) And, a few states (like Arizona) go even further and authorize a police officer to arrest without a warrant if he has <u>probable cause</u> to believe that the suspect committed the misdemeanor, whether or not it was committed in his presence.

(2) **Arrests by citizens:** Arrests by citizens without warrant are usually limited to situations in which a <u>felony</u> has actually been committed and the citizen has probable cause to believe that the person arrested committed the crime.

(a) Some states also allow private citizens to make warrantless arrests for certain types of misdemeanors—usually where a "breach of the peace" is involved.

4. **Use of Force During Arrest**

a. **In general:** A police officer may use <u>reasonable force</u> under the following circumstances:

(1) To overcome the offender's resistance to a lawful arrest;

(2) To prevent his escape;

(3) To retake him if he escapes; and

(4) To protect the police officer from bodily harm.

    b. **What constitutes "reasonable force"**: Reasonable force is that force which a prudent and cautious man would use if exposed to similar circumstances. It is subjective and depends to a large extent upon the circumstances in each case.

    c. **Use of deadly force**

       (1) **In felony cases**: The rules for use of deadly force to effect an arrest in felony cases are basically the same as in cases of self defense:

          (a) The life of the police officer or another person must be in <u>danger</u>, <u>and</u>

          (b) The use of deadly force must be <u>immediately necessary</u> to preserve that life.

          In cases not amounting to self-defense—such as flight from or resistance to arrest—the use of deadly force poses great risks for the police officer and must be resorted to only as an act of <u>last resort</u>.

       (2) **In misdemeanor cases**: The safest advice for the police officer is never to use deadly force in misdemeanor cases. The only exception is when such force is necessary for purposes of <u>self-defense</u>.

    d. **Handcuffing**: The use of handcuffs is left to the <u>sound discretion</u> of the police officer. Such discretion is to be used to protect himself and the public from harm, and to prevent the escape of an arrested person or prisoner. As a general rule, handcuffs are required in felony offenses but not in misdemeanor cases—unless there is some personal danger to the police.

5. **Disposition of Prisoner After Arrest**

    a. **In general**: Statutes or court rules in most jurisdictions require that an arrested person be brought before a magistrate "without unnecessary delay." This is the <u>"initial appearance" stage</u> of the criminal justice process.

       (1) The term "without unnecessary delay" varies in meaning from one jurisdiction to another and is difficult to express in terms of allowable hours or days because the surrounding circumstances must be taken into account.

    b. **Purposes**: The purposes of the initial appearance are:

       (1) To <u>warn</u> the suspect of his rights (including the Miranda warnings, below);

       (2) To <u>determine</u> if there is justification for processing the suspect further through the system or, in the absence thereof, to set him free; and

       (3) If the suspect is to be further processed, to set <u>bail</u> for his release (except in the case of non-bailable offenses).

c. **"Miranda warnings"**: If the police officer does not have to or does not want to ask questions of the suspect (as in cases of arrest by warrant), there is no need to give the Miranda warnings. The magistrate will give these warnings during the initial appearance of the accused.

   (1) However, where the police officer wants to ask questions of the arrested person before the initial appearance with the magistrate, he must give the Miranda warning. I.e., the police officer must tell the suspect that he has the right to remain silent; that anything he says can be used against him in a court of law; that he has a right to counsel; and that if he is an indigent, counsel will be provided by the state. Failure to do so, unless validly waived by the accused, will render the evidence obtained inadmissible in court.

B. **"STOP AND FRISK"**

1. **In General**: A controversial issue in police practice is whether—and under what circumstances—a police officer may <u>stop</u> a person in a public place (or in an automobile), question him as to his identity and activities at the time, and <u>frisk</u> him for dangerous (and perhaps illegally-possessed) weapons. This practice is known as a "stop and frisk".

2. **Authorization for "Stop and Frisk"**

   a. **By statute**: Several states have passed "stop and frisk" laws which allow an officer to stop a person in a public place if the officer has "reasonable suspicion" that the person has committed or is about to commit a felony, and to demand the person's name and address and an explanation of his actions.

   b. **By judicial approval**: Other states, and some federal courts, have upheld such practices in judicial decisions even without statutory authorization.

   (1) **Justification**: Underlying both statutory and judicial approval of "stop and frisk" is the notion that this practice <u>does not constitute an arrest</u> and hence can be justified on less than probable cause for an arrest (discussed earlier).

3. **Guidelines**: The landmark case of *Terry v. Ohio*, 392 U.S. 1, 1968, sets the following guidelines to determine whether a "stop and frisk" is valid:

   a. **Circumstances**: The police officer must observe unusual conduct which leads him reasonably to conclude, in the light of his experience, that:

   (1) criminal activity may be afoot, and

   (2) the person with whom he is dealing may be armed and presently dangerous.

   b. **What police officer must initially do**: In the course of investigating such behavior, the officer must:

   (1) Identify himself as a peace officer;

   (2) Make reasonable inquiries; and

   (3) Find nothing in the initial stages of the encounter that serves to dispel his reasonable fear for his safety or the safety of others.

c. **Extent of what an officer can do:** If these first two requirements are satisfied, the officer is then entitled, for the protection of himself and others in the area to:

(1) Conduct a carefully limited search of the outer clothing of such person;

(2) In an attempt to discover weapons which might be used to assault him.

If, in the course of a frisk under the above circumstances, the officer finds a dangerous weapon, he may seize it; and the weapon may be introduced in evidence against the party from whom it was taken.

4. **Two Separate Acts Involved:** Although the term "stop and frisk" is often used as though one continuous act is involved, there are actually two separate acts in the process—each having its own requirements for legality.

a. A "stop" is justified only if the police officer has <u>reasonable suspicion</u>, in light of his experience, that <u>criminal activity is about to take place</u>. Therefore, the purpose of a "stop" is to prevent criminal activity. A "stop" for anything else is illegal unless it meets the standard of "probable cause" (thus making the act an arrest).

b. And, a "frisk" does not automatically follow a "stop". It should follow only if there is <u>nothing in the initial stages</u> of the encounter after the stop that would dispel reasonable fear about the safety of the police officer or of others. Hence, the purpose of a "frisk" is protection and should take place only if justified <u>after</u> the stop.

5. **Other Considerations in a "Stop and Frisk"**

a. **Extent of risk:** A "frisk" must be limited initially to a pat down of a person's outer clothing; and only an object which feels like a weapon may properly be seized. (The object may not turn out to be a weapon, but if it felt like one the frisk is justified.) Conversely, if the object does not feel like a weapon, it cannot be seized.

(1) **Example:** After a valid "stop" based on reasonable suspicion, a police officer has reasonable fear that the suspect may be armed. He then "frisks" the suspect and in the process feels something soft which cannot possibly be considered a weapon. He cannot validly seize the object in question.

(2) **Note:** Possible confusion over the above rule has arisen because of the decision in *U.S. v. Robinson*, 414 U.S. 218, 1975. In the *Robinson* case, the Supreme Court held that a body search after an authorized arrest for driving without a permit is valid even where the officer admits there was no possible danger to him and therefore no reason to look for possible weapon. However, the *Robinson* case involved an arrest, not a "stop and frisk."

b. **Evidence obtained in a stop and frisk** is admissible in court only if <u>both</u> the "stop" and the "frisk" were justified.

c. **No "fishing expeditions" allowed:** The "frisk" cannot be used to see if some type of evidence can be found on the suspect. Its only purpose is to protect the police officer and others in the area from possible harm.

d. **Drivers are subject to the practice:** "Stop and frisk" also applies to drivers of motor vehicles.

6. **Distinctions Between "Stop and Frisk" and Arrest or Search and Seizure:** The basic differences between "stop and frisk" on the one hand and arrest or search and seizure on the other are shown in the following chart:

|  | | "Stop and Frisk" | Arrest or Search and Seizure |
|---|---|---|---|
| a. | Degree of certainty | "Reasonable suspicion" | "Probable cause" |
| b. | Scope | Very limited—only pat down for weapons | Extensive |
| c. | Purpose | a. Stop—to prevent criminal activity<br>b. Frisk—to protect officer and others | To take person into custody or obtain evidence |
| d. | Warrant | Not needed | May or may not need warrant, depending on circumstances |

## C. OTHER FORMS OF DETENTION

In addition to arrest and "stop and frisk", certain other forms of detention should be mentioned. These include: (1) Station house detention; (2) roadblocks; (3) airport searches; and (4) arrests by bondsmen.

1. **Station House Detention:** This involves a form of detention which is short of arrest but greater than the on-the-street detention in a "stop and frisk".

    a. **Purposes:** Station house detention is used in some jurisdictions for obtaining fingerprints or photographs, police line-ups, administering polygraph examinations, or securing other identification or non-testimonial evidence.

    b. **Can suspect be taken to police station?** It is an open question whether a suspect can be taken into custody and transported to the police station involuntarily for purposes of further investigation when no arrest is made.

    (1) The Supreme Court has implied that such detention for <u>fingerprinting</u> might be made even without probable cause to arrest. [Davis v. Mississippi, 394 U.S. 721, 1969] However, the Court made it clear that "narrowly circumscribed procedures" were required, including at least some objective basis for suspecting the person of a crime, a legitimate investigatory purpose for the detention (such as fingerprinting), scheduling of the detention at a time not inconvenient for the subject, and a court order that adequate evidence existed to justify the detention.

2. **Roadblocks:** Although not strictly a form of detention, roadblocks tend to limit a person's freedom of movement. They are used by the police for a variety of purposes—including spot checks of drivers' licenses, car registrations and violations of motor vehicle laws, and to apprehend fleeing criminals and suspects.

a. **Legality:** The legality of roadblocks has not been directly decided by the Supreme Court. Several states have passed statutes authorizing the practice and specifying guidelines for its use. And, lower courts have generally held that stopping persons at roadblocks on less than probable cause or reasonable suspicion is necessary and helpful for the enforcement of traffic regulations or other administrative rules.

b. **But note:** While roadblocks can be imposed, <u>searches</u> of a motor vehicle during a roadblock cannot validly be undertaken without probable cause.

3. **Airport Searches:** A limited search of air travellers is permissible for the purpose of discovering weapons and preventing hijacking.

a. If an electronic search method (i.e., a magnetometer) is used and the reading indicates a possible weapon, a frisk or pat-down of the traveller's clothing is then justified. Evidence discovered thereby is admissible in court.

4. **Arrests by Bondsmen:** A bondsman who posts bond for the temporary release of an accused has the authority to arrest and deprive a person of liberty should he jump bail.

a. **Status of bondsman:** A bondsman is a private citizen and does not have specific police powers. But the posting of a bond legally transfers custody of an accused from the government to the bondsman on condition that the accused will be present when needed for trial. By virtue of this responsibility, the bondsman has the authority to arrest an accused and deprive him of liberty.

## D. SUMMARY

An arrest is generally an act of the state, carried out through its peace officers, which deprives a person of liberty because of the commission of an offense. It has four essential elements: Intention to arrest, arrest authority, seizure and detention, and an understanding by the individual that he is being arrested. These elements distinguish arrests from other forms of detention.

Arrests are generally of two kinds: With warrant and without warrant. Each form has its own requirements for validity. A police officer is advised to obtain a warrant whenever practicable because this creates a strong presumption of legality for the arrest and thereby helps protect him from subsequent civil suits. However, arrests without warrant are necessary in many instances, and are valid as long as they are based upon probable cause. Private citizens may also make arrests, but usually only for felonies and with probable cause.

The use of force is justified in a number of instances, but it must be reasonable force in the light of the surrounding circumstances. The use of deadly force is generally permitted only in cases of self-defense.

The practice of "stop and frisk" is valid if it satisfies specific conditions. It must be based on "reasonable suspicion", and is used if the police officer suspects that criminal activity is about to take place. Although often discussed as if it constituted one act, "stop and frisk" refers to two different acts, each of which has its own requirements for legality. The primary purpose of the procedure is to prevent harm to police officers and others.

Other forms of detention include station house detention, roadblocks, airport searches, and arrests by bondsmen. Station house detentions and roadblocks have been given implied approval by the United States Supreme Court, while arrests by bondsmen have been authorized because of their obligation to produce the accused during the time set for the trial.

# V. SEARCHES AND SEIZURES

The 4th Amendment of the U.S. Constitution provides that "the right of people to be secure in their persons, houses, papers and effects against unreasonable <u>searches and seizures</u> shall not be violated, and <u>no warrants shall issue, but upon probable cause</u> supported by oath or affirmation, and particularly describing the place to be searched and the persons or things to be seized."

### A. DEFINITIONS

1. **"Search"**: A "search" is any <u>governmental intrusion</u> upon a person's reasonable and justifiable expectation of privacy. It is not limited to homes, offices, buildings, or other enclosed places. Rather, it can occur in any place where a person has a "reasonable and justifiable expectation of privacy".

    a. Example: Police "bugging" of a public telephone booth violated a person's reasonable expectation of privacy within the booth. [Katz v. U.S., 389 U.S. 347, 1967]

    b. Example: Police install a peephole in the ceiling of a public restroom which allows them to observe what occurs in the stalls. Officers observe A and B engaging in illegal sex acts in one of the stalls. This is likewise not a lawful "search" within the meaning of the 4th Amendment . . . because A and B had a reasonable expectation that their acts would not be observed by others (even though the restroom was a "public" place).

    c. Searches and seizures by <u>private persons</u> do not come within the 4th Amendment guarantee, because it applies only to <u>governmental officers</u>. Thus, evidence obtained by private persons is admissible in court as long as the police did not encourage or participate in the private search.

2. **"Seizure"**: A "seizure" is the <u>exercise of dominion or control</u> by the government over a person or thing because of a violation of law.

### B. TYPES OF SEARCH OR SEIZURE

Two basic types exist: (1) Searches with warrant, and (2) searches without warrant.

1. **Search WITH Warrant**: A search warrant is a <u>written order</u> issued by a magistrate, directing a peace officer to search for personal property connected with a crime and bring it before the court.

    a. **General rule**: A search or seizure generally is reasonable under the 4th Amendment <u>only if</u> made with a warrant based on probable cause. Valid searches without warrant (discussed below) are thus an exception to this general rule.

    b. **Basic requirements**: The basic requirements for valid issuance of a search warrant are: (1) Probable cause, (2) supported by oath or affirmation which (3) particularly describes the place to be searched and the person or things to be seized, and (4) is signed by a magistrate.

    (1) The requirements for probable cause are discussed in Chapter III, supra.

    (2) **Support by oath or affirmation**: A warrant is issued based on a sworn affidavit presented to the magistrate establishing grounds for the warrant. The magistrate issues the warrant only if he is satisfied upon the affidavit that probable cause for a warrant exists.

(a) The contents of the affidavit must be sufficient to allow an independent evaluation of probable cause by the magistrate.

(b) The affidavit must establish essential facts: To enable the magistrate to make an independent evaluation, the affidavit must contain more than mere conclusions by the police officer. Rather, it must allege facts showing that seizable evidence will be found in the place to be searched.

(3) **Particular description of place to be searched and person or things to be seized**

(a) **Place to be searched**: The affidavit must remove any <u>doubt or uncertainty</u> as to the premises to be searched. For example, if the premises are an apartment in a multiple-dwelling apartment house, the warrant must specify which apartment is to be searched.

(b) **Items to be seized**: Items for seizure must also be described with <u>sufficient particularity</u> that the warrant server will have little discretion as to what may be seized.

1) Example: The warrant cannot simply provide for the seizure of "stolen goods"; an acceptable identification would be, "a 25-inch Zenith television set."

2) Note that contraband does not have to be described with as much particularity, because it is in itself seizable.

(4) **Warrant must be signed by a magistrate**: The warrant must be issued only by a "neutral and detached" magistrate. Thus, a search warrant issued by the state's chief investigator and prosecutor (who also was a justice of the peace) has been held invalid. [Coolidge v. New Hampshire, 404 U.S. 443, 1971]

c. **Procedure for service of warrant**

(1) The search warrant is directed to a law enforcement officer, and must state the grounds for issuance and the names of those who gave affidavits in support of it.

(2) The warrant usually directs that it be served in the daytime; but if the affidavits are positive that the property is on the person or in the place to be searched, the warrant may direct that it be served at any time.

(3) The warrant must designate the judge or commissioner to whom the warrant is to be returned.

(4) The warrant must be executed and delivered within a specified number of days from the date of issuance. Some states specify 10 days, while others allow less time.

(5) Search and seizure must not excede scope of warrant: The search must <u>not go beyond the premises described in the warrant</u>, and must be limited to locating the item or items described in the warrant. For example, a warrant authorizing search for a stolen television set would not justify a search through locked desk drawers. [Marron v. U.S., 275 U.S. 192, 1927]

(a) Nevertheless, the police may confiscate any seizable evidence which is in "<u>plain view</u>" during a valid search—such as contraband, fruits or instrumentalities of the crime, or "mere evidence".

(b) **Example:** While executing a search warrant authorizing search of a suspect's house for a stolen typewriter, police officer sees powder which he immediately recognizes as heroin on suspect's nightstand. Seizure may be upheld, since this is contraband in "plain view".

(6) The officer executing the warrant must give a copy of the warrant and a receipt for any seized property to the person from whom he takes it, or leave a copy and receipt on the premises. A written inventory must be made; and the return —accompanied by the inventory—must be made promptly.

d. **Announcement requirement for searches and seizures:** The rules here are the same as those for arrests, discussed in Chapter IV, infra:

(1) **Statutory requirement:** Federal (and many state) statutes require that an officer, when making an arrest or executing a search warrant, announce his purpose and authority before breaking into a dwelling. The idea is to allow voluntary compliance and avoid violence.

(a) **Effect of failure to announce:** Under these statutes, breaking into the premises without first complying with the announcement requirement invalidates the entry and any resulting search. Therefore, any evidence obtained must be excluded at defendant's trial.

(b) **Exceptions to requirement**

1) By statute or case law, no announcement is required where it would be dangerous or futile to do so (as where there is danger that contraband or other property sought might be destroyed, danger to life or limb, or danger of escape).

2) Some statutes likewise permit a magistrate to authorize "no knock" searches, particularly in drug cases.

(c) **Breaking into premises after announcement:** Most statutes provide that breaking into the premises is prohibited unless the officer has reason to believe that he has been refused admittance. This requires a showing that the occupant expressly refused to open the door, the occurrence of facts so indicating (such as the sounds of running away, attempted escape through window etc.),–or simply that the door was not opened after adequate time for the occupant to do so.

(2) **Constitutional requirement:** The announcement rule is also required by the U.S. Constitution, but is subject to certain broad exceptions recognized by state law. [Ker v. California, 374 U.S. 23, 1964]

(a) **Exceptions:** The Supreme Court in the *Ker* case did not enumerate all situations in which an announcement could be dispensed with. However, the dissenting (not majority) opinion argued that unannounced police entry into private dwellings should be confined to only three situations, namely:

1) Where the occupants already know of the officer's purpose and authority;

2) Where the officers reasonably believe that persons inside are in imminent peril of bodily harm; or

3) Where persons within are reasonably believed to be engaged in the <u>destruction of evidence</u> or in an <u>escape</u> because they are aware of police presence. (This was the basis on which the Court upheld an unannounced entry in the *Ker* case.)

e. **Oral warrants:** Two states (California and Arizona) permit <u>oral</u> search warrants. Under this procedure, the police apply for the warrant in person or by telephone, stating facts under oath. A recording is made thereof and the judge then orally authorizes the warrant, which is likewise recorded. The practice is valid, since the 4th Amendment does not specify that the supporting affidavit or complaint be in writing.

2. **Searches WITHOUT a Search Warrant:** The general rule is that any governmental search or seizure without a valid warrant is "unreasonable" and therefore illegal. However, there are three basic exceptions to this warrant requirement: (a) Where the search is incidental to a lawful arrest; (b) where the search is with consent; and (c) where special factors justify the intrusion.

   a. **Searches incident to a lawful arrest:** This is by far the most important and most widely utilized exception to the warrant requirement. There are two requirements for such a search, namely:

   (1) **The arrest itself must be lawful**—i.e. there must be an arrest warrant based on probable cause, or the arresting officer must have probable cause to arrest without a warrant; <u>and</u>

   (2) **The search must be limited in scope**—meaning that the search is reasonably required to <u>protect the arresting officer</u> from a possibly armed suspect or to <u>prevent the destruction of evidence</u>. [Chimel v. California, 395 U.S. 752, 1969]

   (a) **Suspect taken into custody—full search of person permitted:** Whenever a suspect is taken into custody, the police may conduct a <u>full search</u> of his person before taking him to the police station. [U.S. v. Robinson, 414 U.S. 218, 1974]

   1) A search of the person includes the right to search the suspect's clothing and any container (such as a cigarette case) carried in his clothing, to prevent destruction of evidence or the smuggling of weapons into jail.

   2) A full search is permitted regardless of the nature of the crime for which the arrest is made. The police do not have to show that they had reason to suspect that the accused was armed or likely to destroy evidence.

   a) Example: X is properly arrested for driving without a valid permit. There is no danger to the police officer, nor is there any danger of destruction of evidence. After the arrest, the officer searches X's person and finds illegal drugs in his pockets. The drug seizure is valid and the evidence can be admitted in court.

   (b) **Suspect taken into custody—search of area within immediate reach permitted:** In addition to a full search of the person of suspects taken into custody, the police may also search <u>any area within the suspect's immediate reach</u> from which he might grab a weapon or destroy evidence. [Chimel v. California, 395 U.S. 752, 1969]

1) **"Area" liberally defined**: Courts tend to be liberal in defining the area into which an arrested person might reach. For example, where an accused was sitting on a bed at the time of her arrest, the area underneath her bed was deemed to be within her "reach". In another case, the fact that D was handcuffed (and his reach thereby limited) was held not to limit the permissible area of search.

2) **Exigent circumstances**: Some courts have permitted the police to search areas in a residence which are beyond a defendant's "reach" <u>if</u> (1) there is some type of emergency requiring immediate action which cannot await the preparation of a search warrant (such as destruction of evidence) <u>and</u> (2) the search is focused on a pre-determined target (such as narcotics in a particular dresser drawer) rather than being a general exploratory search.

(c) **Relevant time frame**: A custodial search may be deemed "incident to arrest" even if carried out <u>later than the time of the arrest</u>, provided there was a valid reason for the delay. Example: A suspect was arrested and jailed late at night. A clothing search the following morning for evidence of the crime was justified, since substitute clothing was not available at the time of booking. [U.S. v. Edwards, 415 U.S. 800, 1974]

(d) **Suspect not taken into custody**: In contrast to situations in which an arrest has been made, where a person is temporarily detained but <u>not</u> taken into custody (as when a person is given a citation instead of being arrested), an ensuing search <u>cannot extend beyond a frisk</u> for weapons and further evidence of the particular crime for which the temporary detention was made.

b. **Searches with consent of accused**

(1) **Consent must be voluntary**: To validate a warrantless search on grounds of consent, the prosecution must show that the accused's consent was "voluntary" and not the result of force or coercion. Voluntariness is determined from all of the surrounding circumstances.

(a) Example: Consent given only after the officer demands entry cannot be deemed free and voluntary. "Open the door" will most likely be interpreted as giving the occupant no choice and therefore as making consent involuntary.

(b) The better practice is for the officer to "request" rather than "demand". Words such as "Would you mind if I come in and look around?" are more likely to result in voluntary consent.

(c) Mere failure to object to a search does not necessarily mean that consent was given. The consent must be <u>clear</u>.

(d) Nor is there valid consent if permission is given as a result of misrepresentation or deception.

1) Example: "We have a search warrant" when in fact none exists.

(2) **Consent to enter does not necessarily mean consent to search**: Thus, for example, consent to enter for purposes of "answering some questions" does not mean consent to a search.

(a) However, the "plain view" doctrine applies—so that any seizable item in plain view after valid entry may be properly seized.

(3) **Warning of rights not required**: The Supreme Court has held that there is no requirement that the police warn the suspect that he has the right to refuse to consent. Rather, the presence (or absence) of such a warning is merely one factor to be taken into account in determining whether the consent was voluntary. [Schneckloth v. Bustamonte, 412 U.S. 218, 1973]

(4) **Scope of search**: The scope of search permitted depends upon the type of consent given. For example, the statement "You may look around" does not authorize the opening of trunks and boxes.

(5) **Revocation of consent**: Consent given may be revoked at any time, even in the course of a search by the person giving it. But evidence obtained before such a revocation is admissible.

(6) **WHO may give consent to search**

    (a) **Landlord—no**: A landlord cannot give valid consent to search property which he has rented to another person.

    (b) **Hotel clerk—no**: Nor can a hotel clerk give effective consent to the search of a guest's room.

    (c) **Co-occupant—yes, with exceptions**: Family members or other persons who share a house can give valid consent.

        1) However, where the co-tenant is present and objects to a search consented to by a co-tenant, evidence recovered from an area that is jointly possessed cannot be used against the non-consenting co-tenant.

        2) And, where a closet, desk, dresser or other area is reserved for the private use of one member of the household, only that person can consent. Example: Stepfather could not effectively consent to police search of personal belongings in adult stepson's room, regardless of the fact that they shared a bedroom. Also, one spouse cannot give effective consent to search the other spouse's personal effects which were not exposed to plain view in their bedroom.

            a) But even as to a person's private belongings, if he allows another person to use same he assumes the risk that the person may show them to police—in which case there is an effective consent. Example: D left his duffel bag at friend's house and allowed the friend to use the bag. By doing so, D assumed the risk that his friend might consent to a police request to search the bag . . . even though D himself would not have consented.

            b) And, where the co-occupant or family member voluntarily gives the absent member's personal belongings to the police (so that they are "in plain view"), evidence so obtained may be admissible. Example: Where police in a murder investigation questioned Wife regarding Husband's guns and clothing, and she spontaneously gave the items to the police in a good-faith effort to clear him, there was no unlawful search or seizure. [Coolidge v. New Hampshire, 403 U.S. 443, 1971]

c. **Situations where special factors justify intrusion without a warrant:** The two broadest grounds upon which search or seizure without a warrant may be justified are incident to a lawful arrest or with valid consent (discussed above). However, there are several more limited grounds upon which warrantless searches are constitutionally permissible—basically where special factors outweigh 4th Amendment considerations and thus justify police intrusion. These include: (1) Emergency searches or searches justified by "exigent circumstances"; (2) automobile searches; (3) searches in "hot pursuit"; (4) search of goods in the course of transit; (5) mail searches; (6) border searches; and (7) "stop and frisk" searches.

(1) **Emergency searches or searches justified by "exigent circumstances":** A warrantless search may be justified when there is reasonable ground to believe that delaying the search until a warrant is obtained would endanger the physical safety of the officers or third persons or allow the destruction or removal of the evidence sought. [Vale v. Louisiana, 399 U.S. 30, 1970]

(a) Example: An officer may enter a dwelling without a warrant in response to screams for help. Once inside, he can conduct a search for the person who cried for help; and may also confiscate whatever seizable evidence is in "plain view".

(b) Similarly, taking a blood sample from a person arrested for drunk driving is proper without a search warrant—and by force if necessary (but with reasonable procedures). "Exigent circumstances" exist because alcohol in the suspect's bloodstream might disappear in the time required to obtain a warrant. [Schmerber v. California, 384 U.S. 757, 1966]

(c) "Exigent circumstances" may also justify the seizure of physical evidence from a person not yet arrested. In one case, the police had probable cause to arrest X for strangling his wife, but had not yet done so. They asked X for permission to take scrapings from his fingernails, whereupon X realized that he was under suspicion and began to destroy such evidence. The police were justified in taking the scrapings by force without a warrant, in view of the highly destructible nature of the evidence. [Cupp v. Murphy, 412 U.S. 291, 1973]

(2) **Automobile searches**

(a) **In general:** Warrantless searches of automobiles have been upheld as reasonable in circumstances where such a search in a home would have been illegal.

(b) **Reasons for permitting auto searches:** Justifications for this distinction are:

1) The inherent mobility of automobiles, which would frequently make strict application of the warrant requirement impossible; and

2) The fact that the expectation of privacy in an automobile is significantly less than in a home or office.

(c) **Specific situations**

1) **Moving vehicles:** Police may search an automobile that is actually moving upon the highway or temporarily stopped, if they have

probable cause to believe that it contains items subject to seizure. [Carroll v. U.S. 267 U.S. 123, 1925]

- a) **"Fleeting target" rationale:** The theory is that an automobile on the highway, as opposed to an automobile parked at a person's home, is a "fleeting target". I.e., it can rapidly move out of the jurisdiction before the police can obtain a search warrant.

- b) **Probable cause as to contents of car:** These searches occur most frequently when officers have probable cause to believe that the car contains contraband, especially illicit drugs or weapons. Such probable cause may be based on traces of the contraband in "plain view", or the odor of same. The presence of contraband may also be inferred if an occupant of the car makes a "furtive gesture" as if to hide something.

- c) **Delayed search of vehicle stopped on highway:** If the police have probable cause to stop and search an automobile on the highway, they may also detain it until a search warrant is obtained—or, where reasonable, may take it to the police station and search it there. [Chambers v. Maroney, 399 U.S. 42, 1970]

2) **Example:** Police, having probable cause, stopped X's car on the highway and arrested him for robbery. At that point, there was also probable cause to search the car for the loot without a warrant. Instead, the police towed the auto to headquarters and searched it there . . . by which point they had had ample time to obtain a warrant and did not do so. Nevertheless, the search was proper, because the police had probable cause to search the vehicle at the time it was first stopped on the highway. [Chambers v. Maroney, above]

3) **Vehicles impounded by police:** When the police lawfully impound a car, they may conduct a routine inventory search of the car (including the glove compartment, at least if unlocked) without a warrant or probable cause to believe that it contains seizable evidence. This is reasonable in order to protect the owner's property, to protect the police against a claim that the owner's property was stolen while impounded, and to protect against vandals finding firearms or contraband. [South Dakota v. Opperman, 428 U.S. 364, 1976—automobile towed to police station for overparking; owner was not available, and a watch and other items of personal property had been observed in "plain view" through the windshield]

- a) Similar reasoning may justify a warrantless search of a car which has been involved in a traffic accident and towed to a private garage for repair. Such a vehicle is neither in the custody nor on the premises of its owner; and a police search may therefore be reasonable if believed necessary for the "safety of the general public". [Cady v. Dombrowski, 413 U.S. 433, 1973—police searched car for revolver because hospitalized driver was police officer and they believed he had been carrying a firearm]

4) **Vehicles parked in driveway or on street—items in "plain view"**: An officer looking through the window of a parked car—and even shining a flashlight into the car to better observe its contents—does not constitute an unreasonable "search". [Cardwell v. Lewis, 417 U.S. 583, 1974]

   a) **Seizure of evidence may require warrant**: However, while shining a flashlight into the car does not constitute a "search", an officer's <u>entering</u> the car and seizing evidence (e.g., contraband observed in back seat) definitely <u>would</u> be a search and seizure, and must meet 4th Amendment standards. Thus, unless there are exigent circumstances justifying an immediate seizure—i.e., probable cause to believe that evidence will be removed or destroyed—the officer must obtain a search warrant <u>before</u> entering the car.

(3) **Searches in "hot pursuit" (or "fresh pursuit") of dangerous suspects**: The police may enter a house without a warrant to search for a dangerous suspect when they are in "hot pursuit" of him and have reason to believe that he is within the premises. [Warden v. Hayden, 387 U.S. 294, 1967]

   (a) Once inside, the police may continue their search as to any other person who might pose a threat to the officers' safety.

   (b) And, any evidence which is in the officers' "plain view" may be seized and is admissible on the theory that the officers had a right to be where they were when they saw it.

(4) **Goods in the course of transit**: The reasoning used to justify warrantless searches of a moving vehicle has also been applied to searches of goods in the course of transit by a common carrier. This means that if there is <u>probable cause</u> to believe that the shipment contains contraband and a search warrant cannot be obtained in time to detain the shipment, a warrantless search may be made.

(5) **Mail searches**: First class letters and sealed packages are fully protected by the 4th Amendment, and hence cannot be searched by the police or postal authorities without a search warrant.

   (a) However, if postal authorities have <u>probable cause</u> to believe that such mail contains <u>contraband or other seizable evidence</u>, they have the <u>right to detain the mail for a reasonable time</u>—i.e., long enough to enable them, acting diligently, to obtain a search warrant. [U.S. v. Van Leeuwen, 397 U.S. 249, 1970]

(6) **Border searches**: The magnitude of smuggling and theft problems at international borders, airports and seaports has led to a relaxation of the "probable cause" requirement for searches at such locations. Hence, a border patrol or customs officer is entitled to search on the basis of a <u>reasonable suspicion</u> that the person is engaged in illegal activity.

   (a) **Persons searched**: The persons searched need not be persons entering the country. Anyone found in a "border area" is subject to search on the basis of reasonable suspicion. This includes visitors, employees, transportation workers, etc.

(b) **"Border area"**: The area in which a border search may be conducted is not limited to the actual point of entry. It may also be conducted at any place which is the "functional equivalent" of the border, such as an established station or intersection near the border, the place where a plane first lands, and all areas immediately adjacent to the point of entry. [Almeida-Sanchez v. U.S., 413 U.S. 266, 1973]

(c) **But note**: None of the foregoing justifies searches by a "roving patrol" of customs officers 20 miles from the border or at a checkpoint 66 miles from the border, where there is no ground to suspect illegal activity. Searches by chance cannot be justified as "border searches", and must be based on probable cause or consent.

   1) Nor may a roving patrol detain persons for questioning in an area near the border solely because occupants of a vehicle "looked Mexican". [U.S. v Brignoni-Ponce, 422 U.S. 873, 1975—patrol must have a reasonable suspicion in order to detain and question occupant]

   2) However, a vehicle may be stopped at an established checkpoint for brief routine questioning of its occupants even though there is no particular reason to believe that the vehicle is carrying aliens. [U.S. v. Martinez-Fuerte, 428 U.S. 543, 1976]

(7) **"Stop and frisk" searches**: No warrant is required for this type of search, if the other requirements therefor are met. (See discussion of "stop and frisk" in Chapter III, supra)

## C. ITEMS SUBJECT TO SEARCH AND SEIZURE

The following items can be searched and seized:

1. **Contraband**—such as narcotics, counterfeit money and plates, etc.—because it is illegal for anybody to have such items.

2. **Fruits of the Crime**—such as stolen goods, forged checks, etc.

3. **Instrumentalities of Crime**—such as weapons, burglary tools, etc.

4. **"Mere Evidence" of the Crime**—such as suspect's clothing containing bloodstains of the victim, suspect's mask, shoes, wig, etc.—provided there is probable cause to believe that the item is related to criminal activity.

## D. GENERAL GUIDE IN SEARCH AND SEIZURE CASES

To avoid confusion in search and seizure cases, the student should ask himself the following questions in any situation involving search and seizure:

1. Is the police activity a "search and seizure", or is it something else (such as "stop and frisk" or "plain view")?

2. Are the circumstances such that a search warrant is required? If so, was a valid search warrant obtained?

3. Are the circumstances such that a search without a warrant is justified (such as searches incident to a valid arrest, searches with consent, or the presence of special or exigent circumstances justifying intrusion without warrant)?

4. What scope of search is permissible; and did the police activity exceed such scope?

E. **SUMMARY**

A "search" is any <u>governmental intrusion</u> upon a person's reasonable expectation of privacy, while a "seizure" is the <u>exercise of dominion or control</u> by the government over a person or thing for a violation of law.

Searches and seizures are of two kinds: Those made <u>with warrant</u> and those made <u>without warrant</u>. The <u>general rule</u> is that searches and seizures are valid <u>only</u> if done with <u>warrant</u>. A warrant is a written order issued by a magistrate, directing a peace officer to search for personal property connected with a crime so that it can be brought before the court.

The basic requirements for issuance of a warrant are probable cause, supported by an oath or affirmation which particularly describes the place to be searched and the persons or things to be seized, and signature of the warrant by a magistrate.

There are three general situations in which searches and seizures can properly be made without a warrant. These are: Searches incident to a lawful arrest, searches with consent; and situations in which special or exigent circumstances justify intrusion without warrant. This last category includes emergency searches, automobile searches, searches in "hot pursuit", goods in the course of transit, mail searches, border searches, and "stop and frisk".

Not all items are subject to search and seizure. Those which can be seized fall into four categories: Contraband, fruits of the crime, instrumentalities of the crime, and "mere evidence".

# VI. PLAIN VIEW, OPEN FIELDS, ABANDONMENT AND ELECTRONIC SURVEILLANCE

Certain other matters relating to searches and seizures deserve separate consideration. These include the "plain view" doctrine, the "open fields" doctrine, abandoned property and electronic surveillance.

### A. "PLAIN VIEW" DOCTRINE

The "plain view" doctrine states that items which are within sight of an officer who has a right to be in the place from which the view is made, and who had no prior knowledge that the items were present, may properly be seized without a warrant—as long as such items are immediately recognizable as property subject to seizure.

1. **Requirements**: As the above definition indicates, there are five basic requirements for reliance on the "plain view" doctrine. These are:

    a. **Items must be within the officer's sight**: This means that awareness of the items must be gained solely through the sense of sight—not through the other senses, such as hearing, smelling, tasting or touching.

    (1) **Example**: While executing a search warrant for a stolen typewriter, the police officer sees vials of cocaine on the suspect's nightstand. Seizure may be made because through his sense of sight the officer knows that the item is contraband and therefore seizable. On the other hand, if the officer senses that there is marijuana in the apartment because of the smell, its seizure in the course of a search cannot be justified under the "plain view" doctrine because it was not discovered through the officer's sense of sight. (Of course, it may be validly seized for "probable cause" or on some other basis if the requirements therefor are met.)

    b. **Officer must legally be in the place from which he sees the items**: The officer must have done nothing illegal to get to the spot from which he sees the items in question. An officer in the place properly serving a search warrant, in the building while in "hot pursuit" of a suspect, on the premises through consent, or making an arrest with or without a warrant would properly be in the "sighting" position.

    (1) **Example**: While executing a search warrant for a stolen TV set, an officer sees illegal drugs on a table. He may properly seize the drugs, even though not included in the warrant, as long as his presence in the premises is legal.

    (2) In contrast, a police officer who forces himself into a house and thereupon sees drugs on the table cannot properly seize the drugs—since he entered the house illegally.

    c. **Officer must have no prior knowledge that such items are present**: The officer must not use the "plain view" doctrine as a pretext for seizing without a warrant items which he already knows are there.

    (1) **Example**: Officer knows that a murder weapon can be found in an apartment where the suspect lives. He asks for and is given permission to enter and look around. If he goes straight to the bedroom and seizes the murder weapon, the seizure cannot come under the "plain view" doctrine.

(a) **Compare:** If the officer knew that the weapon could be found in the suspect's apartment, he can obtain a search warrant or—if properly allowed into the house—can justify the seizure under "consent".

d. **Items must be immediately recognizable as subject to seizure:** Such recognition must be instantaneous, and not the result of further inquiry or prying.

(1) **Example:** Officer is given valid consent by an apartment owner to come in. Once inside, he sees something which he immediately recognizes to be drugs. This is seizable under "plain view".

(2) In contrast, suppose that after a valid entry the officer sees a typewriter which he suspects is stolen. He calls the police station to ask for the serial number of a typewriter earlier reported stolen and, after verification of the number, seizes the typewriter. This seizure cannot be justified under the "plain view" doctrine because the item was not immediately recognizable as subject to seizure.

e. **Items must actually be subject to seizure:** This means that the items must fall within one of the four seizable categories, namely: Contraband, fruits of the crime, instrumentalities of the crime, or "mere evidence" of the crime. Items outside these categories cannot be seized.

2. **Justification for Doctrine:** What the officer does under "plain view" is not considered a "search" within the 4th Amendment because no search for that specific item has been undertaken (although the discovery could be made while the officer is in the process of another search through a warrant, etc.). No warrant is necessary because the officer simply seizes what he sees, not what he has searched for.

B. **"OPEN FIELDS" DOCTRINE**

The "open fields" doctrine states that items in open fields are not protected by the 4th Amendment guarantee against unreasonable searches and seizures, and thus can properly be taken by an officer without warrant or probable cause.

1. **Justification:** Since the 4th Amendment protects only "houses, papers, and effects" against unreasonable searches and seizures, and the term "house" excludes "open fields", the constitutional protection does not apply.

2. **Areas Not Included in "Open Field" Doctrine:** Certain areas come within the 4th Amendment and thus do not qualify for the "open field" doctrine:

a. **"Houses":** The courts have interpreted the term "houses" under the 4th Amendment rather broadly—applying it to homes (owned, rented, or leased), apartments, hotel or motel rooms, hospital rooms, or even sections of places of business which are not generally open to the public.

b. **"Curtilage":** Curtilage means the grounds and buildings immediately surrounding a dwelling. Curtilage is likewise not considered an "open field" and hence is protected against unreasonable searches and seizures.

(1) **Scope of coverage:** "Curtilage" may encompass a variety of places, including the following:

(a) **Residential yards:** Courts disagree on whether this is part of the "curtilage". If members of the public have access to the yard at any time, it is probably not curtilage. But if only members of the family have access thereto, it may be part of the curtilage.

- (b) **Fenced areas**: A fence around a house makes the immediate environs within that fence a part of the curtilage. Here, the owner clearly intended for that area to be private and not open to the general public.

- (c) **Apartment houses**: Areas of an apartment building which are used in common by all tenants are not considered part of any tenants' curtilage. However, if the apartment building is of limited size (such as a four-unit building) and each apartment has its own backyard or frontyard which is not accessible to the general public, such areas would be part of the curtilage.

- (d) **Barns and other outbuildings**: These are usually considered part of the curtilage if they are used extensively by the family, are enclosed by a fence, or are close to the house. The farther such buildings are from the house, the less likely it is that they will be considered part of the curtilage.

- (e) **Garages**: These are usually considered part of the curtilage, unless far from the house and very seldom used.

c. **Areas as to which there is a reasonable expectation of privacy**: Finally, even if something is done or found in an "open field", the 4th Amendment applies if the circumstances are such that a person in that setting would have a "reasonable expectation of privacy".

(1) **Example**: In the case of *Katz v. U.S.*, 389 U.S. 347, 1967, the Supreme Court ruled that attaching an electronic listening device to the outside of a public phone booth (in the "open field") violated defendant's reasonable expectation that his conversations would be private. Therefore, the bugging could not be carried out without a warrant.

3. **Comparison of "Open Fields" and "Plain View"**

a. **Similarities**: In both these situations, there is <u>no need for a search warrant</u> to seize items because both are outside the protection of the 4th Amendment.

b. **Differences**

(1) Under the "open fields" doctrine, the seizable property is <u>not</u> in a "house" or other place to which that term applies (apartments, hotel or motel rooms, hospital rooms, places of business not open to the public, or curtilage)—whereas items under "plain view" are found in just those places.

(2) Under the "open fields" doctrine, <u>items hidden from view may be seized</u>—something not permitted under "plain view", which limits seizure to items within sight of the officer.

## C. ABANDONMENT

Abandonment refers to the <u>giving up of a thing or item absolutely</u>, without limitation as to any particular person or purpose. Abandoned property is not protected by the 4th Amendment guarantee against unreasonable searches and seizures, and thus may be seized without warrant or probable cause.

1. **Justification**: Abandoned property does not belong to anyone because the owner has given it up—in some cases involuntarily (as when items are thrown out of a house or car for fear of discovery by the police). Persons who find such property—including the police—may therefore keep it.

2. **When Items are Considered Abandoned**: This is frequently difficult to determine. However, the two basic guidelines are: (1) The place where the property is left, and (2) intent to abandon.

    a. **Where the property is left**

    (1) **Property left in open field or public place**: Property discarded or thrown away in an open field or public place is considered abandoned.

        (a) **Example**: Drugs discarded by a suspect at an airport rest room when he realizes he is under surveillance, or drugs thrown by the suspect from a speeding car when he realizes that the police are closing in, would be considered abandoned.

        (b) **But note**: The activities of the police which led to the abandonment must be legal, or the seizure cannot be justified under this theory.

            1) **Example**: The police, for no reason whatever, decide to stop a car and frisk the driver. Terrified, the driver throws something out the window which turns out to be prohibited drugs. These cannot be used in evidence because the abandonment was caused by illegal conduct on the part of the police.

    (2) **Property left in private premises**: Property may sometimes be considered abandoned in private premises if circumstances indicate that the occupant has left the premises.

        (a) **Example**: If a suspect pays his bills and checks out of a hotel room, items left behind which are of no apparent value but which the police can use as evidence—such as photographs or clippings—are considered abandoned property and may be seized by the police.

    b. **Intent to Abandon**: This is generally determined objectively—i.e., by what a person does.

    (1) Thus, for example, throwing items away shows an intent to abandon. Failure to claim something over a long period of time also indicates abandonment—and the longer the period, the clearer the intent.

    (2) The prosecution must prove that there was in fact an intent to abandon the item.

3. **Reasonable Expectation of Privacy**: If a reasonable expectation of privacy is apparent from the circumstances, this indicates that there was no intent to abandon.

    a. **Example**: A dilapidated barn at a farm has a recently posted sign reading, "Private Property". This indicates that the barn and items in it have not been abandoned. I.e., the sign means that the owner expects his privacy to be respected.

4. **Comparison of Abandonment and "Plain View"**

   a. **Similarities:** In both cases, there is <u>no need for a search warrant</u>—because both are outside the protection of the 4th Amendment.

   b. **Differences:** Abandonment means that the former owner of the item has <u>given up ownership</u> prior to its being seized by the police. The giving up of ownership may have taken place some time ago (as in the case of abandoned barns) or just seconds before the evidence is obtained by the police (as when contraband is thrown out of a car during a chase). Under the "plain view" theory, on the other hand, ownership or possession has not been given up prior to seizure.

D. **ELECTRONIC SURVEILLANCE**

Electronic surveillance is a type of search and seizure, and can take such forms as wiretapping, bugging, or "false friends". Such surveillance is governed by both the federal constitution and federal and state statutes.

1. **Constitutional Limitations:** The 4th Amendment limitation against "unreasonable searches and seizures" protects a person's <u>conversations</u> from unreasonable intrusion. Therefore, a warrant is needed to wiretap a <u>person's</u> telephone or to conduct electronic surveillance.

   a. **"Search" includes any form of electronic surveillance:** A "search" exists whenever there is police activity which violates a <u>reasonable expectation of privacy</u>. Such activity includes any form of electronic surveillance—<u>with or without</u> actual physical trespass or wiretap.

   (1) **Example:** In one leading case, the police attached an electronic listening device to the outside of a public phone booth which the defendant was using. Although there was no tapping of the line, the listening device still violated defendant's reasonable expectation that his conversations were private. [*Katz v. U.S.*, 389 U.S. 347, 1967]

   (2) **Former rule:** Originally, the Supreme Court held that wiretapping did not violate the 4th Amendment unless there was some <u>trespass</u> into a "constitutionally protected area". Therefore, evidence obtained through a bugging device placed against a wall to overhear conversation in an adjoining office was admissible because there was no <u>actual trespass</u>. This rule was changed by the *Katz* case, above.

   b. **Warrant requirements under 4th Amendment:** The 4th Amendment requires that a warrant authorizing a wiretap or other electronic surveillance meet the following requirements:

   (1) There must be a showing of <u>probable cause</u> to believe that a specific crime has been or is being committed;

   (2) The persons whose conversations are to be overheard must be <u>named</u>;

   (3) The conversations which are to be overheard must be <u>described with particularity</u>;

   (4) The wiretapping or electronic surveillance must be for a <u>limited period of time</u> (although extensions may be obtained upon an adequate showing), and <u>must terminate</u> when the desired information has been obtained; <u>and</u>

(5) A <u>return</u> must be made to the court showing what conversations have been intercepted. [Berger v. New York, 388 U.S. 41, 1967]

    (a) **Exigent circumstances may also be required:** Even with the above procedural safeguards, the court <u>suggested</u> in the *Berger* case that electronic surveillance may only be "reasonable" under exigent circumstances (i.e., when other means of obtaining evidence are inadequate).

c. **Without warrant, police may listen in with consent of either party**: The 4th Amendment does <u>not</u> protect persons against supposed "friends" who turn out to be <u>police informers</u>. Thus, a person assumes the risk that whatever he says to others may be <u>reported</u> by them to the police, there being no police "search" in such cases. It follows that if the supposed "friend" allows the police to listen in on a telephone conversation with the suspect, there is no violation of the suspect's 4th Amendment rights. [On Lee v. U.S., 343 U.S. 747, 1952]

d. **Transmission and recording with consent of either party**: Similarly, there is no 4th Amendment violation where a police informer carries an electronic device into the suspect's home and <u>transmits</u> the conversation to the police outside. The police may <u>record</u> the conversation and the recording itself is admissible: It does no more than assure the accuracy of what was said. [Rathbun v. U.S. 355 U.S. 107, 1957]

    (1) **Limitation under state statutes**: However, some state statutes (below) <u>are more restrictive</u> than required by the 4th Amendment, and prohibit interception of conversations without the consent of all parties thereto.

2. **Statutory Limitations**: In addition to the 4th Amendment limitations just discussed, various federal and state statutes also restrict wiretapping and electronic eavesdropping:

    a. The Federal Wiretap Act (applicable only to the federal government) prohibits interception of any communication spoken in expectation of privacy except by <u>lawful court order or with the consent of either party</u> to the conversation.

    b. Some states have specific statutory restrictions which prohibit interceptions unless all parties consent.

    c. In other states, wiretapping is prohibited altogether.

## E. SUMMARY

There are three notable instances where a search warrant or probable cause need not exist in order to seize items for use as evidence. These are the "plain view" doctrine, the "open fields" doctrine, and abandonment. In all three cases, the items in question are not protected by the 4th Amendment.

The "plain view" doctrine provides that items which fall within the sight of an officer who has a right to be in the place having that view and who had no prior knowledge of the presence of such items may properly be seized without a warrant, as long as the items are immediately recognizable as property subject to seizure.

The "open field" doctrine holds that items in open fields can be legally taken by an officer without warrant or probable cause—because the term "houses" in the Constitution does not include "open fields". The "curtilage"—i.e., grounds and buildings immediately surrounding a dwelling—is considered part of the "house", so that items located therein cannot be seized without a warrant or probable cause. And even if something is in an "open field", a warrant may be required for seizure if there is a "reasonable expectation of privacy".

Abandonment refers to the giving up of a thing or item absolutely. Abandoned property may be seized without a warrant, since at that stage it does not belong to anyone in particular.

Electronic surveillance does require a warrant, because "conversations" in private are protected by the 4th Amendment. The 4th Amendment does not protect against supposed friends who turn out to be police informers. However, the Federal Wiretap Act prohibits interception of <u>any</u> communication spoken in expectation of privacy except by lawful court order or with the consent of either party to the conversation. Some states have statutes prohibiting such interceptions unless all parties consent.

# VII. THE EXCLUSIONARY RULE

The Exclusionary Rule provides that evidence obtained by the government in violation of the 4th Amendment guarantee against unreasonable search or seizure is <u>not admissible</u> in criminal prosecutions against the victim thereof as proof of guilt.

## A. PURPOSE

The purpose of the Exclusionary Rule is to deter police misconduct—the expectation being that if evidence illegally obtained is not admitted in court, there will be no reason for police misconduct in this area. The Exclusionary Rule is therefore one means of enforcing the 4th Amendment.

## B. SCOPE OF RULE

The 4th Amendment applies to any <u>governmental</u> search or seizure. Therefore, evidence illegally seized by federal officers is not admissible in <u>state or federal</u> prosecutions; and vice versa.

1. **Historical Development**

    a. **Federal courts:** Since 1914, evidence illegally obtained by <u>federal officers</u> has been inadmissible in federal criminal prosecutions. [Weeks v. U.S., 232 U.S. 383, 1914]

    (1) From 1914 to 1960, however, evidence of a federal crime which had been illegally obtained by <u>state officers was</u> admissible in <u>federal courts</u>, as long as it had not been obtained in connivance with federal officers. This was the so-called "<u>silver platter</u>" doctrine.

    (2) In 1960, the Supreme Court <u>rejected</u> the "silver platter" doctrine, holding that the 4th Amendment prohibited the use of illegally-obtained evidence in <u>federal prosecutions</u>—whether obtained by federal or state officers. [Elkins v. U.S., 364 U.S. 206, 1960]

    b. **State courts:** In 1949, the Supreme Court held that state courts were <u>not</u> constitutionally required to exclude illegally obtained evidence. [Wolf v. Colorado, 388 U.S. 25, 1949]

    (1) In 1952, the Supreme Court modified this position, finding that some searches were so "shocking" as to require exclusion of the evidence seized. But these were limited to cases involving coercion, violence, or brutality. [Rochin v. California, 342 U.S. 165, 1952]

    (2) Finally, the Court in *Mapp v. Ohio*, 367 U.S. 643, 1961, overruled *Wolf* and held that the 4th Amendment required the state courts to <u>exclude</u> evidence obtained by unlawful searches and seizures.

    c. **Summary:** Thus, since 1961, the Exclusionary Rule has applied to <u>both</u> federal and state criminal prosecutions.

2. **Does Not Apply to Private Searches:** Since the 4th Amendment is a prohibition only as to governmental action, prosecutors may use evidence illegally obtained by <u>private</u> individuals (by methods such as illegal wiretap or trespass)—as long as the police did not encourage or participate in the illegal private search.

3. **Does Not Apply in Grand Jury Investigations**: A person being questioned by the grand jury cannot refuse to answer questions on the ground that the questions are based on illegally obtained evidence (such as information obtained from an illegal wiretap). Reason: Application of the Exclusionary Rule in such proceedings would unduly interfere with the grand jury's investigative function.

4. **May Not Apply to Parole Revocation Hearings**: Although the Supreme Court has not yet ruled on the matter, many lower courts have held that illegally-obtained evidence is likewise admissible in parole revocation hearings. Reason: The unique and critical responsibilities of the parole board in protecting society from recidivist (i.e., "repeater") crime outweigh the interest in deterring police misconduct.

5. **May Not Apply to Post-Conviction Sentencing**: Some lower courts have likewise permitted the trial judge to consider illegally obtained evidence in fixing sentence after conviction, even where the same evidence had been excluded during the trial because it was illegally obtained. Reason: During sentencing, a trial judge should consider any reliable evidence; and the fact that it was illegally obtained does not necessarily affect its reliability.

C. **EXCEPTION TO EXCLUSIONARY RULE—ILLEGALLY OBTAINED EVIDENCE ADMISSIBLE FOR IMPEACHMENT**

Normally, evidence obtained by illegal search or seizure cannot be used for any purpose. However, illegally seized evidence can be used for the limited purpose of impeaching a defendant's testimony if he testifies at the trial. [Harris v. New York, 401 U.S. 222, 1971]

1. **Reason For Exception**: A defendant cannot be allowed knowingly to perjure himself and then claim the protection of the previous suppression of evidence. The fact that the police violated the accused's constitutional right in obtaining evidence does not give him a license to commit perjury.

D. **WHAT IS EXCLUDED UNDER THE RULE**

1. **Illegally Seized Evidence**: Contraband, fruits of the crime (stolen goods, etc.), instruments of the crime (burglar's tools, etc.) or "mere evidence" (shoes, shirt, etc., connecting a person to the crime) which are seized illegally may not be admitted at trial to show defendant's guilt.

2. **"Fruits" of The Illegal Search or Seizure**: Any other evidence (verbal or physical) which is the direct or indirect result of an illegal search or arrest is known as "fruit of the poisonous tree" and must also be excluded.

    a. **Example 1**: The police conduct an illegal search of a house and find a map which shows the location of certain stolen goods. Following the map, they locate the cache and recover the goods. Both the map and the goods are inadmissible as evidence, since the goods are "fruits of the poisonous tree".

    b. **Example 2**: Police officers make an illegal search of D's house and find heroin. They confront D with the evidence and he confesses to possession. D's confession is likewise the "fruit" of the illegal search, and must be excluded.

E. **PROCEDURE FOR INVOKING THE EXCLUSIONARY RULE**

1. **Motion to Suppress**: In both state and federal courts, the basic procedure for excluding evidence on a claim of illegal search and seizure is a motion filed before trial to suppress the evidence.

a. If the accused loses at this pretrial hearing, he can make the motion again at trial. And, if he loses at trial, he can raise the issue once again on appeal.

2. **Burden of Proof:** The burden of proof on a motion to suppress depends upon whether the search or seizure in question was made under a warrant.

   a. If the search or seizure was pursuant to a warrant, there is a presumption of its validity. The burden is therefore on the accused to show that the warrant was issued without probable cause., that the search exceeded the warrant, etc.

   b. If there was no search warrant, the prosecution has the burden of establishing "reasonableness"—i.e., consent, incident to arrest, exigent circumstances, or one of the other exceptions previously discussed.

      (1) However, reasonableness need only be established by a preponderance of the evidence. Proof beyond reasonable doubt is not required.

## F. EFFECT OF VIOLATION OF EXCLUSIONARY RULE

If a motion to exclude was timely made, it is error for the court to receive evidence obtained by illegal search or seizure. Such a mistake requires reversal of any conviction obtained unless admission of the evidence is found to be "harmless error".

1. **Requirements to Demonstrate "Harmless Error":** To prove "harmless error", the prosecution must show beyond a reasonable doubt that the evidence erroneously admitted did not contribute to the conviction.

2. **"Other Sufficient Evidence" Not Enough:** In attempting to demonstrate mere "harmless error", it is not enough for the prosecution simply to show that there was other evidence sufficent to support the verdict. Rather, it must show that there is no reasonable possibility that a different result would have been reached without the tainted evidence. [Chapman v. California, 386 U.S. 18, 1967]

## G. THE FUTURE OF THE EXCLUSIONARY RULE

There has been much dissatisfaction with the Exclusionary Rule, primarily on the ground that it has had little impact on police misconduct while at the same time causing the dismissal of many legitimate prosecutions because the evidence obtained could not be used.

1. **Failure to Deter Misconduct:** A number of reasons are cited for the failure of the Exclusionary Rule to deter police misconduct. Among these are the fact that no effective penalties exist for police misconduct in the search and seizure of evidence, and that only a small percentage of criminal cases (around 10%) actually go to trial. By its nature, the Exclusionary Rule cannot be used—and therefore cannot serve as a deterrent—unless a case is actually filed.

2. **Possible Modifications:** There is a strong move among some courts, as well as law enforcement spokesmen, for modification of the present Exclusionary Rule. Alternative proposals range from adopting the British system—where the illegally obtained evidence is admitted but the erring police officer is penalized—to accepting the evidence but compensating the victim of the illegal search. In a number of recent cases, the vote in the Supreme Court for modification of the Exclusionary Rule has been close. Given this Court sentiment and the mood of the American public, changes in the Exclusionary Rule may be forthcoming.

## H. SUMMARY

The Exclusionary Rule provides that evidence obtained by the government in violation of the 4th Amendment guarantee against unreasonable search or seizure is not admissible in criminal prosecutions (except for purposes of impeachment). There is dissatisfaction with the Rule because it allegedly has failed to deter police misconduct but has led to the exclusion of otherwise trustworthy evidence. There is a move at present to modify the Exclusionary Rule. Given the mood of the public and the Supreme Court, such a change may be forthcoming.

# VIII. ADMISSIONS AND CONFESSIONS; IDENTIFICATION PROCEDURES

The 5th Amendment of the U.S. Constitution provides that "No person shall . . . be compelled in any criminal case to be a <u>witness against himself</u>, nor be deprived of life, liberty or property, without due process of law." This has an important impact on the evidence-gathering methods of law enforcement personnel.

**A. ADMISSIONS AND CONFESSIONS**

1. **Constitutional Requirement of Voluntariness**: As noted, the Constitution prohibits the government from forcing a person to be a witness against himself. The prohibition is designed to discourage law enforcement officers from using force or <u>coercion</u> to secure a confession or admission from a person suspected of a crime.

    a. **What constitutes "coercion"**: The meaning of the term "coercion" has changed over the years. Originally, confessions or statements obtained by <u>physical force</u> (such as beating, whipping, maiming, etc.) were considered involuntary. Later, however, it was recognized that coercion could be <u>mental</u> as well as <u>physical</u>.

    (1) **Current test**: Today, the test of voluntariness is <u>whether, considering all the circumstances surrounding his statements, the accused's confession is the product of a free and rational choice</u>. This is known as the "totality of the circumstances" approach.

    (2) **Relevant factors**: In determining whether or not the suspect's choice was free and rational, the age, intelligence and experience of the accused and the methods employed by law enforcement officers—including length of detention, amount and manner of interrogation, and the fact that defendant could not be interviewed by anyone else—are significant factors. [Clewis v. Texas, 386 U.S. 707, 1967]

    (a) **Example 1**: A 25-year old foreign born man with a history of emotional instability was questioned for 8 straight hours by many officers, while his sympathy was falsely aroused by a childhood friend acting on police instructions. Incriminating statements obtained from the suspect were held involuntary because his will had been overborne. [Spano v. N.Y., 360 U.S. 315, 1959]

    (b) **Example 2**: <u>Promises of leniency</u> or other benefits by police will also make a confession involuntary in most states.

    (c) **Example 3**: Other forms of <u>duress, fraud or trickery</u> may also cause a confession to be deemed "coerced". Thus, a confession obtained from a public employee under <u>threat of removal</u> from office is involuntary. [Garrity v. N.J., 385 U.S. 493, 1967] Likewise, an admission from an attorney under <u>threat of disbarment</u> is involuntary. [Spevack v. Klein, 385 U.S. 511, 1967]

    b. **Procedure for determing admissability of alleged "involuntary" statements**: When the defendant seeks to exclude a confession or admission on the ground that it was coerced or involuntary, there must be a hearing on all the details and circumstances surrounding its execution. This usually takes the form of a <u>motion to suppress</u> filed before the trial. The issue then is whether such evidence should be presented to the jury (which is expected ultimately to pass on the guilt or innocence of the accused) or whether the trial judge alone should make this determination.

(1) **State procedures vary**: In state practice, three different methods have been developed for determining the issue of "voluntariness".

    (a) **New York rule**: Under this approach, the trial judge makes a preliminary determination of the voluntariness of the confession. If he finds the confession involuntary, the confession is excluded. If reasonable men could differ as to the facts, the judge admits the confession but instructs the jury to disregard it if the jury finds the confession involuntary under constitutional standards given in the judge's instructions.

    (b) **California rule**: Here, the trial judge determines voluntariness. The hearing on voluntariness may be held out of the presence of the jury if either party so requests. Once admitted by the judge as voluntary, the jury's only function is to determine the weight and credibility of the confession.

    (c) **Massachusetts rule**: Under this procedure, the judge makes the full determination on admissibility (as in California), but even if the confession is found voluntary and admitted, the jury must also consider the issue of voluntariness if defendant so requests.

c. **Effect of using involuntary or coerced confession—automatic reversal**: An involuntary or coerced confession is inadmissible against the accused for any purpose. Thus if the confession was mistakenly admitted by the trial judge, the rule of automatic reversal applies: I.e., the conviction must be reversed despite sufficient evidence apart from the coerced confession to support conviction. [Rogers v. Richmond, 365 U.S. 534, 1961]

2. **Exclusion of Voluntary Statements**: Even when a confession or incriminating statement is found to be voluntary, it may still be excluded if some constitutional right of the accused has been violated in connection therewith.

    a. **Escobedo Rule**: The Supreme Court has recognized a strong relationship between the 6th Amendment right to counsel and the 5th Amendment privilege against self-incrimination. Thus, when a confession is obtained from the accused at a time when he is denied his constitutional right to counsel, the confession must be excluded.

    (1) **Example**: Danny Escobedo was arrested for murder and interrogated for several hours, during which time he was persuaded to confess. He made repeated but unsuccessful requests to see his lawyer, whom he had previously retained; and the lawyer was simultaneously demanding to see his client. The Court held that this denied Escobedo's right to counsel, and that no statement taken during the interrogation could be admitted against him at trial. [Escobedo v. Illinois, 378 U.S. 748, 1964]

    b. **Miranda Rule**: The case of *Miranda v. Arizona*, 384 U.S. 486, 1966, is the best known and perhaps the most significant case ever decided by the U.S. Supreme Court in the area of criminal procedure.

    (1) **Facts of the case**: Ernesto Miranda was arrested at his home and taken to the police station in Phoenix, Arizona, where he was interrogated by two police officers for two hours. He was not advised of his right to remain silent or his right to an attorney. Miranda signed a written confession, and was later convicted of kidnapping and rape. He appealed his conviction to the U.S. Supreme Court.

(2) **Issue before the Court**: The Supreme Court was asked to decide whether statements by suspects during custodial interrogation, where the suspect was not advised of his right to remain silent or to have an attorney, are admissible in court.

(3) **Decision**: The Court held that the evidence was <u>not</u> admissible, and that Miranda was therefore entitled to a new trial. The heart of the Court's decision read as follows:

> "We hold that when an individual is <u>taken into custody or otherwise deprived of his freedom</u> by the authorities and is subject to questioning, the privilege against self-incrimination is jeopardized. Procedural safeguards must be employed . . . He must be warned prior to any questioning that he has a right to remain silent, that anything he says can be used against him in a court of law, that he has the right to the presence of an attorney, and that if he cannot afford an attorney one will be appointed for him prior to any questioning if he so desires. Opportunity to exercise these rights must be afforded to him throughout the interrogation."

(4) **Aftermath**: Ernesto Miranda was later retried (under an assumed name) for the same offense without using his confession, and was reconvicted on other evidence. After his subsequent release on parole he was killed in 1972 in a skid row card game in Phoenix, Arizona. The police gave his alleged assailant, an illegal alien, the proper Miranda warnings (below).

c. **The Miranda Warnings**: The basic "*Miranda* warnings" which must be given to a suspect or accused are as follows:

(1) You have a right to <u>remain silent</u>;

(2) Anything you say can be <u>used against you</u> in a court of law;

(3) You have a right to the <u>presence of an attorney</u>;

(4) If you cannot afford an attorney, <u>one will be appointed</u> for you.

Note: There are variations in wording among the different states. Most jurisdictions add the following warning: "You have the right to terminate this interview at any time." However, this additional statement is not required in order to make the evidence obtained admissible.

d. **Waiver**: The Miranda warnings can be <u>waived</u> by the suspect (making an incriminating statement or confession admissible), but the prosecution bears a "heavy burden" in proving a valid waiver.

(1) **Waiver must be INTELLIGENT and VOLUNTARY**

(a) Waiver may <u>not be presumed from silence</u> after the defendant has been warned of his rights. I.e., defendant must <u>express</u> the waiver.

(b) The Supreme Court has not yet decided on the type of express waiver necessary—whether the suspect must openly say so, or whether waiver can be implied from the fact that he voluntarily answers questions after receiving the Miranda warnings. The safer practice is for the suspect to openly state that he waives his right(s).

(c) **And note**: Defendant can withdraw a waiver once given. If the waiver is withdrawn, the interrogation must stop. However, evidence obtained before the waiver is withdrawn is admissible in court.

(2) **Proof of voluntary waiver**: Most police departments have a written waiver form which suspects are asked to sign. This written waiver is usually part of the written confession (either before or after the statement by the accused), or is attached to it. If witnesses to the waiver are available (police officers, other police personnel, or private persons), they should be asked to sign the waiver to strengthen the showing of a voluntary waiver. If the confession is typewritten, the defendant should be required to read it and to correct any errors in his own handwriting.

(a) In the absence of a written waiver, the issue boils down to the testimony of the suspect against the testimony of the police officer. This is why a signed, written waiver—although not required to establish voluntariness—is always good strategy on the part of the police.

e. **Stage at which Miranda warnings must be given**: A very important question for the police is: "At what point should the Miranda warnings be given?" The quick answer is, "Whenever there is custodial interrogation." But what constitutes custodial interrogation?

To avoid confusion, simply remember that custodial interrogation, for purposes of the Miranda warnings, covers two general situations: (1) When the person is under arrest; or (2) when he is not under arrest but is deprived of his freedom in any significant way.

(1) **When person is under arrest**: If the 4 elements of arrest—i.e., intent, authority, custody and understanding—are present, there is an arrest and Miranda warnings must be given.

(2) **When person is not under arrest but is "deprived of his freedom in any significant way**: This is more difficult to determine and is best analyzed in terms of specific instances.

(a) **Questioning at the scene of the crime**: Here, a distinction must be made between "general on-the-scene questioning" and questioning after the police officer has "focused" on the individual. "General on-the-scene questioning" for the purpose of gathering information which might enable the police to identify the criminal does not require the Miranda warnings. But questioning after the police officer has "focused" on a particular suspect needs the Miranda warnings, even if the questioning takes place at the scene of the crime.

1) **Example**: Suppose X has been fatally stabbed in a crowded bar. A police officer arrives and questions people at the scene of the crime to determine if anyone saw the actual stabbing. This is considered "general on-the-scene questioning" for which there is no need for a Miranda warning.

2) Assume instead that upon his arrival at the bar, the officer sees Y with a bloody knife in his hands. Here the suspicion of the officer will undoubtedly be "focused" on Y—and any questioning of Y requires that the Miranda warnings be given.

(b) **Questioning at police station:** Police questioning at the station house generally requires Miranda warnings unless there is a "volunteered" statement—i.e., one given spontaneously and not in response to police questions.

1) **Example:** The police invite a suspect to come to the police station "to answer a few questions." This type of interrogation requires the Miranda warnings because a police station lends a "coercive atmosphere" to the interrogation.

2) But if a person enters the station and announces, "I killed a man—here is the weapon," such a statement is admissible in court because it was volunteered.

a) Whether or not the police can then ask questions without giving the Miranda warnings has not been decided by the Supreme Court.

(c) **Questioning in police cars:** Such questioning generally requires Miranda warnings because of its custodial nature and coercive atmosphere.

(d) **Questioning in homes:** Whether or not Miranda warnings must precede questioning in a suspect's home depends upon the circumstances in each case.

1) The Supreme Court has held that the questioning of a suspect in his bedroom by four police officers at four o'clock in the morning needed the Miranda warnings. [Orozco v. Texas, 394 U.S. 324, 1969]

2) On the other hand, the Court has held that statements obtained by Internal Revenue Service agents during a non-custodial, non-coercive interview with a taxpayer under criminal tax investigation, conducted in a private home where the taxpayer occasionally stayed, did not need the Miranda warnings as long as the taxpayer had been told that he was free to leave. [Beckwith v. U.S., 96 S.Ct. 1612, 1976]

(e) **Questioning where defendant is in custody on another offense:** Miranda warnings must be given in connection with this type of questioning.

1) **Example:** D, in jail serving a state sentence, is questioned by federal agents regarding a completely separate offense. D is entitled to Miranda warnings even though no federal criminal charges were contemplated at the time of questioning. [Mathis v. U.S., 391 U.S. 1, 1968]

f. **Situations in which no warnings required:** The Miranda warnings need not be given in the following situations:

(1) **"General on-the-scene questioning"** before the police have focused on a particular suspect (discussed previously).

(2) **"Volunteered confessions"**—meaning spontaneous confessions or statements made without any interrogation (discussed previously).

(3) **Statements or confessions made to private persons:** The right against self-discrimination applies only to interrogation initiated by law enforcement

officers. Hence, incriminating statements made by the accused to friends or cellmates while in custody are admissible regardless of Miranda.

    (4) **Appearance of potential criminal defendant before a grand jury**: Interrogation before a grand jury does not require the Miranda warnings, even if the prosecutor intends to charge the witness with an offense. The theory is that such interrogation does not present the same opportunities for abuse as custodial questioning by police.

g. **Specific applications of the Miranda Rule**: A number of recent cases have further clarified the scope of the *Miranda* decision:

    (1) **Use of statements to impeach the accused**: While the confession of an accused who was not properly given the Miranda warnings is not admissible as part of the prosecution's case, it <u>can</u> be used by the prosecution to <u>impeach</u> (i.e., discredit) testimony of the accused at trial (should he say something different on the witness stand)—provided that the earlier statement was otherwise <u>voluntary</u> and <u>trustworthy</u>. [Harris v. New York, 401 U.S. 222, 1971; Oregon v. Haas, 420 U.S. 714, 1975]

        (a) **Example**: D's confession is obtained by the police after D is given the first two Miranda warnings ("You have the right to remain silent and anything you say can be used against you") but not the third and fourth warnings ("You have a right to the presence of an attorney and if you cannot afford an attorney, one will be appointed for you"). The confession, even if voluntary, cannot be introduced by the prosecution in its own case to prove D's guilt. However, if D decides to take the witness stand and testifies that he was not in town at the time of the murder, the prosecutor can then use the confession (if otherwise voluntary and trustworthy) to show that D had previously admitted to being in town at the time—in order to impeach D's testimony.

    (2) **Subsequent questioning on unrelated offense**: D was arrested for certain robberies and given proper Miranda warnings, after which he declined to discuss the robberies and police questioning stopped. Two hours later, D was given a second Miranda warning and was interrogated about an unrelated murder. During this questioning, D made incriminating statements about the second crime. The Supreme Court held that D's statements were admissible, since his prior invocation of the Miranda rights applied only to the <u>first</u> (unrelated) interrogation. [Michigan v. Mosley, 423 U.S. 96, 1975]

    (3) **Voluntary statements**: As discussed previously, there is no "custodial interrogation" (and thus no need for the Miranda warnings) if a person voluntarily comes to the police station, is told that he is not under arrest, gives a confession, and leaves without hindrance. [Oregon v. Mathiason, 429 U.S. 492, 1977]

h. **Effect of Miranda Rule on the voluntariness rule**

    (1) In the *Miranda* case, the Supreme Court went beyond the "voluntariness" test—i.e., "Is the confession voluntary?"—and applied a formalistic standard—i.e., Were the four Miranda warnings given?—to determine admissibility. Thus, even if the statement or confession is voluntary, the evidence must be excluded if the police fail to give the Miranda warnings.

(2) However, even if Miranda warnings were given, a defendant can still challenge any confession or incriminating statement made to the police on the ground that it was involuntary. Of course, the fact that he was given the Miranda warnings is relevant in determining voluntariness.

   (a) **Example:** The police give X his Miranda warnings, but then force him to give a confession by questioning him continuously for 36 hours. X's confession would undoubtedly be excluded at trial on the ground that it was not voluntary—even though he had been given the Miranda warnings.

(3) In sum, confessions or incriminating statements are admissible only if they are voluntary and if the Miranda warnings have been given.

i. **Unresolved questions on the Miranda Rule:** A number of questions concerning *Miranda* have not yet been clearly answered by the Supreme Court. The more significant of these are:

   (1) Must the Miranda warnings be given to persons arrested for misdemeanor traffic and other minor offenses? Some jurisdictions say yes; others say no.

   (2) If a person goes to a police station and volunteers a confession, must the police give him the Miranda warnings before asking follow-up questions?

   (3) If the suspect has been warned of his rights by one detective and agrees to talk, may other detectives subsequently question him about another crime without again giving the suspect new Miranda warnings?

   (4) If a defendant refuses to sign a "waiver of rights" form, is his oral confession nevertheless valid? Most jurisdictions say yes.

   (5) Are the "fruits" derived from statements obtained in violation of *Miranda* (known as "fruits of the poisonous tree") admissible in court even if the statement itself is not?

   (a) **Example:** The police interrogate D, a murder suspect, without giving him the Miranda warnings. D confesses and states that the murder weapon can be found in the glove compartment of his car. The police find the murder weapon there with D's fingerprints on it. D's confession is inadmissible. But are the murder weapon and fingerprints likewise inadmissible?

   (b) Lower courts have split on this issue, but the trend is to exclude such evidence.

   (6) If a trial judge mistakenly admits into evidence a confession given in violation of Miranda, the conviction will be automatically reversed on appeal because of that mistake. However, the Supreme Court has not decided whether a conviction will be automatically reversed if the statement is merely an admission—i.e., a statement that is incriminatory, but less than an acknowledgement of commission of the crime. Most jurisdictions use the "harmless error" rule—which requires reversal unless the prosecution demonstrates beyond a reasonable doubt that the admission did not contribute to the conviction.

   (7) **Note:** State courts and lower federal courts have given different and sometimes conflicting answers to the above questions on Miranda. Until the U.S. Supreme Court resolves these issues, police officers should follow the decisions of courts in their particular jurisdiction.

B. **IDENTIFICATION PROCEDURES**

The police use a variety of procedures to verify whether a suspect taken into custody is in fact guilty of the offense in question. These identification procedures have the dual function of solving crimes and providing evidence at the suspect's trial.

1. **Basic Types of Procedures**: Three general procedures are used by the police to make certain that the person taken into custody is properly identified. These are:

    a. **Lineups**—at which a victim or witness to a crime is shown several possible suspects at the police station for purposes of identification;

    b. **Showups**—at which only one suspect is shown to the witness or victim, usually at the scene of the crime and immediately following a quick arrest of the suspect; and

    c. **Photographic Identification (rogue's gallery)**—where photographs of possible suspects are shown to the victim or witness.

2. **Rights of Suspects During Identification Stage**: Recent cases have spelled out the rights which suspects have during the identification stage.

    a. **Right to counsel**

        (1) **Lineups—may have right to counsel**

            (a) A suspect in a lineup identification has no right to counsel prior to being charged with a crime. [Kirby v. Illinois, 406 U.S. 682, 1972] Note that this is not the same as interrogation of the suspect, where the Escobedo and Miranda Rules (discussed previously) give the suspect a right to counsel.

            (b) However, a suspect in a lineup held after being charged with a crime—i.e., after an indictment, information, preliminary hearing or arraignment—does have a right to counsel. [U.S. v. Wade, 388 U.S. 218, 1967] If the suspect cannot afford a lawyer, one must be appointed for him by the state.

                1) Reason: A lineup conducted after arrest is considered a "critical stage" in the proceeding, whereas lineups held before any formal charge are not.

        (2) **Other identification procedures—no right to counsel**

            (a) **Photographic identifications**: When the prosecution seeks to identify the accused by displaying photographs to witnesses prior to trial (mug shot identification), there is no right to counsel. [U.S. v. Ash, 413 U.S. 300, 1973]

            (b) **Pretrial interviews**: Likewise, when the prosecutor conducts pretrial interviews of witnesses, the accused has no right to have counsel present.

            (c) **Show-ups**: Similarly, when the police bring a suspect to the scene very soon after commission of the crime for the purpose of identification by the victim or other eyewitnesses, there is no right to counsel.

                1) **Example**: Minutes after a purse is snatched, a suspect fitting the description given by the victim is caught several blocks away and

brought back to the scene of the crime for identification by the victim. The suspect has no right to counsel during this showup.

    (d) **Obtaining physical samples from suspect:** Finally, the taking of a blood sample, fingerprints, etc., from a suspect does not give the suspect a right to counsel.

        1) **Example:** A person taken from the scene of an accident is suspected of being intoxicated. While at the hospital, a blood sample is taken from him to test for alcohol content. The suspect has no right to counsel at this proceeding.

b. **Privilege against self-incrimination:** The accused has a privilege against self-incrimination at <u>all</u> stages of a criminal proceeding—including identification procedures. However, this right can generally be asserted only as to evidence of a <u>testimonial</u> <u>or communicative</u> nature. Thus, while the government cannot force a suspect to <u>say anything which</u> may link him to a crime, it can do the following—none of which are "testimonial" or "communicative":

(1) Draw a blood sample from an unwilling accused.

(2) Make the accused appear before witnesses for possible identification. (This means that a suspect cannot refuse to appear in a police lineup by asserting the privilege against self-incrimination.)

(3) Make the accused give handwriting samples.

(4) Fingerprint suspects.

(5) Make the accused repeat certain words or gestures, or give voice exemplars. (What is being tested here is the quality or level of a person's voice, not the substance of what he ways—so the privilege against self-incrimination does not apply.)

c. **Right to due process of law:** Besides a right to counsel (in certain situations) and the privilege against self-incrimination during identification procedures, a suspect also has the right to due process of law—meaning that the identification procedures must not be unduly unfair.

    (1) **What amounts to "unfairness":** In determining what is "fair" or "unfair" in identification procedures, the court considers <u>all the circumstances</u> leading up to the identification. "Unfairness" will be found only when, in the light of all such circumstances, the identification procedure is so <u>impermissibly</u> suggestive as to give rise to a real and substantial likelihood of irreparable misidentification. [Neil v. Biggers, 409 U.S. 188, 1973]

        (a) **Example:** In a rape case, the victim could give no description of her attacker other than that he was a Black man wearing an orange-colored shirt, and that he had a high-pitched voice. The police arrested D on information supplied by an informer. They showed the victim D's orange-colored shirt, and asked her if she could identify D's voice (from an adjoining room). <u>No other voices were provided for comparison</u>. This procedure was found to be so "inherently suggestive" as to create a substantial likelihood of misidentification.

1) **Compare—necessity for prompt identification**: However, the necessity for a prompt identification is given weight in determining whether a procedure was "fair" or "unfair". Thus, for example, due process was not violated when X was taken to a victim's hospital room for identification, even though he was the only black present—since the victim was near death at the time. [Stovall v. Denno, 388 U.S. 293, 1967]

## C. SUMMARY

The 5th Amendment of the U.S. Constitution provides that no person may be compelled to be a witness against himself. This means that involuntary admissions or confessions cannot be admitted in criminal prosecutions. Involuntariness originally referred only to the use of physical force or coercion. However, this was later extended to mental coercion; and the test of "voluntariness" today is whether—considering all the circumstances—the accused's statement was the product of a free and rational choice.

The *Escobedo* and *Miranda* cases added another dimension to the admissibility of confessions and incriminating statements—namely, that a statement which is voluntary may also be inadmissible if other constitution rights of the suspect have been violated. The *Miranda* decision, perhaps the best-known and most significant case in the field of criminal procedure, requires that in cases of custodial interrogation—i.e., when a suspect is questioned while under arrest or deprived of his freedom in any significant way—the suspect must be given his so-called "Miranda warnings." Failure to do so means that the evidence cannot be admitted in court even if voluntary.

Suspects are usually identified by the police through 3 basic procedures: Lineups, showups, or photographic identification. Suspects have a right to counsel during lineups after (but not before) charges have been filed. There is no right to counsel in showups or photographic identifications. The privilege against self-incrimination is of limited use during identification proceedings, because it protects only evidence of a testimonial or communicative nature. Physical evidence—such as blood or handwriting samples, physical presence, fingerprints, or voice exemplars—are therefore not protected. The right to due process also applies during identification proceedings, and requires that such procedure not be unduly unfair to the suspect.

# IX. THE TRIAL ITSELF—
# CONSTITUTIONAL SAFEGUARDS AND LIMITATIONS

A. **IN GENERAL**

The individual safeguards provided in the Bill of Rights are perhaps most significant during the trial stage of a criminal proceeding. Accordingly, those rights have been extensively developed, refined and protected at this stage. The primary safeguards for the accused in a criminal trial, discussed in this chapter, are:

—Right to Counsel

—Right to a Speedy and Public Trial

—Right to Trial by Jury

—Right to a Fair and Impartial Trial

—Right to Confrontation of Witnesses

—Right to Compulsory Process to Obtain Witnesses

—Privilege Against Self-Incrimination

—Right to Proof of Guilt Beyond Reasonable Doubt

—Right to Protection Against Double Jeopardy

1. **Rights Apply To All Criminal Proceedings**: Each of the safeguards listed above applies in both federal and state criminal proceedings, under the Due Process Clause of the 14th Amendment to the U.S. Constitution. (See earlier discussion of the "incorporation" doctrine, Chap. 1)

2. **Statutes May Supplement Constitutional Safeguards**: The aforementioned rights are constitutional in origin, which means that they cannot be restricted or limited by statutes (either state or federal). However, statutes can create additional safeguards where no constitutional right exists.

   a. **Example**: The constitutional right to a jury trial does not extend to juvenile court proceedings. Nevertheless, some states give juveniles this right under statutory law.

B. **RIGHT TO COUNSEL**

1. **Constitutional Basis for Right**: The 6th Amendment to the U.S. Constitution provides that "in all criminal prosecutions, the accused shall enjoy the right ... to have the assistance of counsel for his defense."

   a. **Effect**: As a result of the 6th Amendment, a defendant has the right to be represented by counsel at "every critical stage" of the criminal proceeding. What is a "critical stage" has been determined by the Court on a case-by-case basis, as indicated below.

   b. **Underlying theory**: The Supreme Court has expressed the reasoning behind a right to counsel in criminal proceedings as follows:

"Even the intelligent and educated layman has small and sometimes no skill in the science of the law. Left without aid of counsel, he may be put on trial without a proper charge, and convicted upon imcompetent evidence, or evidence irrelevant to the issue or otherwise inadmissible. He requires the guiding hand of counsel at every step in the proceedings against him. Without it, though he be not guilty, he faces the danger of conviction because he does not know how to establish his innocence." [Powell v. Alabama, 287 U.S. 45, 1932]

2. **Definition of "Right to Counsel"**: The term "right to counsel" may refer to either: (a) Retained Counsel, or (b) court-appointed counsel.

   a. **Retained counsel**: Retained counsel refers to an attorney chosen and paid by the accused himself. With a few exceptions (such as appearances before a grand jury or certain identification procedures, discussed previously), a person who can afford to retain counsel has the right to have his counsel present at every stage of the criminal proceeding.

   b. **Court-appointed counsel**: This refers to an attorney appointed by the judge and paid by the county or state to represent an indigent accused at a "critical stage" in the criminal proceeding.

      (1) **Who is an "indigent?"** There is no uniform rule to determine indigency. Some standards used by judges to determine indigency are: Unemployment, not having a car, not having posted bail, not having a house, etc. The judge enjoys wide discretion in making this determination; and his decision on this issue is rarely reversed on appeal.

      (2) **How are appointments made?** The method of appointing counsel for an indigent also varies among different courts. Most judges use a list containing the names of available and willing attorneys, who are then assigned to cases on a rotating basis. Others make assignments at random, assigning any lawyer who may be available in the courtroom at the time the appointment is to be made. Still other jurisdictions employ full-time public defenders to handle indigent cases.

      (3) **Indigent has no right to a specific attorney**: An indigent defendant has no right to designate which attorney he wants appointed to represent him. Selection of the attorney is purely within the discretion of the court.

3. **Proceedings in Which Right to Counsel Applies**

   a. **Where felony or actual imprisonment is at issue**: Although the 6th Amendment by its terms extends to "all criminal prosecutions", the Supreme Court has held that the right to counsel applies only (1) if the crime charges is a felony, or (2) if, upon conviction of the offense (whether felony or misdemeanor), actual imprisonment is imposed. [Argensinger v. Hamlin, 404 U.S. 982, 1972]

      (1) The Court has not decided whether the assistance of counsel is constitutionally required where (a) the crime is punishable by imprisonment, but upon conviction no imprisonment occurs, or (b) the crime is not punishable by imprisonment at all.

         (a) In federal courts, however, counsel is required by statute in these cases.

   b. **Effect**: If the trial judge concludes that the offense is punishable by imprisonment, no jail sentence may be imposed unless counsel was provided during the trial.

(1) **Example**: Suppose the law states that punishment for possession of an ounce of marijuana is 10 days in jail and/or a fine of up to $200. If found guilty, defendant cannot be sentenced to jail unless he had counsel during trial. However, a fine could be imposed.

(2) **Juvenile proceedings**: Although juvenile proceedings are not considered "criminal" in nature, a juvenile is entitled to appointed counsel in any such proceeding which may lead to commitment in an institution in which the juvenile's freedom is restricted. [In re Gault, 387 U.S. 1, 1967]

(3) **Parole or probation revocation**: Whether due process requires the state to appoint counsel for indigents at a parole or probation revocation hearing (after trial) must be determined on a case-by-case basis—with considerable discretion allowed to the revocation agency.

   (a) However, the defendant must be informed of his right to request counsel.

4. **Proceedings at Which the Right to Counsel (Retained or Appointed) Does NOT Apply**:

   a. **Grand jury**: A witness called to appear before a grand jury is not entitled to have counsel present. The theory is that such proceedings are only investigative in nature.

   (1) However, to protect the witness' privilege against self-discrimination, a witness who is in doubt whether his answer may incriminate him generally may consult his attorney to obtain advice.

   b. **Purely investigative proceedings**: There is no right to counsel at purely investigative hearings. For example, counsel is not required at a hearing by the state fire marshal to determine if a particular fire was the result of arson.

   c. **Police lineup prior to charges being filed**: There is generally no right to counsel before criminal charges have been filed against a suspect.

   (1) Of course, an accused is entitled to counsel in any custodial interrogation under the Miranda rule. But the presence of counsel in this situation is for the purpose of protecting the 5th Amendment right against self-incrimination—not because of the 6th Amendment right to counsel.

   d. **Prison discipline**: There is likewise no right to counsel in prison disciplinary proceedings. If the prisoner is illiterate or the issue is especially complex, he might be entitled to assistance from a fellow inmate or a member of the prison staff. [Wolff v. McDonnell, 418 U.S. 539, 1974]

   e. **Military proceedings**: Finally, there is no right to counsel in a summary court martial—even where 30 days' confinement at hard labor may be imposed. Reason: Such proceedings are "informal and nonadversary", and thus do not constitute a "criminal prosecution" within the meaning of the 6th Amendment. [Middendorf v. Henry, 425 U.S. 25, 1976]

5. **Stages (as Opposed to Types of Proceedings) at Which Right to Counsel Applies**: The right to counsel applies at "every stage of a criminal proceeding where substantial rights of a criminal accused may be affected". Such "critical stages" where counsel is needed include the following:

   a. **The trial itself.** [Argersinger v. Hamlin, 404 U.S. 982, 1972]

b. **Custodial interrogations**—whether before or after charges have been filed. [Miranda v. Arizona, 384 U.S. 436, 1966]

c. **Noncustodial interrogations after the accused has been formally charged.** Example: Defendant made incriminating statements to a co-defendant whom federal agents had "wired for sound". This was held to violate defendant's 6th Amendment right to counsel, since defendant at the time was out on bail after having been formally charged with the crime. [Massiah v. U.S., 377 U.S. 201, 1964]

d. **A post-indictment "lineup"** where witnesses seek to identify the accused. [U.S. v. Wade, 388 U.S. 218, 1967]

e. **A preliminary hearing** to determine whether there is sufficient evidence against the accused to go to the grand jury. [Coleman v. Alabama, 399 U.S. 1, 1970]

f. **Sentencing.** [Townsend v. Burke, 334, U.S. 736, 1948]

6. **Right to "Effective Counsel":** As a matter of constitutional law, the defendant may challenge his conviction on the ground that his lawyer at the trial was so incompetent as to deprive him of the effective assistance of counsel. However, while this claim is frequently raised, it is rarely upheld by the courts.

   a. **What constitutes "effective counsel":** The Supreme Court has avoided setting any minimum standards of competency for defense counsel in criminal proceedings. Rather, it has indicated that the question is primarily one within the "good sense and discretion of the trial courts." [McMann v. Richardson, 397 U.S. 759, 1970]

      (1) Lower courts have reversed or set aside convictions on the ground that defense counsel was "ineffective" only in extreme cases—as where the services rendered were shocking to the conscience of the reviewing court; where the representation was only perfunctory; or where the services provided were in bad faith, a sham, a pretense, or without adequate opportunity for conference and preparation.

      (2) The mere fact that counsel's advice turns out to be wrong does not mean that the accused was deprived of "effective" counsel. Rather, the question is whether the advice was "within the range of competency" expected of attorneys defending criminal charges.

   b. **Advising defendant to plead guilty:** A guilty plea waives all defenses and most objections. Therefore, the "effectiveness" of counsel's advice to enter such a plea may be more carefully examined.

      (1) Lower courts have held that if counsel unqualifiedly and falsely represents that the state has accepted a plea bargain, where the representation appeared to be supported by acts or statements of state officers, and the defendant justifiably relied on counsel's misrepresentation in entering his guilty plea, the defendant has been denied the effective assistance of counsel and his plea should be set aside.

         (a) However, a mere error of law in advising defendant to enter a guilty plea does not in itself constitute the denial of effective counsel. Again, the test is whether the mistake was "within the range of competency" of most criminal defense lawyers.

   c. **Representation of defendant during trial:** This is the area where counsel's strategy and on-the-spot tactics receive the greatest leeway from reviewing courts.

(1) For example, convictions have been upheld even where it was shown that counsel waived constitutional rights of the accused without consulting with him or advising him of the alternative tactics available.

7. **Effect of Denial of Right to Counsel**

   a. **At trial, plea or sentencing—automatic reversal:** Denial of the right to counsel at the time of trial, at the time defendant is required to plead to the charge, or at the time of sentencing is a fundamental violation of constitutional rights and requires automatic reversal of any conviction.

   b. **At earlier stages-judged by "harmless error" standard:** Denial of counsel at some earlier stage of a criminal proceeding does not always require reversal of a subsequent conviction. In these cases, the issue is whether lack of counsel at that stage was "prejudicial" error (requiring reversal) or mere "harmless" error (which does not require reversal).

   (1) However, the prosecution must prove beyond a reasonable doubt that the error was "harmless"—meaning that it did not contribute to the verdict against the defendant.

8. **Waiver of Right to Counsel**

   a. **Constitutional right to act as own counsel:** An accused has a constitutional right to waive counsel and represent himself in a criminal proceeding. [Faretta v. California, 422 U.S. 806, 1975]

   (1) Note, however, that an accused who elects to represent himself cannot later claim denial of the "effective assistance of counsel."

   b. **Requirements for effective waiver:** Before an accused can be permitted to waive counsel and represent himself, the following constitutional requirements must be met:

   (1) **Accused must be fully advised of right to counsel:** The court must fully advise the accused of his right to be represented by counsel.

   (2) **Waiver must be expressed:** The accused's waiver of counsel cannot be implied from his silence, or from his failure to request the appointment of counsel.

   (3) **Court must determine the competency of the accused:** The trial judge also has the duty to determine whether the accused (a) is competent to waive his right to counsel (i.e., knows and understands the nature of his right, and intelligently intends to waive it) and (b) is competent to make an intelligent choice in the case.

   (a) In determining the defendant's competency to make an intelligent choice, the court must make him aware of the dangers and disadvantages of self-representation.

## C. RIGHT TO A SPEEDY AND PUBLIC TRIAL

1. **Constitutional Basis for Right:** The 6th Amendment provides that "in all criminal prosecutions the accused shall enjoy the right to a speedy and public trial . . . ." Note that there are two spearate rights involved in this provision: A speedy trial and a public trial.

a. **Speedy trial**

   (1) **When right to speedy trial attaches**: By its wording, the 6th Amendment applies only after a person becomes an "accused"—i.e., after he has been formally charged with a crime or placed under arrest and detained for the purpose of answering a criminal charge. Once arrested, a person is deemed an accused and is entitled to a speedy trial, even though he is later released.

   (2) **Determining whether delay is unreasonable**: Violation of the right to a speedy trial is not established by delay alone. Rather, the determination of whether a case must be dismissed for lack of a speedy trial requires a balancing test, in which the conduct of both the prosecution and the defense are weighed and the following factors are considered: (a) Length of delay; (b) reason for delay; (c) defendant's assertion or non-assertion of rights; and (d) prejudice to the defendant. Usually, any one factor alone is not sufficient to justify or condemn the delay in the trial.

   (a) **Length of delay**: The length of delay alone does not establish a violation of the right to a speedy trial. However, a delay of nine months in a case which depended upon eyewitness testimony has been held too long and presumed to be prejudicial to the accused.

   (b) **Reason for delay**: A deliberate attempt by the prosecution to delay the trial weighs heavily toward a violation of the right to a speedy trial. On the other hand, a valid reason—such a missing witness—normally will justify the delay in the absence of prejudice to the accused (discussed below).

   1) If the delay is attributable to wilful tactics by the accused, he will be deemed to have waived his right to a speedy trial.

   2) The mere fact that the accused is serving a jail sentence in another state does not justify a delay of his trial on the pending charge. The prosecution must attempt to have the other state temporarily give up custody for purposes of trial on the pending charge.

   a) To expedite such matters, a number of states have enacted the Uniform Agreement on Detainers, which provides that cases filed against a prisoner in another jurisdiction must, upon request by the prisoner, be tried within 180 days or dismissed.

   (c) **Defendant's assertion or non-assertion of right**: A defendant may at any time waive his right to a speedy trial; but it must be shown that the waiver was knowing and intelligent. It cannot be implied from his silence.

   (d) **Prejudice to defendant**: The nature and amount of prejudice resulting from the delay must be judged by what the right to speedy trial is designed to prevent—namely, oppressive incarceration, loss of evidence, accuracy of witness testimony, anxiety to the accused, and the like.

   (3) **Only remedy is dismissal**: If defendant's constitutional right to a speedy trial has been violated, the only remedy is a dismissal of the prosecution entirely. Such dismissal prevents all further prosecution of the accused for the same offense.

(4) **Statutory provisions**: In addition to the constitutional provision for a speedy trial, some statutes also provide for dismissal of an action when there have been unjustified delays in filing charges or bringing the defendant to trial.

    (a) **Federal Speedy Trial Act**: Under the Federal Speedy Trial Act of 1974, the goal is to bring all federal criminal cases to trial within 100 days following arrest. The Act requires that an information or indictment be filed within 30 days after arrest, arraignment follow within 10 days thereafter, and the trial commence within 60 days after arraignment.

    (b) Similarly, the California Penal Code requires trial within 60 days after the filing of charges against the accused.

    (c) **Compare**: A dismissal for failure to comply with these statutory requirements may not prevent another prosecution for the same offense—unless the statute itself so provides.

b. **Public Trial**: The accused likewise has a constitutional right to a public trial.

  (1) **Exclusion of spectators from courtroom**: The trial judge, in his discretion, may exclude some or all spectators during particular parts of the proceedings for good cause. Under almost no circumstances, however, may the friends and relatives of the accused be excluded from trial.

    (a) Spectators are frequently excluded when "lurid details of a rape must be related by a young lady." The accused's right to a public trial is not violated thereby.

    (b) Likewise, a judge may properly exclude certain persons if it is shown that they are likely to threaten witnesses.

  (2) **Who may object to such exclusions**: There is a split of authority on this issue. Some courts hold that only the accused has the right to object. Others have indicated that the right also belongs to the public—so that members of the public (such as the press) may properly object to being excluded.

## D. RIGHT TO TRIAL BY JURY

1. **Constitutional Basis**: Article III, Sec. 2, cl. 3 of the Contitution provides that "The trial of all Crimes, except in Cases of Impeachment, shall be by jury". The 6th Amendment also provides that "In all criminal prosecutions, the accused shall enjoy the right to a speedy and public trial, by an impartial jury of the State and district wherein the crime shall have been committed".

  a. **Size of jury**: In all federal criminal trials, a jury of 12 is still required by statute. However, a jury of 12 persons is not required by the 6th Amendment. Thus, for example, the Supreme Court has upheld a Florida law providing for a 6-member jury in all criminal cases except those involving capital offenses. [Williams v. Florida, 399 U.S. 78, 1970]

    (1) The Court has not indicated what minimum number of jurors could still properly constitute a jury in a criminal case.

  b. **Unanimous verdict**: In federal criminal cases, the 6th Amendment requires a unanimous jury verdict. But a unanimous jury verdict is not required in state trials.

(1) In *Apocada v. Oregon,* 406 U.S. 404, 1972, a 9-out-of-12 verdict for conviction was upheld as constitutional—although the Court has not decided whether an 8-out-of-12 or a 7-out-of-12 conviction verdict would be constitutional.

    (a) The Court has rejected the argument that permitting a non-unanimous verdict violates the "reasonable doubt" standard for conviction in criminal cases (discussed infra). I.e., the fact that certain jurors disagree would not in itself establish that there was a reasonable doubt as to defendant's guilt.

2. **Serious vs. Petty Offenses:** Since the 6th Amendment guarantees a jury trial only where a <u>serious</u> offense is charged, one must distinguish such offenses from mere "petty" offenses. The Court looks at the <u>maximum potential sentence</u> that could be imposed in making this determination.

    a. **Standard used:** Where the <u>maximum punishment</u> authorized by statute is <u>imprisonment for more than six months</u>, the offense is considered "serious" regardless of the penalty actually imposed—and the accused is entitled to a jury trial. [Baldwin v. New York, 399 U.S. 66, 1970]

        (1) Example: X is tried for theft, the maximum penalty for which is one year in jail. If X is denied a jury trial, convicted, and sentenced to 5 months in jail, the conviction must be reversed as violating his right to trial by jury.

        (2) In contrast, an offense whose maximum penalty is six months or less is "petty" and no right to jury trial exists.

        (3) Where <u>no punishment is prescribed by statute</u>, the offense is considered "petty" if the <u>actual</u> sentence imposed is six months or less.

3. **Waiver of Right:** The right to a jury trial can be waived by the accused, provided this is done <u>expressly and intelligently</u>.

    a. **Prosecution's right to a jury trial:** Note that the prosecution <u>also</u> has the right to demand a jury even if defendant waives it . . . since criminal defendants have no constitutional right to have their cases tried before a judge alone. [Singer v. U.S., 380 U.S. 24, 1965]

4. **Selection of Jurors**

    a. **Must be from fair cross-section of community:** The 6th Amendment requires that trial juries in both federal and state criminal trials be selected from "a representative cross-section of the community". Restricting jury service to special groups is forbidden.

        (1) **Example:** Excluding <u>women</u> from juries, or giving them automatic exemptions with the result that jury panels are almost totally male, is invalid. [Taylor v. Louisiana, 419 U.S. 522, 1975]

        (2) **Example:** Likewise, the exclusion of persons because of race, creed, color or national origin has been held invalid.

## E. THE RIGHT TO A FAIR AND IMPARTIAL TRIAL

1. **Constitutional Basis:** The Due Process Clauses of the 5th and 14th Amendments guarantee the accused a fair trial by an impartial jury.

2. **Prejudicial Publicity**

   a. **The Problem**: Two basic principles of the American system of criminal justice are that a person must be <u>convicted by an impartial tribunal</u>, and that a person must be convicted <u>solely on the basis of evidence admitted at the trial</u>. The publicity given to a notorious case before or during trial may bias a jury or create a significant risk that the jury will consider information other than the evidence produced in court.

   (1) **Example**: Headlines announced that D had confessed to 6 murders and 24 burglaries; and reports were widely circulated that D had offered to plead guilty. Ninety percent of the prospective jurors interviewed expressed an opinion that D was guilty; and 8 out of 12 jurors finally seated, familiar with the material facts, held such a belief. The Supreme Court held that D had been denied due process, stressing that this was a capital case. [Irwin v. Doud, 366 U.S. 717, 1961]

   (2) **Example**: Police arranged to have D's prior confession shown several times on local television. The Court held that D had in effect been "tried" thereby—and that no actual prejudice need be shown to establish a denial of due process under such circumstances. [Rideau v. Louisiana, 373 U.S. 723, 1963]

   b. **Methods of controlling impact of prejudicial publicity**

   (1) **Change of venue**: A defendant claiming undue pretrial publicity or other circumstances that would endanger his right to a fair and impartial trial locally can move for a change of venue—i.e., to have the place of trial changed to another county from which more impartial jurors can be drawn. This is allowable in both felony and misdemeanor cases.

   (2) **Sequestration** (keeping jurors together during trial and strictly controlling contact with the outside world): If there is a danger that jurors will be exposed to prejudicial publicity during the trial, some states permit sequestration at the judge's discretion immediately following jury selection for the duration of the trial. A few states automatically sequester the jury.

   (3) **Continuance** (postponement): If the prejudice is severe, a continuance may be granted to allow the threat to an impartial trial to subside.

   (4) **Control of participating counsel**: One of the most effective means of controlling prejudicial publicity is to prohibit the participating attorneys from releasing information to the press.

   (a) Rule 20 of the American Bar Association Canons of Ethics provides that a lawyer should generally avoid making a statement to the public about a pending case except in "extreme circumstances"—and should never go beyond reference to facts already in the record.

   (5) **Control of the police**: It is generally agreed that police officers connected with a case ought to observe standards similar to those formulated for attorneys (above).

   (6) **Control of the press**: This is a very difficult problem for the judge, because of the 1st Amendment guarantee of freedom of the press.

(a) Generally, attempts to control the news media on the kind of news items they can print in connection with a criminal case are difficult to justify—even where such items may create a "clear and present danger" of unfair trial for the accused. [Nebraska Press Ass'n v. Stuart, 423 U.S. 1327, 1976]

(b) **Television**: Courts usually prohibit the taking of photographs or the televising of courtroom proceedings. In a number of states, however, the televising of courtroom proceedings is <u>discretionary</u> with the trial judge.

1) **But note**: If the judge allows the televising of court proceedings, he must be very careful not to create a carnival atmosphere inside the courtroom. The Supreme Court has already reversed one conviction because the trial against defendant had been televised. The Court found the televising process so distractive to the judge, jurors, witnesses and counsel that it denied the defendant a fair trial.

3. **Remedy if Right is Violated**: Any conviction obtained under circumstances violating the defendant's right to a fair and impartial trial must be reversed.

4. **Right to Competent and Impartial Judge**: The right to a fair trial also includes the right to a competent and impartial judge.

   a. **Competency—legal training**: Even where defendant faces possible imprisonment, there is no constitutional requirement that the judge be a lawyer—provided the defendant, if convicted, can obtain a new trial on appeal before a lawyer-judge and is entitled to release on bail while awaiting the second trial.

   b. **Impartiality**: Due process guarantees a criminal defendant the right to trial before an impartial judicial officer. The right is violated if the judge has either a direct or indirect financial interest in the defendant's conviction.

   (1) **Example**: Judge received part of fines levied against convicted defendant. Conviction was held invalid. [Tumey v. Ohio, 273 U.S. 510]

   (2) **Example**: Judge was mayor of village and fines provided a substantial portion of general funds for municipality. Conviction was held invalid. [Ward v. Village of Monroeville, 409 U.S. 57, 1972]

F. **RIGHT TO CONFRONTATION OF WITNESSES**

1. **Constitutional Basis for Right**: The 6th Amendment provides that "in all criminal prosecutions, the accused shall enjoy the right . . . to be confronted with the witnesses against him."

2. **Proceedings in Which Right Exists**: The right to confrontation exists in all criminal proceedings—including trials, preliminary hearings, and juvenile proceedings where the juvenile is suspected of having committed a crime.

   a. However, the right does not apply to purely investigative proceedings—such as grand jury proceedings, coroner's inquests, and legislative investigations.

3. **Scope of Right**: The right to confrontation includes: (a) The right to cross-examine all opposing witnesses; (b) the right to be physically present during the trial; and (c) the right to know the identity of prosecution witnesses.

a. **Right of cross-examination:** Opportunity to cross-examine all opposing witnesses is an important right of the accused: It is the process whereby any falsehood or inaccuracy in the witness's testimony can be detected and exposed, and through which a skillful lawyer may elicit testimony which can be helpful to his client.

b. **Right to be physically present:** The right to confrontation also means that the accused must have the opportunity to be physically present in the courtroom at the time any testimony against him is offered. However, the right to be present may be waived by the following:

   (1) **Deliberate absence:** If an accused is present at the start of the trial but later voluntarily absents himself, most states hold that the trial may continue in his absence—i.e., he is considered to have waived his right to be present. Note, however, that if the defendant is not present at the beginning, the court cannot proceed without him—even though his absence was deliberate.

   (2) **Disruptive conduct in courtroom:** Likewise, an accused who persists (after a warning) in disorderly or disrespectful conduct in the courtroom will be held to have waived his right to be present and may be excluded from his own trial—at least until he promises to conduct himself properly.

      (a) The Supreme Court has approved the following methods for dealing with a disruptive defendant: (1) Holding him in contempt of court; (2) binding and gagging him in the courtroom; and (3) removing him from the courtroom until he promises to behave properly. [Illinois v. Allen, 397 U.S. 337, 1970]

c. **Right to know identity of prosecution witnesses:** Any witness who testifies against the accused must reveal his true name and address. Such information may be crucial to the defense in investigating and cross-examining the witness for possible impeachment.

## G. RIGHT TO COMPULSORY PROCESS TO OBTAIN WITNESSES

1. **Constitutional Basis for Right:** The 6th Amendment expressly provides that the accused in a criminal prosecution shall have the right to compulsory process for obtaining witnesses in his favor.

2. **Scope of Right:** The right to obtain witnesses includes (a) the power to require the appearance of witnesses, and (b) the right to present a defense—which in turn includes the defendant's right to present his own witnesses and his own version of the facts.

   a. **Intimidation by judge:** Thus, where the trial judge makes threatening remarks to the only defense witness which in effect drive the witness from the stand, the accused is deprived of his right to present a defense. [Webb v. Texas, 409 U.S. 95, 1972]

   b. **Exclusion of crucial evidence:** Similarly, the trial court's exclusion of evidence crucial to the defense, and which bears substantial assurances of trustworthiness, violates the right to present a defense—even where the evidence is technically not admissible under local rules of evidence.

      (1) **Example:** Defendant offered evidence of oral confessions to the crime by another witness. The trial court excluded the evidence because it constituted inadmissible hearsay under the local rules of evidence. This was held to violate

defendant's right to present a defense, since the confessions bore substantial assurances of trustworthiness. [Chambers v. Mississipps, 410 U.S. 289, 1973]

## H. PRIVILEGE AGAINST SELF-INCRIMINATION

1. **Constitutional Basis for Right**: The privilege against self-incrimination springs from the 5th Amendment provision that "No person . . . shall be compelled in any criminal case to be a witness against himself".

2. **Reason for Privilege**: The privilege against self-incrimination is designed to restrain the state from using force, coercion, or other illegal methods to obtain any statement, admission, or confession.

3. **Scope of the Privilege**

    a. **Privilege applies only to natural persons (i.e., human beings)**: Corporations or partnerships (who are considered frequently persons by law) cannot claim the privilege; and the records of such entities cannot be witheld on this ground.

    b. **Protects only against testimonial self-incrimination**: There is no protection where there is no testimonial compulsion. Thus, the accused can be forced to submit to reasonable physical or psychiatric examinations; and the police can introduce evidence obtained thereby—such as fingerprints, footprints, blood or urine samples, or voice identifications—during the trial.

        (1) Likewise, defendant can be forced to stand up for identification in the courtroom, put on certain items of clothing, or give a handwriting sample. [Gilbert v. California, 388 U.S. 263, 1967]

    c. **Does not protect production of records**: The search and seizure of a person's private papers in accordance with legal process (with or without a warrant) does not violate the privilege against self-incrimination—at least where information on the papers was written voluntarily and hence was not obtained by testimonial compulsion.

4. **Two Separate Privileges**: The privilege against self-incrimination is generally considered to guarantee two separate privileges. These are: (1) the privilege of the accused; and (2) the privilege of witnesses.

    a. **Privilege of the accused**: The accused in a criminal case has a privilege not to take the stand and, of course, not to testify. "He may stand mute, clothed in the presumption of innocence."

        (1) **Prosecutor cannot comment on assertion of right not to testify**: No conclusion of guilt may be drawn from failure of the accused to testify during the trial. Therefore, the prosecutor is not permitted to make any comment or argument to the jury suggesting that the defendant is guilty because he refused to testify. Should such comments be made, the conviction will be reversed.

        (2) **When does privilege apply?**

            (a) The privilege applies in all stages of a criminal proceeding—starting with when the suspect is first placed in custody.

            (b) The privilege applies in criminal prosecutions or contempt proceedings, but does not apply where there is no prosecution and no accused—as in grand jury investigations or legislative or administrative hearings. A person cannot refuse to testify in these proceedings, but the witness privilege (below) still applies.

(3) **Waiver by taking the witness stand**: Once an accused takes the witness stand in his own defense, he waives the accused's privilege not to testify.

(a) And, if the accused chooses to testify during the trial, he <u>must answer all relevant inquiries about the charge for which he is on trial</u>.

b. **Privilege of a witness**: <u>Any</u> witness—whether or not an accused—has a privilege to refuse to disclose <u>any</u> matter that may "tend to incriminate" him.

(1) **When privilege applies**: The witness privilege is broader than the privilege of an accused, and extends to <u>all judicial or official hearings, investigations, or inquiries</u> in which persons are formally called upon to give testimony.

(2) **Meaning of "tend to incriminate"**

(a) A question tends to incriminate a witness if the answer would <u>directly or indirectly implicate</u> him in the commission of a crime.

1) The privilege therefore does <u>not</u> extend to any form of civil liability. But if the facts involved would make the witness subject to <u>both</u> civil and criminal liability, the privilege can be claimed.

2) The privilege <u>cannot</u> be claimed merely because the answer would hold the <u>witness up</u> to shame or disgrace (as long as no crime is involved).

3) **Note**: The answer to the question need not <u>prove</u> guilt in order to give rise to the privilege. There need only be <u>a reasonable possibility</u> that the answer would be a <u>link in a chain of evidence</u> against the witness.

(b) **No protection if no danger of criminal liability**: The witness' privilege protects only against the <u>possibility</u> of prosecution. Hence, if a witness could not—or can no longer be—prosecuted, he <u>can</u> be compelled to testify. <u>Examples</u>:

1) If the <u>statute of limitations</u> (statute which provides that a crime must be prosecuted within a certain period of time) has run on the crime, the privilege does not apply.

2) If the accused has been <u>acquitted</u> and therefore cannot be reprosecuted, his testimony can be compelled.

3) If the witness is assured of <u>immunity</u> from prosecution, he may not be able to claim the privilege (see below).

(3) **Who decides whether answer "tends to incriminate"**: This decision is made by the hearing or presiding officer (judge, or administrator or chairman in an administrative hearing).

(4) **Effect of granting immunity**: There are many situations in which the government grants immunity to a witness in return for his testimony. Immunity is usually given where the testimony of the witness is crucial in proving the

government's case or when the government needs further information for investigative purposes (particularly in organized crime cases).

- (a) If the witness is granted proper immunity against prosecution, he may be forced to testify—since the reason for the privilege no longer exists. Once immunity is granted, a witness who still refuses to testify can be held in <u>contempt</u> of court and may therefore be imprisoned.

- (b) Immunity is granted either by <u>law</u> (usually as to a class of witnesses), by the <u>judge</u>, or by <u>prosecutors</u> (in specific cases).

- (c) In a growing number of cases (such as gambling or drug possession), the same act may consitute a crime under both federal and state laws. The question then arises whether a grant of immunity from prosecution under <u>one</u> law (state or federal) is sufficient to prevent the witness from claiming the privilege.

    - 1) If a state granted the witness valid immunity from prosecution and he is thereupon forced to testify in state proceedings, the federal government is <u>not</u> permitted to make use of the forced testimony (or any of its "fruits") in a federal prosecution against the witness. [Murphy v. Waterfront Commision, 378 U.S. 52, 1964]

        - a) **Note**: This does not mean that the federal government cannot prosecute its witness. It simply means that any federal prosecution must be based on independent evidence—<u>not</u> on the forced testimony or its "fruits".

    - 2) The Supreme Court has not expressly decided whether a state would be allowed to use compelled testimony given in federal court under a grant of federal immunity. However, its use would probably be prohibited under the reasoning of the *Murphy* case, above.

(5) **Waiver of witness privilege**: The witness privilege may be waived through the following:

- (a) **Failure to assert**: The witness is the holder of the privilege and only he (or his lawyer) can assert it. If he fails to assert the privilege <u>at the time</u> an incriminating question is asked, the privilege is waived.

- (b) **Partial disclosure**: When the witness discloses a fact that he knows incriminates him, he also waives his privilege as to all further facts related to the same transaction.

- (c) **Accused taking the witness stand**: As stated above, when the witness is also an accused who voluntarily decides to take the stand, <u>he must answer all relevant inquiries about the charge for which he is on trial</u>. He is therefore "fair game" on all such matters during the cross-examination.

## I. RIGHT TO PROOF OF GUILT BEYOND REASONABLE DOUBT

1. **Constitutional Basis for Right**: The Due Process provisions of the 5th and 14th Amendments require proof beyond a reasonable doubt of every fact necessary to establish the crime with which the defendant is charged.

2. **Scope of Right**: The prosecution must prove the following beyond a reasonable doubt:

   (a) The question of guilt, and

   (b) Every element of the crime. For example, in a crime of theft, the element of intent and the fact that the property belongs to another person must be proved beyond reasonable doubt.

      1) However, only those elements of the crime which have to do with defendant's guilt must be established beyond reasonable doubt. For example, questions relating to the admissibility of evidence—i.e., whether evidence was obtained by lawful search, or whether defendant's confession was voluntary—need only be proved by a preponderance of the evidence.

3. **What Constitutes "Reasonable Doubt"**: "Reasonable doubt" is very hard to define. However, the most-widely quoted definition is that contained in the California Penal Code, Sec. 1096a, which states: "It is not a mere possible doubt.... It is the state of the case which, after the entire comparison and consideration of all the evidence, leaves the minds of jurors in the condition that they cannot say they feel an abiding conviction, to a moral certainty, of the truth of the charge."

   a. In practice, an individual juror really determines for himself what is meant by "reasonable doubt". Definitions, like the one above, can only give a general guideline.

4. **Proceedings in Which "Reasonable Doubt" Standard Applies**: The requirement of proof beyond a reasonable doubt applies to every proceeding in which violation of a criminal law is charged, or as a result of which criminal punishment may be imposed (as in a juvenile proceeding where a crime is charged).

5. **Presumptions—"Rational Connection" Required**: A presumption is a statement which can be considered true for purposes of law without further proof. Legal presumptions are usually contained in statutes, an example being a law providing that anyone who cannot explain his possession of recently-stolen property is presumed to know that the property was stolen. The question is whether presumptions can be used to prove guilt.

   a. **Requirement of "rational connection"**: No essential element of a crime can be proved by a presumption "unless it can be said with substantial assurance that the presumed fact is more likely than not to flow from the proved fact on which it is made to depend". This is the "rational connection" requirement.

   b. **Example**: A statutory presumption that any person in possession of marijuana knew that it had been illegally imported into the U.S. (as distinguished from having been grown here) is invalid for a lack of "rational connection" between the proved fact (possession of marijuana) and the presumed fact (knowledge of illegal importation). [Leary v. U.S., 395 U.S. 6, 1969]

J. **RIGHT TO PROTECTION AGAINST DOUBLE JEOPARDY**

   1. **Constitutional Basis for Right**: The 5th Amendment of the U.S. Constitution provides that "no person shall be ... subject, for the same offense, to be put twice in jeopardy of life and limb."

   2. **Scope of Protection**: A person who has committed a criminal act can be subjected to only one prosecution or punishment for the same offense. Accordingly, when a defendant has been prosecuted for a criminal offense and the prosecution has resulted in either a

conviction or an acquittal—or the proceeding has reached a point at which dismissal would be equivalent to an acquittal—any further prosecution or punishment for the same offense is prohibited.

    a.    What constitutes the "same offense" is discussed below.

3. **When Double Jeopardy Attaches**: Double jeopardy attaches when a person is once <u>placed on trial</u> under the following conditions:

    a.    Upon an indictment or information valid and complete in form;

    b.    Before a competent court having jurisdiction of the offense and the accused; and

    c.    When a competent jury has been sworn (or if a non-jury trial, when the first witness is called and sworn).

Therefore, if a case is dismissed <u>before trial commences</u>, it is not a bar to subsequent prosecution for the same offense.

4. **When Double Jeopardy is Deemed to be Waived**: Even though jeopardy attaches under the above conditions, it may be waived in the following instances:

    a.    **In mistrials**: When a new trial is ordered <u>before verdict</u> on motion of the defendant or otherwise with his consent, there is a waiver of the protection against double jeopardy.

        (1)    Thus, if in the course of a trial, defendant moves for a mistrial because of what a prosecutor or a witness did, and the motion is granted by the judge, the case can be tried again.

    b.    **When verdict of conviction is set aside on defendant's motion or appeal**: The general view is that a defendant asking for a new trial or appealing his guilty verdict "<u>waives</u>" his protection against double jeopardy. Hence, in a subsequent trial, he can be tried again for the same offense of which he was convicted in the first trial.

        (1)    **Example**: In the celebrated *Miranda* case (discussed earlier in connection with custodial interrogation of suspects), the defendant Miranda appealed his original conviction for rape on the ground that his confession was obtained in violation of his right against self-incrimination. His conviction was reversed by the Supreme Court, but he was tried again for the same offense in Arizona and was reconvicted based on other evidence. There was no double jeopardy because his appeal of the first conviction "<u>waived</u>" his right against a retrial on the same offense.

            (a)    **But note**: At a second trial following a successful appeal, a defendant <u>cannot be tried on or convicted</u> of an offense which is <u>more serious</u> than the one for which he was originally tried and convicted.

                1)    **Example**: Suppose a defendant is charged with second degree murder, but is convicted of negligent homicide. If defendant appeals the conviction and obtains a new trial, he cannot be charged with first degree murder in the second trial. [See Green v. U.S. 355 U.S. 184, 1957]

    c.    **Where first trial ends in "<u>hung</u>" <u>jury</u>**: If the jury cannot agree on conviction or acquittal, the judge can declare a "hung" jury and the defendant may be tried again before another jury. This is a matter for the judge's discretion; some courts will declare a "hung" jury after several days of deadlocked deliberation, while others require a longer period of stalemate.

5. **Double Jeopardy Applies Only to Prosecution for the "Same Offense":** Once jeopardy attaches, the defendant cannot de prosecuted a second time for the same offense involved in the first trial <u>or for any other offense included in</u> the act charged in the first trial; nor can he receive more than one punishment for the same offense.

   a. **What constitutes the "same offense":** Courts vary in their definitions of what constitutes the "same or an included" offense. However, the usual test is whether the offense charged in the second trial is the <u>same in law and in fact</u> as the offense charged in the first trial. If so, jeopardy attaches.

      (1) On the other hand, if one offense requires proof of some <u>additional</u> fact which the other does not, there are two separate offenses—and jeopardy does not attach.

      (2) Example: D sets fire to V's house, seeking to kill him, but V escapes. D may be tried for both arson and attempted murder, and an acquittal on one charge will not bar prosecution on the other, because attempted murder requires proof of an additional fact—namely, intent to kill.

6. **State Crimes vs. Federal Crimes—Separate Sovereignties:** If the same act may be a crime under both federal and state law, there are <u>two distinct crimes</u>—because there are "separate sovereignties." The acquittal or conviction of defendant on the federal crime in the federal courts generally does not bar his prosecution for the state crime in state courts, and vice versa. [Abbate v. U.S., 359 U.S. 187, 1959]

   a. Example: D robs a federally-insured bank in Ohio. D can be prosecuted for two crimes: The state crime of robbery and the federal crime of robbery of a federally-insured bank.

   b. Note: A number of states have <u>abolished</u> this rule, recognizing the defense of double jeopardy where there was a prior <u>conviction</u> or acquittal in any other state, government or country founded upon the same act or omission.

   c. Moreover, the doctrine of separate sovereignties does not apply to political subdivisions <u>within</u> a state. Thus, if a defendant is convicted under a municipal ordinance, he cannot be tried again in a state court for the same offense. [Waller v. Florida, 397 U.S. 387, 1970]

7. **Limitations on Consecutive Prosecutions—the Doctrine of Collateral Estoppel:** Even though double jeopardy does not prevent a subsequent prosecution for a different offense arising out of the same criminal act, the prosecution may still be barred from relitigating issues of fact which were <u>necessarily determined in defendant's favor</u> in the earlier trial.

   a. Example: Six persons are robbed in a tavern at the same time by the same criminal. D is arrested and prosecuted for the robbery of one of the victims, but is acquitted. If the record establishes that the basis for D's acquittal was a jury finding that D was not the criminal, D cannot later be prosecuted for robbery of any of the other victims because of the doctrine of "collateral estoppel". [Ashe v. Swenson, 397 U.S. 436, 1970]

## K. SUMMARY

The Bill of Rights in the U.S. Constitution is the main source of rights for an accused during trial. These rights were originally applied only in federal criminal proceedings. However, the U.S. Supreme Court has decided that most of these rights should also be applied in state criminal cases. This has been done through a process of "selective incorporation" under the Due Process clause of the 14th Amendment. Hence, except for the right to grand jury indictment and the right against excessive bail, all the protections in the Bill of Rights apply in state as well as federal criminal proceedings.

The right to counsel refers to retained or court-appointed counsel. It applies at every "critical stage" of the criminal proceeding, not just during the trial itself. The right to a speedy and public trial has not received as much attention from the court; but federal and some state statutes now set a time limit within which cases must be disposed of or dismissed. Trial by jury is required in all "serious" criminal cases—meaning cases where the possible penalty is imprisonment for more than six months. Federal cases need 12-member juries and a unanimous conviction; but the Court has decided that states are not constitutionally required to have a jury of 12 (even in felony cases) or a unanimous verdict for conviction.

An accused is entitled to a fair and impartial trial. This means that a person can be convicted by an impartial tribunal, and that the conviction must be based solely on the evidence admitted at the trial—not on other sources, such as newspaper or television. The right to confrontation of witnesses means the right to cross-examine witnesses on the opposing side. However, this right does not apply in purely investigative proceedings.

The accused is also given the right to compulsory process to obtain witnesses. This includes the right to present a defense—meaning that defendant must be given the opportunity to present his own witnesses and his own version of the facts.

The privilege against self-incrimination protects an accused from being forced to testify at all in court, and protects any witness from being compelled to answer a question which would "tend to incriminate" him. The privilege applies only to testimonial evidence, not physical evidence.

In all criminal proceedings, the accused may be convicted only upon proof of guilt beyond a reasonable doubt. Although difficult to define, this requirement insures that flimsy evidence cannot be the basis of conviction.

Finally, the right against double jeopardy insures that once a person has been tried for an offense, he cannot be tried again for the same offense unless he appeals his conviction—in which case he is considered to have waived this right. Collateral estoppel may also prevent a second trial on issues determined in the first trial—even if a separate offense is involved.

# X. SENTENCING

## A. GENERAL CONSIDERATIONS

Sentencing is the formal pronouncement of judgement and punishment upon the defendant following his conviction in a criminal prosecution.

1. **Court Imposes Sentence**: The sentence is always imposed by the court. However, a number of states permit the jury to recommend or determine the punishment for certain offenses.

2. **When Sentence Imposed**: The sentence generally must be imposed "without unreasonable delay." State rules frequently provide a time limit, while recognizing that some period between a verdict of conviction and the sentencing—usually 10 days to 3 weeks— is necessary for the probation officer to prepare a pre-sentence investigation report (which judges use to help them arrive at a fair and appropriate sentence).

3. **Wide Discretion Allowed**: Judges usually have wide discretion in determining the appropriate sentence in a particular case. Such discretion is implied in penal codes which provide a large range between the minimum and maximum penalties for a particular offense, the idea being that the penalty should "fit the offender." In practice, this results in considerable sentencing disparity—with offenders being given different sentences for similar crimes committed under similar circumstances.

    a. **Example**: The Texas Penal Code provides for imprisonment of 5 to 99 years for first-degree felonies. Hence, D can be given 5 years (or even probation) while X can get 30 years for the same type of crime committed under similar circumstances.

    b. **Note**: It is difficult to correct sentencing disparity in individual cases, since as a general rule, the appellate court will not reverse or modify a sentence if it is within the statutory limits, as in the above example.

4. **Pre-Sentence Investigation Report**: When the appropriate punishment is determined by the court, there is usually an investigation by court officers—probation and sometimes parole investigators—and a report to the court which sets forth full details regarding the accused's background, prior criminal record, family and financial circumstances, and the like. This pre-sentence investigation report usually also includes a recommendation on the granting or denial of probation and the amount of sentence. Such reports are required in some states for felony convictions, but are optional with the judge in others.

    a. The convict does not have a constitutional right to see this report; but many judges make it available to counsel for the defendant prior to the sentencing hearing, so that the defendant can contest any alleged factual inaccuracies therein.

    b. Some other states provide by statute that defendant is allowed to see the pre-sentence report.

5. **Types of Sentences**: The sentence imposed by the court usually consists of one or a combination of the following punishments:

    a. Death;

    b. Imprisonment in a jail or penitentiary;

    c. Imposition of a fine;

d. Forfeiture of property; or

e. Probation.

More than one kind of sentence may be imposed for a crime. For example, imprisonment or probation can be imposed with a fine or forfeiture of property.

6. **Sentences Involving Imprisonment**: These may be classified as either determinate or indeterminate sentences.

   a. **Determinate sentences**: Where the period of incarceration is known by the defendant beforehand, according to certain guidelines, the sentence is determinate.

      (1) **Example**: A sentence of five years in the penitentiary for robbery is a determinate sentence.

   b. **Indeterminate sentences**: There are many variations of the indeterminate sentences, but in its purest form it means that the judge does not fix the term of imprisonment but commits the defendant to prison for an unstated period. The date of release is later determined by correctional officers (usually the Parole Board or Adult Authority) subject to the minimum terms fixed by statute for that crime. (This form of sentencing was used in California before the law was changed in 1976.)

7. **Concurrent or Consecutive Sentences**: Where the defendant has been convicted of two or more crimes, or is already serving a sentence on some other offense, it is necessary to determine whether the sentence presently imposed will run concurrently (at the same time) or consecutively (one after the other, or "stacked"). This matter is entirely within the discretion of the judge who imposes sentence, and is obviously of great importance to the accused.

   a. **Example:** X is tried and convicted of two robberies, and is sentenced to five years' imprisonment for each conviction. If the sentences are imposed concurrently, X will serve a total of 5 years. If served consecutively, however, X stays in prison for 10 years.

8. **Rights of Accused During Sentencing**

   a. **Right to counsel**: The accused has a right to counsel because sentencing is a "critical stage" of the criminal proceeding. If he is indigent, an attorney must be appointed for him by the state.

   b. **"Right of allocution"**: Most courts also provide that the defendant is entitled to make a statement on his own behalf as to why the sentence should not be imposed.

   c. **Other rights**: The accused has few other procedural rights during sentencing. Even the rules of evidence are relaxed—so that the judge in determining sentence may rely upon hearsay and unsworn reports (like those contained in the pre-sentence investigation report) and need not afford defendant an opportunity to cross-examine.

B. **CONSTITUTIONAL LIMITATIONS ON SENTENCING**

Even though the accused has limited procedural rights during sentencing, there are constitutional limitations on what the court can do in imposing sentences. The basic limitations are:

(1) The prohibition against "cruel and unusual punishment";

(2) The prohibition against "double jeopardy"; and

(3) The "equal protection" clause.

1. **Prohibition Against Cruel and Unusual Punishment**: The 8th Amendment prohibits the infliction of "cruel and unusual" punishment on a convicted person. What constitutes cruel and unusual punishment has not been precisely specified by the Supreme Court. However, the following standards have been employed in most cases:

    a. **Nature of punishment itself**: One standard is to determine whether the punishment given is excessive, regardless of the crime involved.

       (1) **Example**: Stripping an army deserter of his citizenship is prohibited—since making an accused a stateless person without rights is considered too cruel a punishment for any crime. [Trop v. Dulles, 356 U.S. 86, 1958]

    b. **Whether punishment fits the crime**: A second standard focuses on the degree of punishment compared to the act for which the accused is being punished.

       (1) **Example**: 12 years in irons at hard labor for the crime of falsifying public records is "cruel and unusual punishment" because it is excessive for so minor an offense. [Weems v. U.S., 217 U.S. 349, 1910]

       (2) **Example**: Likewise, jailing a man for being addicted to narcotics has been held "cruel and unusual punishment." Reason: The accused is being punished for a status which he is powerless to overcome—much like prosecuting a person for being physically or mentally ill. [Robinson v. California, 370 U.S. 660, 1962]

          (a) However, the conviction and imprisonment of a chronic alcoholic for being drunk in public has been upheld—at least where there was no showing that the defendant was incapable of refraining from appearing in public while drunk. [Powell v. Texas, 392 U.S. 514, 1968]

    c. **Capital punishment**: The death penalty is not automatically cruel and unusual punishment. It may be imposed if the sentencing authority (judge or jury) is given adequate guidance as to both aggravating factors (that which makes the crime worse) and mitigating factors (that which lessens the gravity of the crime) about the crime and the defendant which are relevant to sentencing, and if there is a review procedure to insure against imposition of the death sentence for discriminatory reasons. [Gregg v. Georgia, 428 U.S. 153, 1976]

       (1) However, statutes which allow imposition of the death penalty without any standard for the exercise of discretion are unconstitutional. [Furman v. Georgia, 408 U.S. 238, 1972]

       (2) And, a law which imposes a mandatory death penalty, without consideration of mitigating circumstances of the crime and the background of the defendant, is also unconstitutional. [Woodson v. North Carolina, 428 U.S. 286, 1976]

2. **Prohibition Against Double Jeopardy**

    a. **Cannot increase sentence during imprisonment**: Although the Supreme Court has not yet ruled on the issue, lower courts have held it to be a violation of the double jeopardy clause for the trial court to increase its original sentence while the defendant is serving that sentence.

(1) In contrast, federal rules give the trial judge a period of 120 days within which he can <u>decrease</u> the sentence imposed.

b. **Can impose longer sentence after retrial**: However, the Constitution does not prohibit the imposition of a longer sentence upon <u>reconviction</u> for the same offense—i.e., where defendant is convicted and sentenced, but thereafter appeals and obtains a new trial—provided the longer sentence is imposed for proper reasons and <u>not</u> for the purpose of punishing defendant for a successful appeal.

(1) If the <u>judge</u> imposes the longer sentence upon reconviction, the reasons and factual <u>data</u> in support thereof must appear on the record and must be based on "objective information concerning identifiable conduct <u>occurring after</u> the time of the <u>original sentencing</u> proceeding." [North Carolina v. Pearce, 395 U.S. 711, 1969]

(a) **Example**: X has been convicted of rape and sentenced to three years in prison. While released on bail pending appeal for this conviction, X is rearrested for and pleads guilty to <u>driving while intoxicated</u>. If given a new trial and reconvicted for <u>rape</u>, the judge can impose a higher sentence. But he must state on the record that the reason for the increase is defendant's conviction for another offense while released on bail.

(2) If a <u>jury</u> imposes the longer sentence, it is valid "so long as the jury is not <u>informed</u> of the prior sentence, and the second sentence is not otherwise shown to be a product of vindictiveness." [Chaffin v. Stynchcombe, 412 U.S. 17, 1973]

c. **Full credit given for time served**: The prohibiton against double jeopardy also requires that a person <u>reconvicted</u> after a new trial be given <u>full credit</u> against the new sentence for the time served (or fine paid) under his original conviction. [North Carolina v. Pearce, 395 U.S. 711, 1969]

(1) **Example**: Suppose X is convicted of robbery and sentenced to 10 years in the state penitentiary. After serving two years, he is given a new trial on the ground that the evidence used against him was obtained by force. If X is retried, reconvicted, and given a six-year sentence, he must be given credit for the two years he has already served—and must therefore serve only four more years.

3. **The Equal Protection Clause**: The Equal Protection Clause of the 14th Amendment provides that people should not be treated differently unless there is <u>valid justification</u> for such discrimination. This is a further limitation on the sentences which may be imposed.

a. **Inability to pay fine**: The Equal Protection Clause prohibits the imposition of a <u>greater</u> punishment on a poor man than a rich man. Thus, indigent defendants cannot be forced to go to jail because they are unable to pay a fine, if non-indigents can pay the fine and avoid imprisonment.

(1) **Example**: A statute which imposes <u>imprisonment plus a fine</u>, and provides that if the fine is not paid the prisoner must <u>remain in jail longer</u> than the prescribed <u>maximum</u> sentence to "work off" the unpaid fine, violates equal protection. [Williams v. Illinois, 399 U.S. 235, 1970]

(2) It is also a violation of equal protection to limit punishment to the payment of a fine for those able to pay it, but to convert the fine to imprisonment

for those unable to pay (such as laws which provide the alternative punishment of "30 days or 30 dollars"). [Tate v. Short, 401 U.S. 395, 1971]

C. **PROBATION**

Probation is the practice of allowing a convicted person to remain free in the community instead of sending him to a jail or penitentiary, subject to court-imposed conditions and generally under the supervision of a probation officer. If the imposed conditions are violated during the specified probation period, the probation can be revoked and the probationer imprisoned.

1. **Convict Not Entitled to Probation as Matter of Right**: In most jurisdictions probation is available at the discretion of the judge (or in some cases, the jury) except when the required sentence is mandatory or where the offense is punishable by death or life imprisonment. Nevertheless, judges hesitate to give probation in serious offenses where stiff penalties are involved.

    a. Some states specify that probation can be given only if the penalty involved is below a certain number of years. E.g., in Texas, it is 10 years or less.

2. **Terms of Probation**: When probation is granted, the judge has broad discretion to impose restrictive conditions aimed at rehabilitating the probationer and protecting society. However, generally the conditions imposed must bear a reasonable relationship to the crime for which the defendant was convicted.

    a. **Example**: D is convicted of driving while intoxicated and is given probation by the judge on condition that he not consume liquor or be found in bars during the term of his probation. Such conditions are valid.

    b. On the other hand, if the judge requires that D not witness any football game during the period of probation, the condition is of questionable validity—because it would be difficult to show any reasonable relationship between the condition and the crime for which D was convicted.

3. **Need For Acceptance by Probationer**: Since conditions are attached to probation, they must be accepted by the probationer. Most states require that the probationer be given and sign a copy of the conditions of probation.

4. **Revocation of Probation**: Probation can be revoked for two basic reasons:

    a. **Commission of a new criminal offense**—whether felony or misdemeanor.

    b. **Technical violation** of the conditions of probation. This does not involve a crime, but the violation of other conditions—such as a prohibition against consumption of alcoholic beverages, or association with persons of "questionable reputation."

5. **Rights of Probationer Concerning Revocation**: Until recently, probation could be revoked arbitrarily by the court. But in a series of decisions, the Supreme Court has held that probationers are entitled to the following rights before revocation—the same rights given in parole revocation cases and later extended to probation revocation in *Gagnon v. Scarpelli*, 411 U.S. 778, 1973:

    a. **Minimal procedural due process** which includes:

        (1) Written notice of the claimed violation;

(2) Disclosure to the probationer of the evidence against him;

(3) Opportunity to be heard in person and to present witnesses and documentary evidence;

(4) Right to confront and cross-examine adverse witnesses, unless the hearing officer specifically finds good cause for not allowing cross-examination;

(5) A neutral and detached hearing body; and

(6) A written statement of the findings of fact and the reason for the revocation.

b. **Two-step procedure for revocation** involving:

(1) A preliminary (or on-site) hearing; and

(2) A final hearing.

6. **Time which must be Served upon Revocation**: If probation is revoked, the original sentence imposed must be carried out. No credit need be given for the time served on probation, although the judge may reduce the original sentence if he so desires.

## D. SUMMARY

Sentencing is the formal pronouncement of judgment upon the defendant after his conviction in a criminal prosecution. It is always imposed by the court, although some states permit the jury to recommend or determine the punishment for certain offenses. Sentences for serious offenses are usually imposed after the judge receives a pre-sentence investigation report, usually prepared by the probation officer. Judges enjoy wide discretion in determining the appropriate sentence. While this has the advantage of making the penalty "fit the offender" instead of the crime, it also causes sentencing disparity whereby offenders are given different sentences for similar crimes committed under similar circumstances.

Sentences may consist of death, imprisonment, fine, forfeiture of property, probation, or a combination of same. Sentences that involve imprisonment may be determinate or indeterminate. Although the defendant has limited procedural rights during sentencing, certain constitutional provisions restrict the type and severity of sentences that can be imposed. These are the prohibition against cruel and unusual punishment, the prohibition against double jeopardy, and the Equal Protection Clause.

Probation is a form of sentence which has been increasingly used in less serious and first-time offenses. This allows the defendant to stay out of jail or prison under conditions specified by the judge and under the supervision of a probation officer. Should the conditions imposed be violated, the probation may be revoked; but the probationer must be afforded certain basic rights concerning such revocation.

# XI. KINDS OF EVIDENCE;
# PROCEDURE FOR ADMITTING OR EXCLUDING EVIDENCE

A. **EVIDENCE DEFINED**

Evidence is the means by which an alleged fact is either proved or disproved. It includes testimony, documents, material objects and anything else presented to the senses of the jury (or other trier of fact) to prove the existence or non-existence of the fact in question.

1. **"Admissible" vs. "Inadmissible" Evidence:** The above definition of evidence includes anything offered at the time of trial—regardless whether the evidence may properly be admitted or not. Hence, the terms "admissible evidence" and "inadmissible evidence" are used to distinguish the evidence which would be accepted from the evidence which would be rejected at trial.

2. **"Evidence" vs. "Proof":** These two terms are often confused, but they are two different concepts. Evidence is the means by which an alleged fact is either proved or disproved, while proof is the effect of the evidence.

3. **"Evidence" vs. "Testimony":** Testimony is a form of evidence which consists of oral statements made by live witnesses under oath in court (see discussion below). Evidence is a broader term which includes testimony.

B. **FORMS OF EVIDENCE**

There are four basic forms of evidence, namely:

   (1) Real evidence;

   (2) Documentary evidence;

   (3) Testimonial evidence; and

   (4) Judicial notice.

1. **Real Evidence** (also known as "demonstrative" or "physical" evidence): consists of tangible objects (objects which can be touched) presented for inspection to the trier of fact. This is usually the most trustworthy form of evidence, and its admissibility is favored.

   a. **Examples:** Bullets, guns, knives, heroin, television sets, etc., are real evidence.

   b. **Need for Identification:** Although real evidence is said to "speak for itself" (meaning that "seeing is believing"), its significance depends upon proper identification. Such identification is generally based on testimonial evidence.

2. **Documentary Evidence:** Documentary evidence is like real evidence, but consists of writings rather than tangible objects.

   a. **Examples:** Letters, wills, contracts, telegrams, notes, etc., are documentary evidence.

   b. **Need for Identification:** As in the case of real evidence, someone's testimony is usually needed to identify the document or to establish its authenticity.

3. **Testimonial Evidence:** Testimonial evidence is oral evidence presented by live witnesses under oath in court.

4. **Judicial Notice:** The trial judge is entitled—and under certain circumstances may be compelled—to determine certain facts as a matter of common knowledge, without the introduction of any evidence. This process is referred to as "judicial notice."

   a. **Examples:** The public laws of a state, the territorial jurisdiction of a state, the judicial system of a state, the fact that the U.S. has 50 states, the fact that the world is round, and the fact that Monday follows Sunday are each matters as to which a court could take judicial notice.

C. **TYPES OF EVIDENCE**

There are also four basic types of evidence, namely:

   (1) Direct evidence;

   (2) Circumstantial evidence;

   (3) Cumulative evidence; and

   (4) Corroborative evidence.

1. **Direct Evidence:** Direct evidence is that which proves the fact in issue through the personal knowledge of a witness who relates what he saw, heard, felt, touched, or tasted. It is testimony unaided by any intervening fact or inference.

   a. **Example:** In a murder case, W testifies that he saw X take aim at and shoot Z despite Z's plea for mercy. The testimony of W is direct evidence—relying upon his sense of sight and hearing.

2. **Circumstantial Evidence:** Circumstantial evidence is that which proves the fact in issue indirectly by proving another fact from which an inference or presumption may be drawn as to the fact in issue.

   a. **Example:** D is accused of killing his wife with a pistol. Nobody actually saw D fire the gun, but E testifies that he saw D run from the house with a gun in his hand immediately after he heard a shot. E's testimony is circumstantial evidence of the fact in issue, which is whether D killed his wife. This cannot be proved directly, since no one saw D fire the gun. But D's guilt could be inferred from the fact that E saw him run from his house with gun in hand after a shot had been heard.

   b. **Admissibility:** The admissibility of circumstantial evidence is determined initially by whether the evidence is sufficiently related to a fact in issue that an inference as to the fact may legally be drawn.

3. **Cumulative Evidence:** Cumulative evidence is additional evidence on matters as to which direct or circumstantial evidence already has been admitted. Since it merely repeats or verifies evidence already admitted, the court may exclude such evidence as merely causing delay or wasting time.

   a. **Example:** Suppose 10 people observe X shoot and kill Y. It is probably not necessary for the prosecution to have all 10 witnesses testify to the shooting, since after the first few witnesses the testimony will likely be cumulative.

   b. The judge determines the point at which evidence becomes cumulative and therefore unnecessary.

4. **Corroborative Evidence**: Corroborative evidence is that which has no direct bearing on the facts in issue, but tends to strengthen other evidence by showing the reliability of the sources from which the other evidence was obtained.

   a. **Example**: W is the state's main witness in a robbery case, and his eyewitness testimony concerning the robbery is direct evidence. However, any evidence presented by the state to establish the credibility of W—such as the testimony of other witnesses establishing W's good character and reliability—is corroborative evidence.

### D. BASIC REQUIREMENTS FOR ADMISSIBILITY OF EVIDENCE: RELEVANCY AND MATERIALITY

To be admissible in court, evidence must be both <u>relevant</u> and <u>material</u>.

1. **Relevancy**: The relevancy of an item of evidence can be determined by asking this question: Does the evidence offered <u>tend to prove</u> the fact for which it is being offered? If the answer is yes, the evidence is relevant. If not, it must be excluded as irrelevant.

   a. **"Tend to prove"**: The phrase "tend to prove" covers a broad area. However, there are certain identifiable limits.

      (1) **Example**: Defendant's possession of burglar's tools is certainly <u>relevant</u> as evidence in a prosecution for <u>burglary</u>. But it would be irrelevant in a prosecution for forgery, since possession of such tools would in no way "tend to prove" any fact related to a forgery charge.

   b. **Only relevant evidence is admissible**: A fundamental rule of evidence is that only relevant evidence is admissible. This is because irrelevant evidence may be confusing and misleading. Conversely, all relevant evidence is admissible <u>unless excluded by other rules of evidence</u>. Therefore, the law of evidence is largely an inquiry into two matters: (1) Is the evidence relevant and, if it is (2) is it excluded by other rules of evidence (such as the hearsay rule, privileged communication, coerced confession, etc., discussed infra).

2. **Materiality**: The materiality of evidence can be determined by asking this question: Is the evidence being offered <u>directed to some fact properly in issue</u>?

   a. **When is a "fact properly in issue"**: In general, a fact is properly in issue if it is raised by the pleadings (the formal written allegations by the parties of their respective accusations and defenses) or by pretrial orders. Again, the phrase "raised by the pleadings" covers a broad area.

3. **Modern Trend**: Traditionally, a distinction has been made between relevancy and materiality. However, modern rules of evidence treat these terms as <u>two aspects of "relevancy"</u> (meaning that materiality is really a degree of relevancy). Thus for practical purposes, the distinction between relevancy and materiality has little importance today.

### E. HOW EVIDENCE IS INTRODUCED

There are two general ways to introduce evidence at trial, depending upon the type of evidence involved.

1. **Testimonial Evidence**: Testimony is introduced by placing the witness on the witness stand and asking him a question or a series of questions.

2. **Real or Documentary Evidence**: To introduce objects, items, documents or other forms of tangible evidence, the person seeking to introduce such evidence must do the following:

   a. Have a proposed exhibit marked by the clerk for identification (this identification becomes its reference number, such as "Exhibit 1 for the state").

   b. Authenticate the object or writing. Authentication (also known as identification) means a showing that the evidence is what it purports to be.

      (1) **Example**: A showing that the gun sought to be introduced by the prosecutor is in fact the same gun found by the police officer at the scene of the crime.

   c. Submit the offered evidence to opposing counsel for inspection. It is at this stage that opposing counsel raises any objections to admissibility.

   d. Present the evidence to the judge as an offer in evidence. Once the object or item is admitted in evidence, it may be (subject to the court's discretion) be exhibited, read to the jury, or even taken to the jury room.

## F. HOW QUESTION OF ADMISSIBILITY ARISES

Questions on the admissibility of a particular item of evidence arise when one party offers the evidence and an objection is made by the opposing party.

1. **"Objection Sustained"**: If the objection is sustained, the evidence is excluded (if testimony, the witness does not have to answer the question).

2. **"Objection Overruled"**: If the objection is overruled, the evidence is received (if testimony, the witness must answer the question).

3. **Purposes Served by an Objection**: An objection during the trial serves the purpose of excluding evidence from the trial (if sustained) and establishing a basis for an appeal (if overruled).

## G. RULINGS ON ADMISSIBILITY OF EVIDENCE IN TRIAL COURT

The admissibility of evidence is determined solely by the trial judge, who alone decides whether an item of evidence may be considered by the jury. This determination is made on the basis of the preponderance of evidence.

1. **Example**: X is called to testify as an expert witness for P. P's lawyer must convince the trial judge that the witness in fact has expert qualifications. If X's qualifications are challenged by the opposing party, the judge must decide on the preponderance of the evidence whether X qualifies as an expert or not.

2. **Weight and Credibility**: In contrast, the weight and credibility of evidence once it is admitted are always up to the jury to decide. A judge may admit a piece of evidence to which the jury may give no weight at all. But the weighing process does not begin until the evidence has been admitted by the judge.

3. **Where No Objection is Made**: If no objection is made, any kind of evidence may be received. Failure to object is considered a waiver of any existing ground for objection. The trial judge has no obligation to raise objections on his own—based on the concept of the "adversary system" where the two parties oppose each other and the judge serves as a neutral referee.

a. **Exception**—the "plain error" doctrine: However, if an error in failing to object to certain evidence is so fundamental that it deprives the accused of his constitutional right to a fair trial, it is a ground for reversal on appeal even if the accused failed to object in the trial court.

(1) **Example**: Suppose counsel for defendant X fails to object to the introduction of a coerced confession during his trial. This evidence is so fundamental that its admission constitutes a ground for reversal on appeal—despite the absence of any objection at trial.

## H. APPELLATE REVIEW OF TRIAL COURT RULINGS ON ADMISSIBILITY

The trial judge's rulings admitting or excluding an item of evidence are reviewable on appeal from the final judgement in the case. This means that the trial continues despite an erroneous ruling by the judge; and only after final judgement can an appeal on the ruling be made.

1. **Evidence Erroneously Admitted—Requirements for Reversal on Appeal**: In order for an appellate court to reverse a trial court judgment on grounds that some item of evidence was improperly admitted at the trial, the following must be shown:

    (a) A specific objection;

    (b) Timely made;

    (c) Valid ground for objection; and

    (d) Prejudicial error in overruling objection.

    a. **Specific objection**: First of all, the record must show that the party complaining on appeal made a specific objection to admission of the evidence in the trial court.

        (1) **A "specific" objection** requires that counsel have stated the particular legal ground or reason why the evidence was not admissible.

            (a) **Example**: After a question is asked, opposing lawyer says: "Objection. Question calls for hearsay answer."

        (2) **Reason for Requirement**: Specific objections are required to enable the lawyer offering the evidence to cure defects, if possible, and to allow the trial judge to rule intelligently on all phases of the questions before him.

            (a) **Example**: Opposing lawyer says: "Objection. Counsel is leading the witness." Judge: "Sustained. Rephrase the question."

    b. **Timely made**: The objection must also have been timely—i.e., made before the evidence was received. This means before the witness answers (in oral testimony) or before real or documentary evidence is shown to the trier of fact.

        (1) **Motion to strike**: A motion to strike is an objection to the evidence after it has come in. Such a motion is proper only where there was no opportunity or basis for objection at the time the evidence was received.

            (a) **Examples**: A motion to strike is proper in the following cases:

                1) When the witness answers an objectionable question before counsel has opportunity to object to the question.

2) When the question istseIf is not objectionable, but the answer is not responsive to the question. Example: Question: "When you reached the scene of the crime, what did you see?" Answer: "The accused immediately confessed that he committed the offense."

(b) **Time of making motion**: Like an objection, a motion to strike must be made as soon as the ground for such a motion appears. Failure to make a motion to strike constitutes a waiver and the answer or item of evidence stays in the record.

c. **Ground for objection must be valid**: The evidence must in fact have been inadmissible on the ground stated in the objection. If another ground for objection existed, it cannot be raised on appeal for the first time.

(1) **Example**: Opposing lawyer objects to a question during trial on the ground that it calls for a hearsay answer. If admitted anyway by the judge because it is not hearsay, the lawyer cannot challenge its admissibility later on appeal based on the fact that it was a leading question (even if it were).

d. **Prejudicial error in overruling objection**: Finally the trial court judgement will be reversed only if the court's overruling of the objection and admission of the evidence constituted prejudicial error—meaning that it probably had a substantial influence on the verdict or otherwise affected a substantial right of the party objecting to the evidence.

2. **Evidence Erroneously Excluded—Requirements for Reversal on Appeal**: Here, the person appealing (usually the accused) alleges that certain evidence excluded by the trial judge should have been admitted.

   a. **Example**: An accused in a homicide case seeks to introduce the arrest record of the deceased in order to establish that the killing was in self-defense. If the evidence is excluded by the trial judge, exclusion can be challenged by the defendant on appeal, if convicted.

   b. **Requisites for reversal**: It is not easy to obtain reversal of a conviction based on the erroneous exclusion of evidence. To secure a reversal on this ground, the party appealing must establish the following:

   (1) **No valid ground for the exclusion**: The person appealing must first establish that the evidence was in fact legally admissible and that its exclusion was therefore erroneous.

   (2) **Offer of proof made at trial**: Secondly, it must be shown that following the sustaining of the objection made by the opposing lawyer, the party seeking to introduce the evidence made an offer of proof to the trial judge—showing the substance of the evidence and the purpose for which he sought to introduce it.

   (a) **Reason for requirement**: The function of an offer of proof is to establish a record for appellate review. Therefore, the offer must show the relevancy of the evidence (i.e., how it ties into the issues of the case) and its admissibility under the rules of the evidence (e.g., if hearsay, how it could be admitted anyway under an exception to the hearsay rule).

   (3) **Prejudicial error**: The sustaining of the objection (meaning the exclusion of the evidence) must have caused "prejudicial" error.

## I. SUMMARY

Evidence is the means by which an an alleged fact is either proved or disproved and includes anything presented to establish the existence or nonexistence of an alleged fact (regardless of whether or not the evidence is admissible).

There are four basic <u>forms</u> of evidence. <u>Real evidence</u> consists of tangible objects, such as bullets, guns, drugs, television sets, etc. <u>Documentary evidence</u> consists of writings, such as letters, wills, contracts, telegrams, etc. <u>Testimonial evidence</u> is oral evidence given by a witness under oath in court. <u>Judicial notice</u> refers to the practice under which a trial judge may determine certain facts as a matter of common knowledge, without introduction of any evidence on the issue.

There are also four basic <u>types</u> of evidence. <u>Direct evidence</u> proves the fact in issue through witnesses who saw the acts done or heard the words spoken. In contrast, <u>circumstantial evidence</u> proves the fact in issue indirectly by using another fact from which an inference or presumption may be drawn. <u>Cumulative evidence</u> merely repeats or verifies other evidence already in the records and thus may be excluded. <u>Corroborative evidence</u> has no direct bearing on the facts in issue, but strengthens other evidence by showing the reliability of the sources from which that evidence was obtained.

Only <u>relevant</u> and <u>material</u> evidence is admissible in a trial. Evidence is relevant if it tends to prove the fact for which it is being offered and it is material if directed to some fact properly in issue through pleadings or pretrial orders. Testimonial evidence is introduced by placing the witness on the witness stand, while the introduction of real or documentary evidence involves a slightly more complex procedure.

Questions on admissibility are raised when one party offers evidence to which an objection is made by the opposing party. If the objection is "sustained," the evidence is excluded; if "overruled," the evidence is received. The <u>admissibility</u> of evidence is determined solely by the trial judge, while the <u>weight and credibility</u> of the evidence are determined by the jury. If no objection is made, any kind of evidence can be received. The erroneous decision of the trial judge in admitting or excluding evidence is reviewable on appeal, but only after <u>final judgement</u> in the trial court.

# XII. WITNESSES AND PRIVILEGED COMMUNICATIONS

A. **COMPETENCY TO TESTIFY**

1. **General Rules on Competency**

    a. **Old English law**: Under old English law, a person could be disqualified from giving testimony on a number of grounds. These included: Having a financial interest in the outcome of the suit, being married to one of the parties, lack of religious belief, conviction of a felony, race, infancy, or mental derangement.

    b. **Modern law**: The trend in modern law is to abolish all such grounds for disqualification. For example, the federal rule provides that in federal trials, "every person is competent to be a witness, except as otherwise provided by these rules." Most states have followed this trend.

2. **Basic Qualifications to be a Witness**: Despite the trend in modern law to abolish common law grounds for disqualifications, a person must still have certain basic qualifications in order to be a witness. These basic qualifications are:

    a. **Ability to communicate**: The witness must be capable of expressing himself so as to be understood by the jury—either directly or through an interpreter.

    b. **Understanding of duty to tell the truth**: The judge must also determine that the witness understands his duty to tell the truth. Witnesses always take an oath to "tell the truth, the whole truth, and nothing but the truth" before taking the witness stand.

    c. **Personal knowledge of the facts**: Personal knowledge means a present recollection of an impression derived through any of the witness' five senses—i.e., sight, touch, smell, hear, and taste.

3. **Specific Examples of Competency**

    a. **Children**: Age is not a decisive factor in determining competency of child witnesses. A child of any age may be permitted to testify as long as the trial judge is satisfied that the child possesses the ability to observe, recollect, and communicate.

    b. **Mentally impaired persons**: Similarly, a person with a mental impairment may testify as long as the trial judge is satisfied of his capacity to communicate and understand the duty to tell the truth.

    c. **Criminals**: A convicted felon may also be competent to testify. However, the fact of conviction may be used to impeach his testimony.

B. **METHOD AND SCOPE OF EXAMINING WITNESSES**:

The order of examination in a court trial is as follows:

—**Direct Examination**: The first questioning of a witness by his own lawyer.

—**Cross-Examination**: Examination of the witness by the opposing lawyer following the direct examination.

—**Redirect Examination**: The further examination of the witness by his own lawyer after the cross-examination.

—**Recross Examination**: Examination of the witness by the cross-examiner following the redirect examination.

1. **Direct Examination**

    a. **How presented**: Testimony from witnesses on direct examination is presented by placing the witness on the stand, having him sworn, and then asking him a series of questions.

    b. **Form of questioning**: On direct examination, the lawyer is usually limited to questions calling for specific responses by the witness, such as questions preceded by "who", "where", "when" or "how." Certain forms of questioning are considered <u>objectionable</u> on direct examination. These include:

    (1) **Questions calling for conclusions**: "Did the defendant in this case see the injured person on the sidewalk?" calls for the witness' <u>opinion</u> as to what the defendant did or did not see: Likewise, "Why did the defendant shoot the deceased?" calls for a conclusion as to defendant's state of mind.

    (2) **Repetitive questions**: These are questions designed to bolster or emphasize what has already been established. Example: "Tell us again whether you saw the accused beat up the victim or not?"

    (3) **Narrative questioning**: Questions which allow the witness to tell a narrative are not permitted in many courts. Example: "Tell this court everything that happened in the evening of the accident."

    c. **Use of leading questions prohibited**: The use of <u>leading</u> questions on direct examination is also prohibited. A leading question is one which <u>suggests</u> to the witness the answer which the examining lawyer desires;

    (1) **Example**: Lawyer asks: "The accused had a pistol in his hand when you saw him, did he not?" Or, "The argument was followed by a violent fight, was it not?" In both cases, the lawyer has suggested to the witness the answer he wants—and all the witness need do is say yes.

    (2) **Exceptions**: In some instances, leading questions are <u>permitted</u> in direct examination—either because there is little danger of improper suggestion, or because such questions are necessary to obtain relevant evidence. These are:

    (a) With respect to <u>preliminary or collateral</u> matters that are not in issue. Examples: Name, address, occupation, date, etc. "You are a detective in the Police Department, are you not?"

    (b) To <u>revive or refresh a witness'</u> memory. Example: "To refresh your memory, Officer Jones, you in fact arrested the accused on March 15, 1978, did you not?"

    (c) In examination of <u>handicapped, timid, or confused</u> witnesses.

    (d) In examination of <u>expert witnesses</u>.

    (e) In examination of <u>hostile witnesses</u>.

    d. **Effect of lack of memory**: If the witness on direct examination has <u>absolutely no recollection</u> regarding the matter at issue, he obviously is not competent to testify.

More often, however, his memory is merely <u>incomplete</u>: I.e., he remembers the event in general, but not the essential details. In such cases, the direct examiner may seek to aid the witness' memory by using two different concepts—"<u>present recollection revived</u>" and "<u>past recollection recorded</u>".

(1) **"Present recollection revived":** This concept permits a testifying witness to refer to a writing or something else to refresh or revive his memory, so that he will thereafter be able to testify from memory.

    (a) **Anything may be used:** This rule is not limited to use of a writing. The examining attorney may use anything which legitimately revives the witness' memory—such as a picture, an object, shorthand notes, photographs, or the like. A few courts even allow the use of hypnosis to revive a witness' memory.

(2) **"Past recollection recorded":** Where the witness has no independent recollection whatsoever of the contents of a document (even after being shown the document), he will not be permitted to testify by relying on the writing—since he does not recollect anything. However, the <u>contents</u> of the writing itself might be admissible in evidence, provided certain requirements are met. The contents of the writing may then usually be read to the jury.

(3) **Example:** A retired police captain is called to testify in court concerning an official report which he wrote, based on personal knowledge, and submitted to his superior years ago concerning the involvement of the accused in a crime. His memory of the report is incomplete, and he is shown the report in court (reviving his recollection), after which he proceeds to testify based on his recollection. This is a case of "<u>present recollection revived</u>."

    (a) On the other hand, if the captain is shown the report but has no recollection of what has been recorded, he cannot testify on the report. But the report itself might be read into the record as evidence of what the witness once knew—i.e., as a case of "<u>past recollection recorded</u>."

(4) **Distinctions between the above concepts:**

| "<u>Present recollection revived</u>" | "<u>Past recollection recorded</u>" |
|---|---|
| (a) Something is shown to revive witness' memory and he recollects. | (a) Something is shown to revive witness' memory but witness does not recollect. |
| (b) After memory is revived, witness testifies on the matter. | (b) Witness does not testify on the matter because memory is not revived. |
| (c) Material used to revive memory is not admitted in evidence, but other party has right to inspect it. | (c) Contents of material used to revive memory may be read into the record. |

(Where the witness uses the writing to refresh his memory <u>before testifying</u>—as when a police officer looks at documents at the police station or prosecutors office before coming to court, which is indeed a good practice—most courts hold that the other party has <u>no right to inspect</u> the document. But the court has discretion to order its production).

2. **Cross-Examination**

   a. **Method of cross-examination:** On cross-examination, a lawyer is permitted to use any type of question which would be allowed on direct examination—plus certain types which are <u>not</u> allowed on direct examinations.

      (1) **Leading questions permitted:** For example, a cross-examiner may use leading questions which suggest an answer. Examples: "Isn't it true that the accused and you have had fights in the past?" or "You did not actually see the accused stab the deceased, did you?"

      (2) **Improper questions:** Despite the wide leeway given lawyers on cross-examination, certain types of questions still are not permitted:

         (a) **Misleading questions:** A question which cannot be answered without making an unintended admission is not permitted. The classic example is, "Have you stopped beating your wife?"

         (b) **Compound questions:** A question which requires a single answer to more than one question is not allowed. Example: "Did you see and hear the explosion?"

         (c) **Argumentative questions:** Similarly, a leading question which also reflects the examiner's interpretation of the facts is impermissible. Example: "Why were you driving so carelessly?"

         (d) **Questions which assume facts not in evidence:** A question which assumes that a disputed fact is true although it has not yet been established in the case is not permitted. Example: "Since the wound inflicted by the accused was what caused the death of the deceased in this case, why did you . . .?"

         (e) **Conclusionary questions:** And, questions calling for an opinion or conclusion that the witness is not qualified or permitted to make may not be asked. Example: "Did your wife understand what was going on?"

         (f) **Note:** These types of questions are also prohibited on direct examination.

   b. **Scope of cross-examination**

      (1) **Majority view—restricted scope:** A majority of states restrict the scope of cross-examination to <u>matters put in issue on direct examination</u>.

      (2) **Minority view—wide open:** However, a minority of states retain the old English rule that a witness may be cross-examined on <u>all relevant matters,</u> whether or or not they were covered in direct examination.

3. **Redirect Examination:** Redirect examination is used to explain or rebut adverse testimony or inferences developed by opposing counsel on cross-examination, and to rehabilitate the witness if his credibility has been damaged on cross-examination.

a. **Scope of redirect examination:** Those states which follow the restricted view on direct examination (above) usually also limit the redirect to matters covered on cross-examination.

   (1) Conversely, those which follow the minority view allow any matter to be inquired into on redirect—subject only to the court's power to limit the scope of questioning.

4. **Recross Examination:** After the redirect examination, the trial judge may allow recross-examination of the witness. The purpose is to overcome the other party's attempts to rehabilitate a witness or his attempts to rebut damaging evidence brought out on cross-examination.

   a. Such examination is generally within the trial court's discretion, although some states allow it as a matter of right.

C. **OPINION TESTIMONY**

An opinion is defined as an inference derived from facts observed. An inference, in turn, is a rational connection deduced from facts proved.

1. **General Rule—Opinion Testimony Not Admissible:** Witnesses must testify only as to facts within their personal knowledge. It is the function of the jury to draw conclusions from the facts brought out by the witnesses. Therefore, testimony which expresses the opinion or conclusion of the witness generally is not admissible because it usurps this jury function.

2. **When is Witness' Statement an "Opinion":** The content of the witness' testimony—rather than the use of such phrases as "I think" or "I believe"—determines whether a statement is an opinion or a conclusion. The test is whether the testimony is a statement of the witness' personal observations or an inference or conclusion therefrom?

3. **Types of Opinion Testimony:** There are two general kinds of opinion testimony, corresponding to the two basic kinds of witnesses. These are opinion testimony by lay witnesses (i.e., persons with personal knowledge of the facts of the case) and opinion testimony by expert witnesses (i.e., persons who have special knowledge, skill, etc., beyond that of the average person as to the subject on which he is testifying).

   a. **Opinion testimony by lay witnesses:** As noted above, opinions by lay witnesses generally are not admissible. However, most states recognize a number of exceptions in which lay opinions are admissible. These include:

      (1) **Physical conditions:** A witness may give his opinion in describing the appearance or apparent condition of another person. Thus, descriptions such as "drunken", "angry", or "sad" are admissible.

         (a) **Reason:** It is much easier for a witness to say that someone looked "drunk" than to describe the person's way of walking, eyes, breath, or speech at that particular time.

      (2) **Physical descriptions:** If the opinion concerns the matter upon which normal persons consistently form reasonably reliable opinions, the opinion likewise is generally admissible. Examples: Opinions about the speed of a car, size and weight of a person, color, sound, smell, distance, etc.

      (3) **Identity of a person:** The identity of a person is generally established through opinion testimony. The witness can testify that he recognized a person's face

or voice; or he may base identity upon a person's physical characteristics or marks, the sound of his footsteps, etc.

(4) **Sanity**: In most jurisdictions, a lay witness may also state his opinion as to the sanity of a person who is an intimate acquaintance.

(5) **Handwriting**: The opinion of a lay witness is admissible to identify handwriting <u>if</u> the witness has personal knowledge of the alleged writer's handwriting.

b. **Opinion testimony by experts**: Opinions by an expert are generally admissible, as long as they are limited to matters within his expertise.

(1) **Procedure to qualify witness as an expert**: The qualifications of a proposed expert witness must be established before he is allowed to testify. This determination is made by the <u>judge</u> and is binding on the jury. The party seeking to use the expert has the burden of establishing his expert qualifications.

(a) **Factors considered**: The factors considered in determining whether a witness is an expert include: Special skill and knowledge, training and education, experience, familiarity with standard references and authorities in the field, membership in professional organizations and societies, etc.

1) **Technical expertise and high education are <u>not</u> always required**: Any special experience may qualify a person to give an expert opinion. In effect, an expert is one who is believed to be such by the judge (as long as his decision has some basis in fact).

2) **Key factor is helpfulness to jury**: The trend is toward liberalizing the rules governing qualification of expert witnesses. Thus, the determinative issue is whether the witness has sufficient skill or experience in a particular field so that his <u>testimony would be likely to assist the jury</u> in its search for the truth.

(2) **Areas in which expert opinion may be needed**: There are literally hundreds of instances where expert opinion is needed and oftentimes required. In criminal trials, the more common areas are: Specific cause of death; effect of drugs or certain forms of medication; identification of physical evidence (such as hairs, fibers, or blood; fingerprint identification; ballistics comparisons; and identification of narcotics or other dangerous substances.

(3) **Effect of expert opinion**: The general rule is that the jury is <u>not</u> bound to accept an expert's opinion—even if uncontradicted—as long as there are grounds for objecting to it. The theory is that an expert's opinion is no better than the reasons and factual data upon which it is based; and the trier of fact may choose to disagree or disbelieve such supporting reasons or data.

(a) **Limitation**: However, jurors may not arbitrarily disregard uncontradicted expert opinion on <u>matters as to which lay witnesses are not qualified</u> to render valid opinions. If they do so, their verdict may be set aside as unsupported by the evidence.

D. **IMPEACHMENT OF WITNESSES**

1. **Definition and Effect**: Impeachment means <u>discrediting</u> the witness. However, the fact that a witness has been impeached does not mean that his testimony will be stricken

from the record or disregarded. The jury may still choose to believe the witness—since the weight and credibility of the evidence is for the jury, not the judge, to decide.

2. **Methods of Impeachment**: A witness may be impeached either by

   a. **Cross-examination**—eliciting facts from the witness which discredit his own testimony; or

   b. **Use of extrinsic evidence**—i.e., outside evidence, such as other witnesses, records, etc., which discredit that testimony.

3. **Grounds for Impeachment**: There are six basic grounds for impeachment, namely:

   —Bias and interest.

   —Lack of character for honesty or truthfulness.

   —Prior inconsistent statements.

   —Defects of capacity.

   —Lack of knowledge.

   —Contradictions.

   a. **Bias and interest**: Evidence that a witness is biased or has an interest in the outcome of the case tends to discredit his testimony. Examples of bias or interest are:

      (1) The fact that the witness is being paid to testify, or that he has a financial interest in the outcome of the case.

      (2) The witness is a member of the family or has some other relationship with a part in the case (such as business relationship or friendship).

      (3) The fact that the witness has been promised immunity from punishment for testifying.

   b. **Lack of character for honesty or truthfulness**: A witness may be impeached by showing that his character is such that he is likely to lie. The following evidence is admissible for this purpose:

      (1) **Conviction for any felony**: Conviction for any felony generally can be used to impeach a witness. A few states admit evidence of conviction of any crime, whether felony or misdemeanor, for this purpose. In either case, however, there must be a conviction; Mere arrest is not sufficient.

         (a) **Effect of juvenile adjudication**: Juvenile offenses are generally not admissible for impeachment. This is because juvenile proceedings are not criminal proceedings. Moreover, most states either expunge or seal juvenile records after the juvenile reaches the age of majority.

         (b) **Effect of pardon**: In most states evidence of a conviction may be used for impeachment even though the witness was later pardoned.

      (2) **Misconduct not the subject of criminal conviction**: A witness may also be impeached by proof of specific acts which reflect on his poor credibility.

Examples might include lying, cheating at poker or other card games, defrauding others, etc.

- (a) Most American courts allow cross-examination in this area, subject to the <u>discretionary control</u> of the trial judge.

(3) **Poor reputation for truthfulness**: Similarly, a witness may be impeached by showing that he has a poor reputation for truthfulness.

- (a) The usual method of impeachment here is to ask other persons about the witness' general reputation for truth and veracity <u>in the community in which he lives</u>. The modern view also permits evidence of reputation in <u>business circles</u>, which may extend outside the community or neighborhood in which the witness resides.

c. **Prior inconsistent statements**: Proof that a witness previously made statements inconsistent with his present testimony casts doubt upon his truthfulness or accuracy:

(1) **"Laying a foundation"**: Before extrinsic evidence can be introduced to prove a prior inconsistent statement, the witness usually must be given an opportunity to say whether or not he made the statement, and to explain it if possible. This is usually done by asking the witness whether he in fact made the statement (after giving its substance and naming the time, place, and person to whom it was made). This is known as "laying a foundation" (for contradicting him).

d. **Defects in capacity**: A witness may be impeached by showing that his perception and recollection are or were so impaired as to make it doubtful that he could have perceived the facts to which he testifies.

(1) **Example—poor memory**: Thus, a witness can be impeached by showing that he has a poor memory of the events about which he testifies. This is done by asking the witness about related matters—to suggest that if his memory of related matters is poor, his recollection of the events to which he is testifying is likewise doubtful.

e. **Lack of knowledge**: A witness may also be impeached by showing that he has an insufficient knowledge of the facts to which he testifies. This can be done with either lay or expert witnesses.

f. **Contradiction**: Finally, the testimony of a witness may be impeached by introducing rebuttal evidence to disprove the facts to which he testified.

(1) **No impeachment on a collateral matter**: However, where the witness makes a statement <u>not directly relevant</u> to the issues in the case, his opponent is <u>prohibited</u> from proving that the statement is false. The purpose of this rule is to avoid unfair surprise, confusion of the issues and waste of time resulting from attempts to prove and disprove facts which are not directly relevant.

- (a) **Example**: State's witness testifies: "I saw the accident on the way home from church." If it is conceded that the witness in fact saw the accident, defendant will not be allowed to show that the witness was on his way home from a pool hall rather than a church—since this is a collateral matter.

- (b) **Judge determines whether matter is collateral**: Trial judges have a wide range of discretion in this area.

4. **Rehabilitation**: When an attack has been made upon the credibility of a witness, the party who introduced the witness may try to rehabilitate him by introducing evidence to rebut the discrediting evidence, or to reflect favorably on the witness' credibility.

   a. However, rehabilitation is allowed only if the witness' credibility has been attacked. Otherwise, there is nothing to "rehabilitate."

E. **PRIVILEGED COMMUNICATIONS**

   1. **"Privilege" Defined**: "Privilege" is a rule of law which allows a witness to refuse to give testimony which he might otherwise be compelled to give, or to prevent someone else from testifying on the same matter.

   2. **Purpose**: The purpose of privilege is to protect a particular relationship or interest which society considers more important than the testimony which the witness might otherwise give.

   3. **Waiver of Privilege**: All of the privileged communications discussed below may be waived in either of two ways:

      a. **Failure to claim**: This constitutes a waiver of privilege, except where there was no opportunity for the holder to claim the privilege or where disclosure was erroneously compelled by the trial court.

      b. **Voluntary disclosure or consent**: Likewise, if the holder of the privilege discloses, without coercion, any significant part of the communication or consents to such disclosure by anyone else he has waived his right to the privilege.

   4. **What Communications are Privileged**: There are seven basic privileged communications, namely:

      — Lawyer-client privilege

      — Privilege not to testify against spouse

      — Privilege for confidential marital communications

      — Physician-patient privilege

      — Psychotherapist-patient privilege

      — Clergyman-penitent privilege

      — Identity-of-informer privilege

      a. **Lawyer-client privilege**

         (1) **Basic rule**: A client may refuse to disclose, and may prevent another person (usually the attorney) from disclosing, a confidential communication made for the purpose of helping his attorney give proper legal services to the client.

            (a) **Reason for privilege**: The attorney-client privilege is designed to encourage full disclosure by the client to his attorney of all pertinent matters, so as to further the administration of justice and the giving of legal advice.

         (2) **Who is "holder" of privilege**: The holder of the privilege is the client, or his authorized representative if the client is incompetent or deceased.

(a) The lawyer is not a holder of the privilege and cannot claim it on his own behalf. However, an attorney is required to claim the privilege <u>for his client</u>—unless otherwise instructed by the client or his authorized representative.

(3) **Requirements for exercising lawyer-client privilege**

(a) "**Client**": The client must be a person who consults a lawyer for the purpose of retaining the lawyer or securing legal advice from him.

(b) "**Lawyer**": The lawyer must be a person <u>authorized</u> (or reasonably believed by the client to be authorized) to practice law. The rules of several states require that the attorney be a member of the bar of that state.

(c) "**Communication**": The communication must be made <u>in the course of the lawyer-client relationship</u>.

1) **Consultation enough**: However, the client need not actually employ the attorney. The privilege attaches to any communication made while consulting the attorney—even though the attorney declines the case or the client decides not to hire him.

2) **Documents**: "Communications" include written documents intended to provide information to the attorney. However, a suspected murder weapon is not a communication and thus is not protected by the privilege.

(d) "**Confidential**": Finally, the client's communication to the attorney must be confidential.

1) **Presence of third persons**: A communication made in the presence of another person will still be confidential if that person is present to further the interest of the client in the consultation (such as business associate or consultant of the client).

2) **Employees of attorney**: The privilege also applies to communications made by the client to those who confidentially aid the lawyer in performing his work—including secretaries, interpreters, clerks, or accountants. Such persons may also be prohibited from testifying.

(4) **Exceptions to privilege**: The lawyer-client privilege can<u>not</u> be claimed:

(a) If the aid of the lawyer is sought to <u>perpetrate a crime or a fraud</u>; or

(b) As to communications relevant to a claim by the client of <u>breach of duty</u> arising out of a lawyer-client relationship—as when a client sues a lawyer for malpractice, or the lawyer sues his client for fees.

b. **Privilege not to testify against spouse**

(1) **Basic rule**: A married person whose spouse is the defendant in a <u>criminal</u> case <u>may not be called as a witness</u> or <u>be compelled to testify against</u> the spouse in any criminal proceeding.

(a) **Reason for privilege**: The privilege against spousal testimony is designed to protect the marital relationship from the disruption which would follow from allowing one spouse to testify against the other.

(2) **Holder of the privilege**

    (a) The majority view is that the privilege belongs to the <u>accused</u> spouse. He can therefore prevent the witness spouse from testifying.

    (b) The minority view is that the privilege belongs to the <u>witness</u> spouse—so that if the witness spouse wants to testify, the party spouse cannot prevent it.

(3) **Requirements for the use of privilege**

    (a) There must be a <u>valid marriage</u>.

    (b) The privilege lasts only <u>during the marriage</u> and terminates upon divorce or annulment.

        1) If a marriage exists, many states allow the privilege to be asserted even as to matters that took place <u>before</u> the marriage. Thus, an accused could effectively seal a witness' lips by marrying the witness.

(4) **Exceptions**: There is no privilege—and one spouse can therefore testify against the other—in the following cases:

    (a) When one spouse is charged with crimes against the person or property of the other spouse or a child of either.

    (b) When one spouse is charged with bigamy or adultery.

c. **Privilege for confidential marital communications**

(1) **Basic Rule**: Either spouse has a privilege to refuse to disclose, and to prevent another from disclosing, a confidential communication made between the spouses while they were husband and wife.

    (a) **Reason for privilege**: The protection of confidential communications between spouses is designed to encourage open communications and trust between spouses.

(2) **Distinguished from privilege against special testimony**: What is involved here is confidential information between spouses; whereas the privilege on spousal testimony prevents the spouse from testifying against the accused spouse on <u>anything</u> (not just confidential information).

    (a) Moreover, this privilege may be claimed even after the marriage has terminated; whereas the privilege against spousal testimony lasts only during the marriage.

(3) **Holder of the privilege**: <u>Both spouses</u> jointly hold this privilege. Thus, either can prevent the other from <u>disclosing</u> confidential marital communications, even after the marriage has terminated.

(4) **Requirements for use of privilege**:

    (a) The communication must have been <u>made</u> at the time when the parties were husband and wife—even though the privilege may be <u>claimed</u> forever.

(b) The communication must have been made confidential. However, most states presume that communications between spouses are confidential; and the party objecting to the claim of privilege therefore has the burden of showing that it was not privileged.

(c) Only "communications" are privileged: Thus, for example, observations by one spouse as to the actions or conditions of the other spouse are not privileged.

1) But note: Some states hold that nonverbal conduct which is private or confidential is also privileged. Thus, if a wife sees her husband hide a gun in their bedroom, the husband's conduct may be treated as a form of communication—on the theory that if the husband did not trust his wife he would not have hidden the gun while she could see him do it.

(5) **Exceptions to privilege**: The privilege for confidential marital communications cannot be claimed in the following cases:

(a) When one spouse is charged with crimes against the person or property of the other spouse or a child of either.

(b) When one spouse is charged with bigamy or adultery.

(c) If the communication was made to enable or aid anyone to commit (or plan to commit) a crime or fraud.

(d) When one spouse is a defendant in any criminal proceeding (not necessarily one between the spouses) and he wants to testify to a communication between him and his spouse because such evidence is material to his defense.

d. **Physician-patient privilege**

(1) **Basic rule**: A patient has a privilege to refuse to disclose, and to prevent anyone else from disclosing, any confidential communication between himself and his physician.

(a) In many jurisdictions, however, the exceptions to this privilege are so broad as to make the rule almost meaningless.

(2) **Holder of the privilege**: The holder of the privilege is the patient or his authorized representative.

(a) The privilege does not belong to the physician, and cannot be claimed by him independently. However, as in the attorney-client privilege, the physician is required to assert the privilege on behalf of his patient unless the privilege has been waived.

(3) **Requirements for exercise of the privilege**

(a) "Communication": In most jurisdictions, the privilege applies only to confidential communications to a physician in the course of consultation for treatment.

1) Thus, communications made to a physician who examines the patient in order to testify at trial—as when an accused is sent by the prosecutor to a physician for examination—are not privileged. However, if the doctor is employed by the patient's attorney, such communications may be privileged.

(b) **"Physician"**: The physician must be a person authorized (or reasonably believed by the patient to be authorized) to practice medicine.

(c) **"Confidential"**: Confidential communications include any information obtained by a physician in the course of a physician-patient relationship which would be normally regarded as confidential. Hence, the results of physical examinations, blood or urine tests, etc. would be privileged.

(4) **Exceptions to privilege**: The physician-patient privilege cannot be claimed in the following cases:

(a) In criminal proceedings (as when X goes to a physician for treatment after a shootout with the police and X is later accused of that crime).

1) This often makes the physician-patient privilege virtually meaningless in criminal cases. In fact, some states require physicians to report to the authorities any treatment made for a gunshot wound.

(b) Any proceedings in which the condition of the patient has been put in issue by the patient: Suppose P sues Y for damages based on Y's recklessness. P here is placing the extent of his injury in issue, and thus he has no physician-patient privilege.

(c) Where the services of the physician were sought or obtained to assist anyone to commit a crime or civil damage to another person.

(d) Communications concerning breach of duty arising out of a physician-patient relationship: This is like the similar exception for the attorney-client privilege—e.g., malpractice cases brought by patients against physicians.

(e) Where information is of a type that the physician or patient is required to report to a public employee—provided such reports are open to public inspection.

e. **Psychotherapist-patient privilege**: The physician-patient privilege has been extended in a few states to patients of psychotherapists, on the ground that full disclosure between doctor and patient is even more necessary for the treatment of mental and emotional illnesses.

(1) However, it is still uncertain how many other jurisdictions will adopt this privilege.

f. **Clergyman-penitent privilege**

(1) **Basic rule**: A person may refuse to disclose, and may prevent the clergyman from disclosing, any confidential communication made by him to the clergyman who was acting in his professional capacity as a spiritual adviser.

(2) **Holders of the privilege**

    (a) **The penitent**: who can also prevent the clergyman from disclosing information.

    (b) **The clergyman**: Most states also allow a clergyman independently to refuse to disclose such information—even if the penitent wants him to. Reason: Clergyman's religious beliefs may require him to maintain secrecy regardless of penitent's wishes.

(3) **Requirements for exercise of the privilege**

    (a) The clergyman must be a practitioner or functionary of a church or religious organization who is authorized or accustomed to hearing penitential communications and who is under a duty to his church to keep such communications secret. (Some states limit this privilege to confessions.)

    (b) Only communications are privileged. Therefore, observations by the clergyman are not.

    (c) The communication must be made in confidence.

g. **Identity-of-informer privilege**

(1) **Basic rule**: The state has the privilege of refusing to disclose, or of preventing another from disclosing, the identity of an informer.

    (a) **Exception**: When the informer's identity is material to the issue of guilt or innocence, the identity must be revealed. Refusal by the state to reveal the identity of the informer in this situation requires dismissal of the case.

        1) The circumstances in which identity is material to the issue of guilt or innocence is a matter to be determined by the judge.

    (b) When the identity of the informer relates to a narrower issue—such as determining probable cause for the search or arrest—the state is not required to reveal the identity of the informer in order to establish the legality of the search or arrest.

## F. SUMMARY

Under old English law, there were a number of grounds upon which a person could be disqualified from giving testimony. However, the modern trend is to abolish these disqualifications and allow every person to be a witness as long as he possesses certain basic qualifications.

These qualifications are the ability to communicate, an understanding of the duty to tell the truth, and personal knowledge of the facts in the case.

The order of the examination in any court trial is as follows: Direct examination, followed by cross-examination, followed by redirect examination, followed finally by recross examination. The form of questioning on direct examination is limited; and leading questions are specifically prohibited (although there are some exceptions).

If the witness' memory on direct examination is incomplete, the examiner may use the practice of "present memory revived" or "past memory recorded". Greater leeway is permitted to the lawyer on cross-examination, since it is designed to expose weaknesses or falsehood in the witness' testimony.

The obligation of the witness is to tell the facts to the jury, letting the jury draw any conclusions therefrom. Therefore, the opinions or conclusions of witnesses are generally not admissible. There are generally two kinds of witnesses—lay and the expert. A lay witness is any person who has personal knowledge of the facts of the case; while an expert witness is one who has special knowledge, skill, experience, training, or education on the subject on which he is testifying. Opinions of expert witnesses may be permitted on subjects within their area of expertise.

Witnesses may be impeached (discredited) by cross-examination or through the use of extrinsic evidence. There are several grounds for impeachment, the basic ones being bias and interest, lack of character for honesty or truthfulness, prior inconsistent statements, defects of capacity, lack of knowledge, and contradiction. If the witness' credibility has been impeached, he may be rehabilitated by the party who introduced him.

"Privilege" is a rule of law which allows the witness to refuse to give testimony in court which he could otherwise have been compelled to give, or permits him to prevent someone else from testifying on such matters. The rule basically prevents disclosures of confidential communications made in the course of a professional or marital relationship. It extends to the relationships between lawyer and client, spouses, physician and patient, psychotherapist and patient, clergyman and penitent, and state and informer. However, the privilege can be waived by failure to claim it or through voluntary disclosure or consent.

# XIII. THE HEARSAY RULE AND ITS EXCEPTIONS

A. **STATEMENT OF THE RULE**

If a statement is hearsay, that evidence must be excluded upon an appropriate objection to its admission <u>unless</u> it comes within one of the many exceptions to the Hearsay Rule.

1. **What Constitutes "Hearsay":** Hearsay is a statement, other than one made by a witness while testifying at the trial or hearing, which is being offered to prove the truth of the matter asserted.

2. **Reasons for Excluding Hearsay:** The usual reason given for excluding hearsay is that in cases of oral declarations, there is danger of inaccurate reporting by the witness who is repeating what he heard. However, the <u>real reason</u> for excluding hearsay is that the opposing party is denied the opportunity <u>to cross-examine</u> the person who originally made the statement—since that person is not on the witness stand.

3. **Forms of Hearsay:** Contrary to popular belief, the term <u>hearsay</u> is not limited to spoken words. There are actually three basic forms of hearsay:

    a. **Oral statements:** For example, witness testifies that "Y told me that Z has threatened to kill him."

    b. **Writings:** A written document offered in evidence may also be hearsay. Example: Witness introduces a letter or telegram in court from Y wherein Y writes: "Z has threatened to kill me."

    c. **Assertive conduct:** Finally, conduct intended by the actor to be a substitute for words may be hearsay. Example: The nod of Y's head indicating consent when Witness asked him whether Z had threatened to kill him, where Witness later recounts the nod of the head.

4. **Test to Determine Oral Hearsay:** In the case of oral hearsay, the test is this: If the statement being repeated by the witness is offered to prove the <u>truth of what somebody else has said</u>, the statement is hearsay.

    a. **Example:** Witness says: "One of my neighbors told me that he saw the accused beat up his wife that morning." If the statement is offered to prove that the accused did in fact beat up his wife that morning, the statement is hearsay and therefore not admissible.

    b. However, if that same statement is offered to prove something else—such as that someone talked to the witness that morning or that the witness can hear—the statement is not hearsay and is therefore admissible.

B. **EXCEPTIONS TO THE HEARSAY RULE**

Certain kinds of hearsay have elements of special reliability which make up for the absence of cross-examination. Therefore, a number of exceptions to the Hearsay Rule have been recognized. In these cases, the hearsay evidence is admissible if the trial judge determines that it falls within one of the exceptions.

The seven exceptions which are used most often in criminal trials are:

—Confessions

—Dying Declarations

—Spontaneous Declarations

—Previously Recorded Testimony

—Past Recollections Recorded

—Business Records

—Official Records

1. **Confessions**

    a. **Definition**: A confession is a <u>direct acknowledgement</u> of criminal guilt by an accused. The acknowledgement may be oral or in writing. Most courts regard out-of-court confessions as heresay if offered to prove the truth of the matter confessed.

    b. **Reason for admission**: People do not ordinarily admit to a criminal act. Thus if they do so, their statement can be considered reliable.

    c. **How presented in court**: Confessions are presented in court through testimony by the person to whom the confession was made.

    d. **Requirements for admissibility**: The following requirements must be present in order to admit hearsay evidence of a confession:

       (1) **Confession must be voluntary**: Voluntariness is determined by the judge on a case-by-case basis.

       (2) **No violation of defendant's rights**: Even if otherwise voluntary, the confession must be excluded if it was obtained in violation of the accused's constitutional rights. Examples: Accused not advised of his Miranda rights; accused not given counsel; accused illegally arrested; accused denied speedy arraignment.

2. **Dying Declarations**

    a. **Definition**: A dying declaration is a statement made by a dying person concerning the cause and circumstances of his impending death. It is admissible in evidence as an exception to the Hearsay Rule.

    b. **Reason for admission**: A person who knows he is about to die would probably not wise to do so with a lie on his lips. Therefore, the declaration is trustworthy.

    c. **How presented in court**: Dying declarations may be testified to by any witness who heard or witnessed the declaration.

    d. **Form**: No particular form of declaration is required. While most dying declarations are oral, they can also be written or given by a sign of the hand or a nod of the head.

e. **Type of action in which admissible**: The general rule is that dying declarations are admissible only in homicide cases. However, several states now admit dying declarations in all civil and criminal cases.

f. **Requirements for admissibility**: The following must be present:

   (1) **Victim must have given up hope of surviving**: The declaration must have been made by the victim while he believed that his death was imminent and therefore had given up hope. However, it is not necessary that the victim die immediately after making the dying declaration.

       (a) **Example**: P was seriously wounded. En route to the hospital in an ambulance, he told the police officer, "X shot me"; but he also told the ambulance driver to "get me to the nearest hospital immediately." P's statement that "X shot me" is not admissible as a dying declaration, because his statement to the ambulance driver indicated that he had not given up hope of surviving.

   (2) **Declaration must concern the cause of death**: Example: "W stabbed me" is admissible. However, declarations by the victim about previous quarrels or statements about the character of the alleged assailant would not be admissible.

   (3) **Victim's personal knowledge**: The statement must concern facts within the personal knowledge of the victim. I.e., statements of opinion are not admissible. Example: "I think D tried to poison me" is not admissible.

   (4) **Victim must be dead**: Most courts require that the victim must be dead when the evidence is ultimately offered. If he is alive, he can testify himself; and there is no need for the dying declaration.

   (5) **Note**: The above requirements for admissibility are rather strict. However, statements of the victim which do not comply with all of the above requirements may still be admissible . . . not as a dying declaration, but as a spontaneous statement (below).

g. **Rebuttal and impeachment**: Once admitted in court, the dying declaration is subject to all the objections and impeachment which could be asserted if the victim were on the witness stand testifying. Thus, for example, the declaration can be impeached by showing that the victim had withheld relevant facts or had made prior inconsistent statements, by proof of his lack of perception, or by evidence contradicting the declaration.

3. **Spontaneous Declarations** (also known as "Excited Utterances", "Spontaneous Statements", or "Res Gestae Statements")

   a. **Definition**: Spontaneous declarations are statements made under the stress of some shocking or exciting event, concerning something related to that event. Such declarations are admissible in evidence as an exception to the Hearsay Rule.

   b. **Reason for admission**: The spontaneity of such statements, and the consequent lack of opportunity for reflection and deliberate fabrication, provide an adequate guarantee of their trustworthiness.

   c. **How presented in court**: Spontaneous declarations are testified to by the person who heard the declaration. Example: M heard O say "That sports car ran the red light" right after the accident. That statement can be testified to by M.

d. **Requirements for admissibility**: The following requirements must be met:

   (1) **Startling event**: There must have been an occurrence startling enough to produce shock and excitement in the observer. Examples: Crash of a car, shooting of a person, sudden explosion, beating up of a person, snatching of a handbag, etc.

   (2) **Declaration made contemporaneously**: Secondly, the statement must have been made while the declarant was under the stress of the event and before he had time to reflect upon it.

   (a) The time element is very important. There is no mechanical test, but courts usually limit admissibility to statements made <u>contemporaneously</u> (i.e., while the event is taking place) or <u>immediately after</u> the exciting event. But courts conflict as to whether <u>this means seconds</u>, minutes or even hours after the event.

   (3) **Personal knowledge of the facts observed**: The statement must also relate to the circumstances of the event and must represent declarant's personal observations of the facts. Example: Right after an accident, the declarant was heard by the witness to say: "That sports car ran a red light." This is admissible. However, "That guy must have been driving fast" would not be admissible.

e. **The following are not required for admissibility**:

   (1) **Declarant need not be competent**: The person who makes the spontaneous declaration need not be competent as a witness, as long as he had personal knowledge of the facts and powers of perception and recollection. <u>Reason</u>: The declarant himself is not a witness. The <u>one who heard</u> him is the one testifying.

   (2) **Declarant need not be unavailable**: The spontaneous declaration testified to by someone who heard it is probably better testimony than what the declarant could presently recall on the stand.

   (3) **Declarant need not always be identified**—as long as his existence can be established by inference from the circumstances. Example: A witness testifies that he heard somebody yell, "That man in a white shirt fired the shot." This is admissible even though the witness cannot identify who said it.

f. **Distinguished from "res gestae"**: Although spontaneous declarations are often referred to as "part of the <u>res gestae</u> (literally, the "thing done"), it is really only a small portion of the whole res gestae concept. Res gestae includes not only declarations, but also conduct or any physical object which can be considered an integral part of a crime or an event. The two terms should not be confused since they are used interchangeably.

4. **Previously Recorded Testimony**

   a. **Definition**: Previously recorded testimony refers to depositions or transcripts of testimony given under oath by a witness at some former hearing or trial in the same case of another case. Such testimony is considered hearsay in most jurisdictions because it was not given at the present trial or hearing, but is admissible as an exception to the Hearsay Rule.

(1) **Example**: X was convicted of rape, but given a new trial. Before the new trial starts, one of the state's main witnesses dies. His former testimony may be admissible in evidence.

b. **Reason for admission**: Former testimony is admitted because of the presence of certain elements insuring reliability—such as the oath, the solemnity of the occasion, and, most important, the opportunity for cross-examination at the former hearing.

c. **How presented in court**: The usual method of proving the prior testimony is by introducing a certified transcript of the prior proceedings. The court reporter can be called to the witness stand to read the entire testimony of the dead or unavailable witness—including the direct, cross, redirect, and recross examinations.

d. **Type of previous proceeding**: The prior proceeding in which the testimony was given may be judicial, legislative, or administrative.

(a) However, grand jury hearings or coroner's inquests do <u>not</u> qualify because the opportunity to cross examine did not exist.

e. **Requirements for use in criminal proceedings**: Previously recorded testimony can be used in criminal proceedings as long as the following requirements are met:

(1) The accused or his attorney must have been present and <u>had the opportunity to cross-examine</u> at the time the testimony was given (whether in a preliminary examination, former trial for the same offense, etc.); and

(2) The witness whose reported testimony is involved must now be <u>unavailable</u>. The term "<u>unavailable</u>" can mean:

(a) That the witness is dead; or

(b) That the witness is insane, out of the court's jurisdiction, or cannot be found despite sincere efforts to produce him.

1) Temporary physical disability or illness is <u>not</u> sufficient to establish unavailability.

2) And, a mere showing that the witness is incarcerated in a prison outside the state is insufficient if there is no showing that he could not be produced. [Barber v. Page, 390 U.S. 719, 1968]

5. **Past Recollection Recorded**

a. **Definition**: Past recollection recorded refers to the <u>contents</u> of writings made at or near the time of event which may be introduced in <u>evidence</u> if a witness' recollection is not revived even after having been shown the writing on the witness stand. Use of the contents of the writing to prove the facts contained therein raises a hearsay problem. But if a proper foundation can be laid, the contents of the writing may be introduced into evidence under an exception to the Hearsay Rule.

(1) **Example**: A retired police captain is called to the witness stand to testify on a report he submitted to his superiors years before, based on his personal knowledge and concerning involvement of the accused in a crime. If the witness has no present recollection of the facts contained in the report even after being shown the document on the witness stand, its contents may be read into the record.

b. **Reason for admitting**: A writing made by an observer when the facts were still fresh in his mind is probably more reliable than his testimony on the witness stand —even though there was no opportunity to cross examine him on that document.

c. **How presented in court**: The general view is that the writing itself is not admissible. Rather, it must be read to the jury and thereby becomes a part of the court's record. The justification for this practice is that juries tend to overvalue documents.

d. **Requirements for admissibility**: The following must be present:

(1) **No present recollection**: The witness must have no present recollection of the facts recorded in the document.

(2) **Recording made when events were fresh in mind**: The document must have been made at a time when the facts recorded therein actually occurred or when they were still fresh in the witness' memory. What this means in each particular case is determined by the judge.

(3) **Recording made by or under direction of witness**: In general, the writing must have been made (a) by the witness himself or under his direction, or (b) by some other person for the purpose of recording the witness' statement at the time it was made.

(4) **Verification**: The witness must testify that the recording was a true statement of the facts when it was made.

(5) **Authentication**: And, the document must be authenticated as an accurate record of the statement.

6. **Business Records**

   a. **Definition**: Business records are official records kept by a person or an organization in the regular course of business. They are considered heresay, but are admissible as one of the exceptions to the Hearsay Rule.

   b. **Reason for admission**: Business records tend to be trustworthy because of the source of the information contained therein and the method and time of their preparation.

   c. **How presented in court**: Business records are introduced through a witness who is acquainted with the record and business procedure in the particular organization or company whose records are to be introduced. Example: The head accountant of a corporation can testify concerning the business records of the company, or the head physician in a hospital as to medical entries.

   d. **Requirements for admissibility**: The following requirements must be present for admission of business records:

   (1) **A business**: Most statutes define "business" very broadly to include every association, profession, occupation, and calling, whether conducted for profit or not. Thus, the definition would include records made by churches, hospitals, schools, etc.

   (2) **Entry made in the regular course of business**: It must also appear that the record was made in the course of a regularly conducted business activity.

Example: Entries in hospital records—such as records of the kinds of medicine administered or notes of the attending physician are admissible.

(3) **Personal knowledge**: The business record must consist of matters within the personal knowledge of the entrant or within the personal knowledge of someone with a business duty to transmit such matters to the entrant.

   (a) **Rule on police reports**: Police reports based on the personal knowledge of the reporting officer are admissible. But those based on statements of bystanders would not be admissible—because the bystanders had no business duty to report the facts to the officer.

(4) **Entry made at or near time of event**: The entry must have been made at or near the time of the transaction, while the entrant's knowledge of the facts was still fresh.

(5) **Authentication**: Finally, the authenticity of the records must be established. The usual method of authentication is to have the custodian of the records or some other qualified witness (not necessarily the person who made the entry) testify at the trial to the identity of the record, the mode of preparation, and the manner of its safekeeping.

7. **Official Records**:

   a. **Definition**: Official records are statements and documents prepared by a public officer in the performance of his official duties. They are heresay, but are admissible as exceptions to the Hearsay Rule.

      (1) **Examples**: Record of birth, death, marriages, and court judgments are official records.

   b. **Reason for admission**: This exception is necessary in order to avoid having public officers leave their jobs constantly to appear in court and testify to acts done in their official capacity. Also, such records are presumed to be trustworthy because public officials are under a duty to properly record what they do.

   c. **Distinguished from "business records" exception**: The official records exception can be considered a part of, and is in fact usually covered by the provisions of, the business records exception. The only major difference is that the judge may admit an official record without requiring anybody to testify in court as to its identity and mode of preparation.

   d. **How presented**: Official records must be presented in court through the use of a certified copy. However, as just noted, the keeper of the record need not appear.

8. **Other Exceptions to the Hearsay Rule Not Discussed**: Over the years, many exceptions to the Hearsay Rule have developed by statute or judicial decisions. These exceptions can be added to or eliminated at any time.

   a. Among the exceptions not discussed in this text are: Admissions, declarations against interest, declarations re state of mind or physical condition, prior identification, judgment of previous conviction, family history, ancient writings, family records, vital statistics, and reputation as to character.

C. **SUMMARY**

Hearsay is a statement, other than one made by the witness while testifying at the trial or hearing, which is being offered to prove the truth of the matter asserted. The Hearsay Rule provides that hearsay evidence must be excluded, unless it comes under one of the many exceptions to the Rule. The real reason for excluding hearsay is that the opposing party is denied the opportunity to cross-examine the person who originally made the statement. Contrary to popular notions, hearsay evidence is not only in the form of oral statements: It also includes writings or assertive conduct.

There are numerous exceptions to the Hearsay Rule which make evidence which is otherwise hearsay admissible in court. These exceptions are justified on the ground that they have elements of special reliability which make up for the absence of cross-examination. The basic exceptions for purposes of a criminal trial are: Confessions, dying declarations, spontaneous declarations, previously recorded testimony, past recollection recorded, business records, and official records. Each exception has its own specific requirements for admissibility.

These exceptions have developed over the years through legislation and judicial decisions. They are not fixed and may be increased or decreased, depending upon future legislative or judicial needs.

# XIV. USE OF DEMONSTRATIVE, SCIENTIFIC AND DOCUMENTARY EVIDENCE AT TRIAL

In Chapter XI, we identified the four general forms of evidence. This chapter focuses on three of these forms—demonstrative, scientific and documentary evidence—and discusses admissibility and uses of such evidence in a criminal trial. Judicial notice, the fourth form of evidence, is discussed in Chapter XV.

A. **DEMONSTRATIVE EVIDENCE (ALSO KNOWN AS REAL EVIDENCE OR PHYSICAL EVIDENCE)**

1. **Definition**: Demonstrative evidence consists of tangible things (things which can be touched) presented to the jury for inspection. Examples would include: weapons, whiskey bottles, clothing, money, shoes, jewelry, etc.

2. **Statement of the Rule**: Demonstrative evidence is admissible in court. This form of evidence is usually trustworthy, and its use is favored. Once introduced in court, it "speaks for itself"—in that members of the jury can see, touch, feel or inspect it.

3. **Requisites for Admissibility**: In order for demonstrative evidence to be admissible in court, it must be shown to be relevant and authentic.

    a. **Relevant**: First, the evidence must tend to prove the fact for which it is being offered.

        (1) **Example**: If the stolen things are introduced in a burglary prosecution it must be shown that a burglary took place and that these items were stolen.

    b. **Authentic**: Secondly, it must be shown that the object introduced in evidence is what the person introducing it says it is—i.e., that the gun found near the scene of the crime is the same gun that is now being introduced; or that the blood tested really came from the accused and not from someone else.

        (1) **Types of authentication**: There are two methods of authenticating demonstrative evidence. These are:

            (a) **By testimony**: If the demonstrative evidence is a type which can readily be identified by a witness, the witness' testimony will be sufficient for authentication.

                1) **Example**: Where a model of the murder scene is presented, the witness must testify that the model, as constructed, accurately represents what is sought to be depicted.

            (b) **By establishing chain of custody**: On the other hand, where the demonstrative evidence is difficult to identify or could easily be tampered with—as is true of much of the demonstrative evidence obtained by police—the person introducing the evidence must establish its chain of custody.

                1) **Example 1**: A gun is found at the scene of the murder. The gun is likely to pass from the hands of the police officers to others in the police department for purposes of testing and inspection. The police officer who testifies to the finding of the gun must therefore know who else had access to it, when, and for what purpose. This is known as establishing the chain of custody.

2) **Example 2**: Before evidence of a blood alcohol test will be admitted, a <u>chain of custody</u> must likewise be established—from the taking of the blood to the testing and exhibiting of the sample. A system of identification and custody must be shown to prove that no tampering with the evidence has taken place.

(2) **Purpose of authentication**: Authentication is necessary for two reasons, namely:

(a) To prevent the introduction of another object different from the one testified about; and

(b) To insure that there have been no significant changes in the condition of the evidence.

4. **Types of Demonstrative Evidence**: There are four general types of demonstrative evidence. These are:

   a. **Direct evidence**—meaning evidence which can prove directly the fact for which it is being offered. Example: A badly scarred arm or mutilated face to show the nature and extent of an injury would be direct demonstrative evidence.

   b. **Circumstantial evidence**—where facts about the object are proved as the basis for an <u>inference</u> (conclusion) that other facts are true.

      (1) **Example**: The prosecutor introduces a piece of cloth found near the scene of a strangulation which matches a bigger piece of cloth found hidden in the defendant's home. The evidence here is circumstantial, because the jury must infer that the defendant committed the crime (i.e., if only he had access to both pieces of evidence).

   c. **Original evidence**—meaning evidence which has some connection with the transaction at issue in the trial. Example: A butcher knife allegedly used in a murder, or burglary tools used in a burglary.

   d. **Prepared evidence**—meaning evidence which has been produced specifically for the trial. Examples: Sketches, models, charts, drawings, graphs, etc.

5. **Discretionary Power of the Court to Admit or Exclude Evidence**: Even if the demonstrative evidence is clearly relevant and properly authenticated, it is subject to the same limitations as any other form of evidence. Therefore, it may be excluded if the trial judge determines that its value is outweighed by danger of prejudice, inflaming the jurors, etc.

   a. **Example**: In a capital murder case, blown-up photographs of the badly-mutilated, nude and decomposed body of the victim are clearly relevant. But such evidence could be excluded if the photographs are so gruesome that they would likely create prejudice against the accused.

   b. **Seldom reversed if admitted**: If the trial court decides to admit the evidence, however, its decision is seldom reversed on appeal.

      (1) **Example**: In one Texas case, the trial judge allowed the plaintiff, stripped to the waist, to display a shriveled arm dangling as though suspended by a string. The appellate court questioned the propriety of allowing the repeated exhibition of such gruesome evidence; but this was not enough to justify a reversal.

6. **Admissibility of Specific Types of Demonstrative Evidence**

   a. **Diagrams, drawings, graphs, charts, models, casts, etc.**: These are usually admissible for the purpose of illustrating testimony. Since they are all reproductions, they must be authenticated by testimonial evidence showing that they are faithful reproductions of the object depicted.

      (1) **Example**: In a homicide case, a model of the embankment and river from where a small boy was pushed by the accused is admissible.

   b. **Photographs**: As a general rule, a photograph is admissible only if identified by a witness as a correct representation of the person or object depicted. It is generally sufficient if the witness who identifies the photograph is familiar with the scene or object represented.

      (1) However, a few courts require the testimony of the person who actually took the picture, describing the camera angle, speed and lighting, development process, and the care and custody of the negative (to show that there was no retouching or tampering).

   c. **X-ray pictures, electrocardiographs, etc.**: A more complex procedure is required for admission of this type of evidence.

      (1) First, it must be shown that the process used is accurate.

      (2) It must then be shown that the machine itself was in working order, and that the operator was qualified to operate it.

      (3) Finally, a custodial chain must be established—i.e., who took the X-ray, to whom it was given, for what purpose, and when.

   d. **Tape recordings**: A tape recording may be used to revive a witness' memory, to impeach by showing a prior inconsistent statement, or to serve as direct evidence.

      (1) Proper preliminary facts must be established as a condition for admissibility. These include authenticity, identification of the speakers and, under some circumstances, evidence that the conversation was not improperly induced.

   e. **View of the scene**: The trial court may allow the jury to visit the scene of the crime if this is considered necessary. This is a part of the formal trial, so the judge, the parties and the lawyers must be present.

   f. **Exhibit of child in paternity suits**

      (1) Almost all courts permit exhibition of a child for the purpose of showing whether or not it is one of the <u>same race</u> as the alleged father.

      (2) However, the courts are divided with respect to the propriety of exhibiting the child in order to prove its <u>physical resemblance</u> to the alleged father. Some courts allow it, while others do not.

   g. **Demonstrations**: The court in its discretion may permit demonstrations (such as those to show the extent of bodily injury) or scientific experiments in the courtroom.

## B. SCIENTIFIC EVIDENCE

1. **Statement of the Rule**: Testimony concerning controlled scientific experiments is admissible under the following circumstances:

    a. **Substantially similar conditions**: The experiment must have taken place under conditions substantially similar to those existing at the time the facts in issue occured. Example: In a skid test, there must be a showing of same size of car, same type of pavement, same weather conditions, etc.

    b. **Done by expert if complicated**: If the experiment or test was of a complicated nature, it must have been conducted by qualified experts in the field who must then testify as to (1) the way the test was conducted, and (2) the reliability of the testing procedures. Examples: Blood analysis, shot test patterns, ballistics, etc.

    c. **Probative value**: The probative value of the experiment must be greater than the danger of misleading the jury or confusing the issue.

2. **Where and When are Experiments Conducted**: Scientific experiments may be performed:

    a. **In the courtroom during trial**: For example, a physician may be allowed to swallow certain tablets at the beginning of the testimony and to testify an hour later that he was not drowsy.

    b. **Outside the courtroom before trial**: More frequently, tests are conducted outside the court prior to trial and the results are offered as testimonial evidence by an expert. Examples: Comparison of fingerprints, firearms, blood tests, hair samples, voiceprints, etc., done in the crime laboratory of the police department.

3. **Qualifications of Witness**: Some scientific tests are simple, and testimony concerning them may be given by lay witnesses. In most cases, however, a witness testifying as to scientific evidence must first be qualified as an expert.

4. **Discretionary Power of the Court**: Even if the scientific evidence is admissible, courts have the discretion to exclude it if it is likely to be prejudicial.

    a. **Example**: Evidence from lie detector tests might be excluded because of the fear that a jury would give too much weight to this type of evidence.

5. **Judicial Notice**: Once a particular scientific test or principle has been sufficiently well established, courts no longer require proof of the underlying basis of the test. Rather, judicial notice will be taken that the test is accurate.

    a. **Example**: In some jurisdictions, courts take judicial notice that radar testing is an accurate method of measuring speed. (Of course, it must still be shown that the test was properly administered in the present case.)

6. **Conclusiveness of Scientific Evidence**: In some cases, the weight of scientific evidence is so great that it becomes conclusive. Example: When blood tests exclude the possibility of paternity and there is no contention that the test has been improperly conducted, such blood test are frequently held conclusive on the issue of paternity. As a result, evidence to the contrary will not be admitted in court.

7. **Admissibility of Specific Scientific Evidence**

   a. **Lie detector (polygraph) tests**

      (1) Most courts exclude results: Until recently, most courts refused to admit the results of lie detector tests in either civil or criminal proceedings, unless admissibility was agreed to by both parties.

      (a) Similarly, statements made by a person under the influence of drugs ("truth serum") or hypnosis have generally been excluded unless agreed to by both parties.

      (2) Today, more and more courts are beginning to accept lie detector tests because of their improved scientific reliability.

      (3) However, even where lie detector tests are admissible, their use is limited by the fact that the prosecution cannot require the accused to take a lie detector test.

      (a) Reason: The 5th Amendment privilege against self-incrimination prohibits a person from being compelled to testify against himself. (However, it does not protect a person from having to submit to a blood test or a breath test under proper conditions—because these tests are physical rather than testimonial.)

   b. **Breath or blood tests for intoxication**: The results of such tests are admissible in evidence but are usually not conclusive of intoxication. I.e., the jury can accept or reject the results; and the accused can present contrary evidence that he was sober.

      (1) Some state statutes call for corroboration of test results. Such corroboration may be in the form of testimony by anyone who saw the person drinking, or by a police officer who saw and witnessed the person's erratic behavior.

   c. **Radar speedmeter to determine speed**: The results of such checks are generally admissible in evidence. Admissibility is provided for by statute in some states—meaning that expert testimony in court concerning the scientific validity of radar speed checks is not necessary. However, it is usually necessary to prove the following:

      (1) That the person operating the equipment had proper training;

      (2) That the equipment had been properly checked and tested;

      (3) That the speeding in fact took place as observed in the radar speedmeter; and

      (4) That the speeding vehicle was driven by the defendant.

      (5) In other states, there is no statute providing for admissibility, but courts take judicial notice of the reliability of such checks and therefore admit them.

   d. **Blood grouping tests**

      (1) **To show identity**: Evidence of blood tests has always been held admissible for the purpose of identifying a party.

      (a) For example, evidence that blood found on an assault victim was of the same type as the blood of the accused could be used as evidence tending to show that the accused was the assailant.

(b) Note that some blood test evidence may not be very helpful. For example, blood tests may show that the blood in question is Type O, the type found in approximately 45 per cent of the population. Most courts have admitted such evidence even though it establishes only a possibility or probability of identification.

(2) **To show paternity**

(a) Many courts have been reluctant to admit blood tests in paternity actions where the tests indicate only the possibility of paternity—for fear that juries would give undue weight to such tests.

1) Example: Suppose the blood tests show that both the child and the alleged father are Type O. This merely shows that the defendant <u>could</u> be the father of the child: He is not necessarily the father, because millions of other males also have Type O blood.

(b) However, when blood tests <u>disprove</u> paternity, the results are admissible.

1) Example: If the tests show that the child has Type O blood and the alleged father has Type B, the evidence is admissible to show that defendant could not be the father of the child.

C. **DOCUMENTARY EVIDENCE**

1. **Definition**: Documentary evidence consists of <u>writings</u> rather than <u>testimony</u>. Examples: Contracts, wills, extortion notes, suicide notes, bookmaking records, letters, etc.

2. **Statement of the Rule**: Documentary evidence is admissible as long as it is <u>relevant</u> and <u>authentic</u>.

   a. **Relevant**: This means that the documentary evidence must tend to prove the fact for which it is being offered. Example: A list of names found in the "date book" of a call girl is relevant if it is introduced to prove that it is in fact a list of "customers", and tends to prove the charge of prostitution.

   b. **Authentic**: This requires that the person offering the evidence prove that the document is genuine and is what it purports to be. Example: If a letter from the accused threatening to kill the deceased is introduced in court, it must be shown that it is indeed a threatening letter and that it was written by the accused.

3. **How to Authenticate Evidence**: Authentication is generally accomplished in one of two ways: By <u>direct</u> evidence or by <u>circumstantial</u> evidence. Let us discuss each of these.

   a. **By direct evidence**: Direct evidence may be introduced in the following ways:

   (1) **Through the testimony of a subscribing witness**: A writing may be authenticated by the testimony of one who sees it executed or hears it acknowledged, and thereupon signs his name as a witness.

   (a) Example: A Howard Hughes will (if one exists) could be authenticated by the testimony of one who saw the will made and whose signature as a witness appears on the will.

   (2) **Through the testimony of other witnesses**: A writing may also be authenticated by anyone who saw the writing made or executed, even if he did not sign it.

(a) **Example**: Cards mailed to promote the business of a house of ill-repute may be authenticated by one who helped the accused produce and mail the cards.

(3) **Through handwriting verifications**: A writing likewise may be authenticated by evidence establishing the genuineness of the handwriting of the maker. This can be done through:

(a) **Nonexpert opinion**: Any person who has personal knowledge of the handwriting of the supposed writer may state his opinion as to whether the document is in that person's handwriting.

(b) **Expert comparison of writings**: An expert witness or the trier of fact can determine the genuineness of a writing by comparing the questioned writing with another writing proved to be genuine.

(4) **Voice identification**: Any person familiar with the voice of an alleged speaker may authenticate a recording of the voice by giving his opinion as to the identity of the speaker.

b. **By circumstantial evidence**: Authentication may also be accomplished through the use of circumstantial evidence, in two basic ways:

(1) **Admissions by an opposing party**: A writing may be authenticated by evidence that the party against whom the writing is offered either admitted its authenticity or acted upon the writing as though it were authentic.

(2) **Contents of the document**: A writing may also be authenticated by showing that it contains information, or was written in a manner, peculiar to the person who is alleged to have written it.

(a) **Style**: Thus, a writing may be authenticated by identifying a style, appearance, or manner of expression which is distinctive to the alleged writer. This includes the use of certain words, phrases, abbreviations, or idioms which are shown to have been unique to the person who is claimed to have written it.

1) **Example**: A threatening note sent by a former boyfriend who usually signed his letters, "Yours till death do us part."

(b) **Reply letter doctrine**: A writing also may be authenticated by evidence that it was written in response to a communication sent to the alleged author. The content of the letter must make it unlikely that it was written by anyone other than the alleged author.

1) **Example**: X mails a letter to Y. A reply is received in which reference is made to X's letter. This is sufficient evidence to authenticate the reply letter as having actually come from Y.

4. **Self-Authenticating Documents**: Certain documents require no independent proof of authenticity—i.e., merely producing the document establishes its authenticity. It is then up to the other party to prove that the document is not what it purports to be or that it is not authentic. Self-authenticating documents include:

a. **Public documents**: Documents bearing the seal of a governmental agency or the signature of an authorized official may be received without independent proof of authenticity.

b. **Certified copies**: Copies of public records are also self-authenticating if the original writing was recorded or filed in a public office and is certified as correct by its custodian.

c. **Notarized documents**: Writings likewise are presumed authentic when acknowledged before a notary public.

5. **The Best Evidence Rule** (also known as the Original Document Rule or Primary Evidence Rule)

    a. **Statement of the rule**: The Best Evidence Rule states that in order to prove the contents of a private writing, the original writing should be produced.

        (1) But while the original writing is required if available and is strongly preferred, the Best Evidence Rule does not exclude the introduction of secondary evidence if the original writing is shown to be unavailable.

    b. **Reason for the rule**: Requiring that originals be produced is designed to minimize the possibility of misinterpretation and to prevent fraud in the use of documentary evidence.

    c. **What constitutes a "writing" under Best Evidence Rule**: The term "original writing" is not limited to writings alone. It applies to any tangible form of communication, and thus includes contracts, wills, letters, notes, photographs, x-rays, motion pictures, tape recordings, and the like.

    d. **"Duplicate originals" may qualify under the rule**: Duplicate originals are admissible as originals in many jurisdictions. These would include a xerox copy, a carbon copy, a photostatic copy, or a microfilm reproduction.

    e. **Exceptions to Best Evidence Rule**: In the following cases, the original writing need not be produced:

        (1) **Official records**: The Best Evidence Rule applies only to private writings. Therefore, properly authenticated copies of an official document or recorded writing (such as a recorded deed) may be used instead of the originals.

        (2) **"Collateral" writings**: The Rule applies only where secondary evidence is offered to prove the contents of an original writing. It does not apply where the "writing" itself is "not closely related to the controlling issues."

            (a) **Example**: P alleges an oral employment contract. In the course of the direct examination, he testifies that he met D by responding to a newspaper advertisement. The advertisement is not in issue, the main question being whether there was in fact an oral contract. Therefore, the newspaper advertisement is "collateral" and need not be produced.

        (3) **Where opposing party admits contents of writing**: The contents of a writing may be proved by the testimony or written deposition of the party against whom it is being introduced, or by his written admission acknowledging the existence of the document and the validity of its contents.

(a) **Example**: In his formal answer to the complaint, defendant admits that the contract which is the basis of the suit against him exists and that it obligates him to pay $10,000 to the plaintiff, but that defendant is asking for more time to be able to pay it. Here, the original of the contract need not be produced.

f. **Secondary evidence may be admissible**: The Best Evidence Rule allows the introduction of secondary evidence as long as the failure to produce the original writing is satisfactorily explained.

g. **When secondary evidence may be introduced**: Secondary evidence may be introduced in the following instances:

(1) **When original writing is lost or destroyed**: Secondary evidence is admissible as long as the loss or destruction was not the fault of the party offering the secondary evidence. Example: Where an original contract is lost in a fire which destroys plaintiff's house.

(2) **When original writing is unobtainable**: Where the original writing is in the possession of a third person who is outside the state, and therefore outside the court's subpoena power secondary evidence is admissible.

(3) **When original writing is too voluminous**: Similarly, where the original writing is so voluminous that it would be impractical to produce it in court, the trial court may allow secondary evidence (such as a summary) to be introduced—provided the originals are available for inspection by the other party. Examples: Multi-volume books, accounting entries, or invoices.

(4) **When original writing is in possession of opposing party**: And, the Best Evidence Rule does not apply when the original writing is in the control or possession of the adverse party, and he fails to produce it upon reasonable advance notice.

h. **What type of secondary evidence is preferred**: Where secondary evidence is admissible, such evidence could conceivably be furnished (1) by producing a copy of the writing in question, provided it is shown to be a true copy of the original writing, or (2) through the testimony of witnesses.

(1) **Majority view**: Most courts require a copy of the original writing, if available, rather than oral testimony as to the content of the document.

(2) **Minority view**: Some courts allow the use of any kind of secondary evidence—either a copy of the original writing or mere oral testimony by persons who have read it.

6. **The Parol Evidence Rule**: The Best Evidence Rule must not be confused with another rule of evidence involving documents, the so-called Parol Evidence Rule.

a. **Statement of the Rule**: The Parol Evidence Rule provides that when the parties have executed a written instrument (such as a contract, deed or will) as a complete and final embodiment of the terms of their agreement, other evidence which would add to, alter or contradict the terms of the written instrument cannot be considered. The written instrument therefore becomes the only evidence admissible in court as proof of the terms of the contract.

b. Comparison of Best Evidence Rule and Parol Evidence Rule

| Best Evidence Rule | Parol Evidence Rule |
|---|---|
| (1) States that original writing must be produced, unless not available but satisfactorily explained | (1) States that no other evidence can be introduced except the written instrument |
| (2) Issue involves availability of original writing. If original is not available but satisfactorily explained, secondary evidence may be introduced. | (2) Availability of written instrument is not in issue because written instrument is available. Issue is whether other evidence (written or oral) can be introduced to supplement it. |
| (3) Used in both criminal and civil cases. | (3) Used primarily in civil cases involving contracts, deeds, wills, etc. Seldom used in criminal cases. |

D. **SUMMARY**

Demonstrative evidence consists of tangible things. It is admissible in court, and its admissibility is in fact favored because of trustworthiness. To be admissible, the demonstrative evidence must be relevant and requires authentication. Even if otherwise admissible, demonstrative evidence may be excluded by the trial court if its value is outweighed by the danger of prejudice or of inflaming the jury.

Scientific evidence is likewise admissible. Scientific experiments sought to be introduced in evidence may be done in the courtroom during the trial, but are more often done outside the courtroom (as in a police crime laboratory) before trial. Once a particular scientific test or principle has been sufficiently well established, courts may take judicial notice of it—thereby dispensing with the need to establish its scientific worth. Radar speedmeters to determine speed are in this category in most jurisdictions.

Documentary evidence consists of writings rather than testimony, and is admissible if proved to be relevant and authentic. There are documents which need no authentication, because producing the document in itself establishes its own authentication. This category includes public documents, certified copies, and notarized documents.

An important rule governing the admissibility of documentary evidence is the Best Evidence Rule. The Rule states that in order to prove the contents of a private writing, the original writing itself must be produced—unless it is shown to be unavailable. The term "writing" covers all tangible forms of communication.

The Best Evidence Rule should be distinguished from the Parol Evidence Rule, which provides that when the parties have executed a written instrument as a complete and final embodiment of the terms of their agreement, other evidence cannot be considered which would add to, alter, or contradict the terms of the written instrument. The Parol Evidence Rule applies most often in civil (rather than criminal) cases.

# XV. JUDICIAL NOTICE, BURDEN OF PROOF AND PRESUMPTIONS

Judicial notice, presumptions and burden of proof help to simplify and expedite the disposition of cases. These three concepts may appear related, but are in fact independent from one another.

**A. JUDICIAL NOTICE**

1. **Definition:** Judicial notice is the process by which the trial court accepts certain facts or propositions as true without the necessity of formal proof. I.e., No witness need be called nor any evidence presented in order to prove them.

2. **Nature:** Judicial notice is a substitute for evidence—i.e., an evidentiary shortcut which relieves the parties of proving facts which any reasonably intelligent person knows are true. Thus, contradictory evidence disputing a fact noticed by the court is <u>not</u> admissible at the trial.

3. **Reason for Judicial Notice:** Judicial notice expedites trials and avoids a result contrary to well-known facts.

    a. **Example:** Judicial notice of the fact that the sun rises in the east and sets in the west (instead of having one party in the case prove it) obviously saves time. Purported evidence to the contrary would be absurd.

4. **Procedure for Judicial Notice**

    a. **Request usually made:** A request for judicial notice may be made by a motion (oral or written), or in any of the written pleadings in the case. However, a request is not essential (see below).

    b. **Procedural safeguards**

    (1) If the trial court intends to take judicial notice of a matter that has a substantial bearing on the ultimate determination of the action, the trial judge must advise the parties that he proposes to take such notice and give them a reasonable opportunity to argue the point.

    (2) Similarly, if the judge denies a request to take judicial notice of any matter, he must advise the parties at the earliest practicable time and indicate for the record that he is denying the request.

5. **Effect of Judicial Notice**

    a. **In civil cases:** A fact which is judicially noticed in a civil case is binding on the jury and the judge will so instruct them.

    b. **In criminal cases:** In a criminal case, however, the judge will instruct the jury that it <u>may</u>—but is not required to—accept facts which are judicially noticed.

    (1) **Reason:** Binding the jury in criminal cases as to any fact in issue may violate an accused's 6th Amendment right to a jury trial. Only the jury can decide which facts are conclusive.

6. **Matters Judicially Noticed:** In most states, judicial notice is <u>mandatory</u> as to certain matters and <u>discretionary</u> with respect to others.

a. **Mandatory judicial notice**: This means that the court <u>must</u> take notice <u>even if not requested</u> by one of the parties in the case. Judicial notice of the following matters is generally mandatory:

   (1) **Universally known and indisputable facts**: A fact is universally known if it is known among all persons of average intelligence and knowledge. This includes a wide range of matters.

       (a) **Examples**: A person dies if he cannot breathe; Monday comes after Sunday; fire can burn one's fingers.

   (2) **All federal and state law**: Including constitutions, charters, statutes, and decisions.

       (a) Municipal ordinances are subject to judicial notice, but only by the municipal courts in that particular municipality.

   (3) **Federal and state rules on practice and procedure.**

   (4) **Documents published in the Federal Register.**

   (5) **The true significance of all English words and phrases, and all legal expressions.**

       (a) **Examples**: The meaning of the words "kill", "steal" or "forge"; or the meaning of such legal expressions as "arrest", "lineup" or "sentencing".

b. **Discretionary judicial notice**: The court may also take notice of certain other matters even without request from any of the parties; but <u>if</u> an appropriate request is made by one of the parties, the court is <u>required</u> to take <u>notice</u> thereof—provided the requesting party furnishes the court with sufficient information. Discretionary judicial notice therefore becomes mandatory if a request is made. Judicial notice of the following matters is generally discretionary:

   (1) Facts of such common knowledge within the area of the court's jurisdiction that they cannot reasonably be disputed.

       (a) **Examples**: A court sitting in New Orleans can take judicial notice of the fact that the Louisiana Superdome is located in downtown New Orleans, or that at 5:30 p.m. during the month of July, it is still daylight in Louisiana.

   (2) Verifiable facts—i.e., indisputable facts immediately ascertainable by referring to sources of reasonably indisputable accuracy (such as almanacs, encyclopedias, books of information, etc.).

       (a) **Examples**: That the Bill of Rights became part of the U.S. Constitution in 1791, that the Statue of Liberty is found in New York City, or that Alaska is the largest state in the United States.

       (b) **Note**: Judicial notice of verifiable facts is a rapidly expanding area of the law. Trial courts have increasingly taken judicial notice of matters which formerly had to be proved at the trial. Examples include, radar speed-tests, ballistics, and paternity blood tests—which are now almost universally recognized as valid scientific tests and no longer require expert testimony to establish their validity. (Polygraph test results and voiceprints may also be appropriate subjects of judicial notice in the near future.)

(3) The laws of sister states, including constitutions, statutes and case decisions.

(4) Administrative regulations and orders of any agency of the state or federal government.

(5) Court rules and court records of any state or federal court.

(6) Official acts of any branch of the U.S. government or of any state of the United States.

7. **Matters Which Cannot be Judicially Noticed**

   a. **Personal knowledge of the judge**: The judge cannot take judicial notice of facts within his own peculiar personal knowledge. Rather, the test of "common knowledge" and "verifiability" must be satisfied.

   (1) **Example**: Suppose a judge sees two cars collide at an intersection, and a case for driving while intoxicated arising out of that incident is now before him. The judge may not take judicial notice of the facts therein even though he saw what happened—because the latter falls within his own peculiar personal knowledge. It does not meet the test of "common knowledge" and "verifiability."

   b. **Essential elements of a crime**: An essential element of a crime is rarely proved by judicial notice—and in some states cannot be. This is because taking judicial notice of an essential element of a crime violates the requirements of procedural fairness, due process, and trial by jury.

   (1) **Example**: In a theft case, the value of the stolen article is often an essential element to determine whether the crime is a misdemeanor or a felony. Most courts will require independent evidence rather than take judicial notice of the value of the stolen items—even though their worth obviously exceeds a certain amount. I.e., a brand-new 25-inch television set is worth more than $50 and its theft is therefore a felony; but this can easily be established by having the owner testify thereto in court.

## B. BURDEN OF PROOF

1. **Definition**: The term "burden of proof" has been the subject of confusing interpretations by courts and writers. For our purposes, "burden of proof" is not a single concept but two closely-related but separate concepts, namely:

   a. The "burden of producing evidence"; <u>and</u>

   b. The "burden of persuasion".

   a. **"Burden of producing evidence"** (also known as "burden of going forward with the evidence"): The burden of producing evidence is the obligation of a party in a case to introduce evidence which is sufficient to avoid a ruling against him on the issue.

   (1) Allocation of burden: The initial burden of producing evidence on a particular issue falls on the party which will suffer from an adverse ruling on that issue if the burden is not met.

(a) Once that party has introduced sufficient evidence, the burden of introducing evidence shifts to the other party to introduce rebutting evidence or evidence establishing some defense to avoid the risk of a ruling against him on the issue.

(2) In a criminal case, the prosecutor has the burden of producing evidence on all the material elements of the crime charged. Once this burden has been met, the accused has the burden of producing evidence in support of his affirmative defenses—such as insanity, intoxication, self-defense, or coercion.

(3) **Example**: In a homicide case, the prosecutor must prove beyond reasonable doubt that someone was killed and that the accused did it. Thus, evidence must be produced in court to prove these elements. If no such evidence is produced, there can be no conviction—because the prosecutor failed to carry the burden of producing evidence.

(a) However, once the prosecutor has introduced evidence on which a jury could find beyond a reasonable doubt that someone was killed and that the accused did it, the burden of producing evidence shifts to the accused. The accused must then introduce evidence that he is not the killer, that he was justified in killing the victim, etc.

(b) If the accused fails to introduce any evidence, the jury must decide whether the prosecution's evidence warrants conviction.

b. **"Burden of persuasion"** (also loosely known as "burden of proof"): The burden of persuasion is the obligation of a party to establish by evidence the required degree of certainty in the mind of the jury about a matter in issue.

(1) **Satisfaction of burden**: A party therefore satisfies the "burden of persuasion" when he convinces the jury of a proposition to the required degree of certainty sufficient for him to win the case.

(2) **Differentiation of degree**: The required degree of certainty varies from a mere "preponderance of the evidence" to "proof of guilt beyond reasonable doubt".

(3) **Allocation of burden**: Each party bears the "burden of persuasion" on all issues which are essential to his side of the case. The burden of persuasion, unlike the burden of introducing evidence, does not shift.

(4) **Degrees of certainty**: The burden of persuasion requires a party to establish in the mind of the jury a required degree of certainty concerning a fact. Four different degrees of certainty are generally recognized and applied. These are:

(a) **Preponderance of evidence**: This means that the trier of fact must believe from the evidence that it is more probable than not that the fact in question exists. This is the usual degree of certainty required in civil cases, and is also used for proof of certain affirmative criminal defenses—such as self-defense, insanity, intoxication, or coercion.

(b) **Clear and convincing evidence**: This requires the trier of fact to be persuaded that there is a high probability that the fact in question exists. This is the degree of certainty usually required in civil cases involving an oral contract to make a will or issues of fraud, deceit, etc.

(c) **Beyond a reasonable doubt**: This refers to "that state of the case in which, after the entire comparison and consideration of all the evidence, leaves the minds of jurors in the abiding conviction, to a moral certainty, of the truth of the charge."

1) **In criminal cases**—the jury must be convinced beyond a reasonable doubt as to the issue of guilt. This means that <u>all the material elements of the offense charged must be proved beyond reasonable doubt</u>.

   a) **Example**: There are usually six elements of the crime of larceny, namely:

      1/ A trespassory

      2/ taking and

      3/ carrying away of the

      4/ personal property

      5/ of another

      6/ with specific intent to permanently deprive the owner thereof.

   b) The accused can be found guilty of larceny only if all six elements above are proved beyond a reasonable doubt. Failure on the part of the prosecutor to prove any one of these elements to that degree of certainty means that the accused cannot be convicted.

2) **Note**: Factual issues in a criminal case other than those pertaining to the guilt or innocence of the defendant are met by proof on a preponderance of evidence (rather than beyond a reasonable doubt).

   a) Examples of such matters would include lawfulness of a search, voluntariness of a confession, effectiveness of consent, whether the statute of limitations has run out, and the like.

(d) **Creating "reasonable doubt"**: The defendant in a criminal action may have the burden of persuasion as to certain issues. However, the defendant generally satisfies this burden by raising a reasonable doubt as to the existence of the fact.

1) **Example**: In a narcotics possession case, the defendant is not guilty if the narcotics are possessed pursuant to a prescription. Although the burden of persuasion is upon the defendant to show that he possessed a prescription, this burden is satisfied if the defendant merely raises a reasonable doubt as to whether he had a prescription.

2. **Significance of Two-Part Concept**: Where a party does not meet his burden of producing evidence on an issue, the court will direct a verdict against him on that issue ... and if the issue is essential to his case, the party loses. However, even where the party meets his burden of producing evidence, the jury may still find against him if that party fails to meet his burden of <u>persuasion</u> to the required degree of certainty.

a. **Example**: In a homicide case, the prosecutor has carried the <u>burden of producing evidence</u> by introducing evidence in court to prove that a killing took place and that the accused did it. However, he may fail to carry the <u>burden of persuasion</u> in that the evidence presented may not come up to the required degree of certainty needed in criminal cases—which is guilt beyond reasonable doubt. I.e., the evidence may constitute only a preponderance of the evidence or clear and convincing evidence. In this case, the prosecutor loses.

b. In a criminal case, therefore, if the prosecutor cannot establish his case "beyond a reasonable doubt", there must be an acquittal—even if the defendant produces <u>no</u> evidence in his defense.

3. **Comparison of Burden of Producing Evidence and Burden of Persuasion**

| <u>Burden of Producing Evidence</u> | <u>Burden of Persuasion</u> |
|---|---|
| a. Function is to introduce evidence. | Function is to persuade the trier of fact. |
| b. Purpose is to avoid a directed verdict. | Purpose is to convict (for prosecution) or to acquit (for the accused). |
| c. No varying degrees of certainty. Only test is whether reasonable man could find for the non-moving party on that issue. | Involves varying degrees of certainty—guilt beyond reasonable doubt for prosecution and usually preponderance of evidence for defense. |
| d. Judge determines if burden has been met. | Jury determines if burden has been met. |
| e. Burden usually shifts once met by one party. | Burden does not shift. |

C. **PRESUMPTIONS**

1. **Definition**: A presumption is a deduction which the law requires to be made from particular facts in evidence, in the absence of sufficient evidence to the contrary. Example: A person who has been absent and not heard from for seven years is presumed dead for legal purposes.

   a. **Uses of presumptions**: Presumptions are designed to expedite court procedures based on considerations of:

   (1) **Probability**—the high probability that certain conclusions are true based on given facts;

   (2) **Practical convenience**—saving of time and effort; and

   (3) **Public policy**—protection of certain relationships and status (such as the legitimacy of a child born in marriage).

b. **Sources**: Presumptions may arise from <u>laws</u> passed by the legislature or from consistent <u>judicial practice</u>.

2. **Requirement of "Rational Connection" in Criminal Cases**: Where a presumption is created by statute and made applicable in criminal proceedings, there must be a "rational connection" between the basic fact proved and the ultimate fact presumed.

   a. **Example**: The Congress of the United States passed a law creating a presumption that any person caught possessing marijuana (the basic fact proved) <u>knew</u> that it was illegally imported (the ultimate fact presumed) and could therefore be convicted for transporting and concealing the drug with knowledge of its illegal importation. The Supreme Court held that this statutory presumption was not rational and the statute was therefore invalid. [Leary v. United States, 395 U.S. 6, 1969]

   b. **What constitutes a "rational connection"**: A connection is rational only if it can be said with <u>substantial assurance</u> that the presumed fact is <u>more likely than not</u> to flow from the proved fact on which it is made to depend. In the *Leary* case, above, it could not be said with substantial assurance that knowledge of importation is more likely than not to flow from possession of marijuana.

3. **Operation of Presumptions**: Before a presumption can operate, the party seeking its benefit must establish the existence of a "basic fact" which is a condition to the "ultimate fact presumed".

   a. **Example**: To invoke the presumption that a person missing for seven years is dead, the "basic fact"—that the person has been missing and unheard from in seven years—must be established before the "ultimate fact presumed" (death) can arise.

   b. **How proved**: The basic fact may be established by the pleadings in the case, by evidence introduced at trial, or by judicial notice.

      (1) **Examples**: In their answer to a complaint, those representing the estate of an absent person may admit that he has been absent and unheard from for seven years. Or, this fact may be proved by the plaintiff by presenting evidence to that effect—such as testimony of the wife or other member of the family.

4. **Classification of Presumptions**: Presumptions may be classified in two general ways. These are: (a) conclusive presumptions or rebuttable presumptions, and (b) presumptions of fact or presumptions of law.

   Note: Presumptions may also be cross-classified. I.e., a conclusive presumption may also be a presumption of law; or a rebuttable presumption may also be a presumption of fact.

   a. **Conclusive and rebuttable presumptions**

      (1) **Conclusive presumptions**: Conclusive presumptions are really rules of substantive law rather than presumptions. They differ from rebuttable presumptions in that conclusive presumptions cannot be contradicted and no evidence to the contrary is admissible in court. There are very few such conclusive presumptions. Examples:

- (a) In most states, a child born to a married woman is conclusively presumed legitimate if she was living with her husband at the time of conception and her husband was not impotent.

- (b) Likewise, some states provide that a child under a certain age (usually 10) is not capable of commiting a felony and therefore cannot be prosecuted for it.

(2) **Rebuttable presumptions** (also known as "disputable presumptions"): Rebuttable presumptions are deductions which the law requires the jury to make unless disproved by contrary evidence. This is generally the kind of presumption referred to when the term "presumption" is used.

- (a) **Examples**: Rebuttable presumptions are many, and vary from state to state. However, some of the more commonly-used presumptions are:

    1) That a couple presenting themselves to be husband and wife are in fact validly married.

    2) That an accused is innocent until proved guilty.

    3) That persons are sane and logical, and intend the logical consequences of their act.

    4) That past legal proceedings have been legally and properly carried out.

    5) That a person is of good moral character, law-abiding, and honest in his dealings with others.

    6) That a person found dead did not commit suicide.

    7) That a person who exercises ownership over property is presumed to be its owner.

    8) That people obey the law.

    9) That an unlawful intent is presumed from the doing of an unlawful act.

    10) That a letter properly addressed, stamped and deposited in a mail box has been delivered to the addressee.

    11) That a person owns what he possesses.

    12) That a writing was executed on the date it bears.

b. **Presumptions of fact and presumptions of law**

(1) **Presumptions of fact**: These are presumptions which the experience of mankind has shown to be valid. They are founded on general knowledge, information and common experience. Examples are:

- (a) That a couple representing themselves to be husband and wife are in fact validly married.

(b) That persons are sane and logical and that they intend the logical consequences of their acts.

(c) That a person found dead did not commit suicide.

(2) **Presumptions of law**: These are presumptions that the law requires be drawn from the existence of certain basic facts, in the absence of evidence to the contrary. Examples are:

(a) That a person who has been absent and unheard from in seven years is presumed dead.

(b) That an accused is innocent until proved guilty.

(c) That if a certain percent of alcohol is found in a person's blood, that person is legally drunk.

5. **Inferences**

   a. **Definition**: An inference is a rational conclusion deduced from facts proved. It is the reasoning process by which the jury comes to conclusions on the significance of the evidence presented in court. The process of inference is usually necessary when the evidence presented is circumstantial rather than direct.

   (1) **Example**: In a prosecution for murder, the evidence shows that the deceased was last seen picking up a hitchiker, that the hitchiker was identified as the defendant, that the car of the accused was later recovered from the defendant, and that a lead pipe with the deceased's blood stains was found inside the trunk of the car. On these facts, the jury may well draw an inference (although they do not have to) that the accused is the murderer.

   b. **Discretion of trier of fact**: The drawing of inferences is largely a matter of discretion for the jury.

   (1) When evidence is offered, it is up to the court to decide whether it is admissible. Once the evidence is admitted, however, it is ordinarily for the jury to decide what inference, if any, should be drawn therefrom.

   c. **Comparison of inference and presumption**

   | Inference | Presumption |
   | --- | --- |
   | (1) A function of the jury. | A function of the judge. |
   | (2) Optional—may or may not be made from an established set of facts. | Required, if the law so states. Must be made once a set of facts has been established. |
   | (3) Usually applies if evidence is circumstantial rather than direct. | Has nothing to do with direct or circumstantial evidence. |

D. **SUMMARY**

Judicial notice, burden of proof and presumptions help simplify and expedite the disposition of cases. These concepts may appear interrelated, but are in fact independent from one another.

Judicial notice refers to the process by which the trial court accepts certain facts or propositions as true without the necessity of formal proof. It is an evidentiary shortcut, and exists because certain facts are so well known that the introduction of proof is not necessary. In most states, judicial notice is mandatory as to certain matters and discretionary as to others.

Mandatory notice means that the court must take notice of a law or fact even if this has not been requested by one of the parties. Discretionary notice means that the court may take notice of certain matters without a request from any of the parties. Certain matters cannot be judicially noticed—basically matters within the personal knowledge of the judge and matters constituting the essential elements of a crime.

Burden of proof is a term which is made up of two closely-related concepts: The "burden of producing evidence" and the "burden of persuasion". The burden of producing evidence is the obligation of a party in a case to introduce evidence which is sufficient to avoid a ruling against him on the issue. The burden of persuasion refers to the obligation of a party to establish by evidence the required degree of certainty in the mind of the jury about a matter in issue. This degree of certainty varies from preponderance of the evidence to guilt beyond reasonable doubt. Once a party has met the burden of producing evidence, the burden usually shifts to the other party. However, the burden of persuasion does not shift and must be discharged by the party obligated to establish an issue to a required degree of certainty.

A presumption is a deduction which the law requires be made from particular facts in evidence, in the absence of sufficient evidence to the contrary. It is a legal tool designed to expedite court procedures, and may arise from law or judicial practice. Presumptions in criminal cases require a "rational connection" between the basic fact proved and the ultimate fact presumed. Presumptions may be classified into conclusive or rebuttable presumptions, and presumptions of fact or presumptions of law. An inference (sometimes confused with a presumption) is a rational conclusion deduced from facts proved. It differs from a presumption primarily in that an inference may or may not be made from an established set of facts, while a presumption must be made if so required by law.

# NOTES

# NOTES

# NOTES

# NOTES

# NOTES